VIRGINIA

WINE
COUNTRY

HILDE GABRIEL LEE & ALLAN E. LEE

BETTERWAY PUBLICATIONS, INC.
WHITE HALL, VIRGINIA

Published by Betterway Publications, Inc.
Box 87
White Hall, VA 22987

Cover design by Deborah Chappell
Book design by Josef Beery
Cover painting © 1983 by Karen Singel
Illustrations by Pamela Poole (except Charlottesville Book Gallery & Restaurant by R. J. Kirchman)
Typography by TechType, Kent Lester

The "Tours" symbol is adapted from the "Winery Tour" signs posted by the Highways and Transporatation Department, Commonwealth of Virginia.

Library of Congress Cataloging-in-Publication Data)

Lee, Hilde Gabriel
    Virginia wine country

    Includes index.
    1. Wine and wine making-- Virginia. 2. Restaurants, lunch rooms, etc.--Virginia--Guide-books. 3. Cookery--Virginia. I. Lee, Allan E.   II. Title.
TP557.L443 1987   662'.22'09755   87-15923
ISBN 0-932620-89-2
ISBN 0-932620-87-6 (pbk.)

Printed in the United States of America
09876543

Preface

Why a book on the Virginia wine industry? The simplest answer is that one is needed since none has been written. We felt that those who enjoy wine and are fortunate enough to visit or live near the Virginia Wine Country would benefit from a book that describes the people and heritage of this unique community of Virginians.

It goes deeper than that, however. Hilde grew up and lived in southwestern Virginia and considers it her home state. The opportunity to write this book was, therefore, like a homecoming to Hilde.

It also provided us with an opportunity to make a small contribution to the Virginia wine industry. We found the winemaking community of Virginia, like its counterparts everywhere, a friendly, interesting, and exciting group of people. As an added attraction, Mother Nature has been gracious enough to make the Virginia landscape, beautiful, a suitable place to grow grapes. It was a thrilling experience to see vineyards on top of the Blue Ridge, on the Eastern Shore, on the rolling hills of northern Virginia Hunt Country, around Monticello, near Colonial Williamsburg, and in the historic Shenandoah Valley.

As it turned out, the timing of the book was fortuitous. The Virginia wine industry is rapidly blossoming into a formidable competitor in the mid-Atlantic wine market. As we became acquainted with those involved, we found an almost missionary-like zeal that conveys a sense of sure success for their efforts.

The initial suggestion to undertake this book came from Leon Adams, who had also sensed the dynamics at work in the Virginia wine community and felt that it was time to record what was being accomplished. Leon's book, *Wines of America*, has been a sort of national bible of the American wine scene since it was first published in 1973.

At the time we decided to embark on this effort in November of 1986, Hilde had just completed publishing, *Vintners Choice*, which describes the lives, recipes, and wines of 125 small California family wineries. Her thesis had been that those who know how to make fine wine also know how to cook good food. This assumption proved correct and, in fact, brought out many of the ethnic nuances frequently overlooked when viewing such a large group of people.

For books such as these to be truly useful, they must be up-to-date. This means the information must be gathered and the book written and published in a matter of months. Consequently, once we decided to write *Virginia Wine Country*, we immediately began to contact publishers, and other persons knowledgeable about the Virginia wine industry. Fortunately, we came in contact with Bob and Jackie Hostage, of Betterway Publications, who immediately became interested in publishing the book.

As a consequence, we found ourselves touring the Virginia wine country throughout the month of February of 1987, meeting and interviewing all of the 35 vintners. As the research proceeded, it became clear that many of the restaurants in the wine country play an intimate role in the industry by featuring local wines, holding "meet the vintner" dinners, and generally helping to promote the industry. We decided, therefore, to add 28 wine country restaurants to the book and provide the reader with information about them.

It is our premise that good wine and good food go together. The combination of the stories of the people who make up the Virginia wine community and a sampling of their favorite recipes provides a unique insight into their lifestyles and their wines.

All of the vintners and restaurateurs in the book were interviewed personally at their facilities. This was no minor accomplishment in February, since it involved more than one visit in snow or sleet – plus a number on lovely, crisp, sunny days.

We want to express our deep gratitude to the vintners, restaurateurs, and their families and staff who graciously gave of their time and shared their experiences and family recipes. Without their enthusiastic help and support this book would not have been possible.

We also want to thank Bruce Zoecklein, state enologist at VPI, Blacksburg, and Dr. Tony Wolf, state vitaculturist, at the Fruit Research Laboratory in Winchester, for their invaluable assistance. Our thanks also to Jim and Sharon Livingston of Hartwood Vineyard in Falmouth for their valuable information about the industry and comments during the writing process. The Wine Marketing Program office, as well as the Agricultual Statistics Service, of the Virginia Department of Agriculture and Consumer Services were very helpful in getting us started and providing statistical data.

While we have provided a bibliography of reference material, there are several of these publications that warrant special mention. *The Vinifera Wine Growers Journal*, which started in 1974, provides a unique chronicle of events and developments of the Virginia wine industry. A research report published by the Accokeek Foundation (Maryland), entitled, "Heaven's Favourite Gift" contains a wealth of material on vitaculture in colonial Virginia. Three booklets written by Hudson Cattell and Lee Stauffer Miller are excellent descriptions of the three types of wine grapes grown in the eastern United States and Canada. Finally, the two books by Philip Wagner are invaluable guides to grape growing and wine making in the East.

We both hope that *Virginia Wine Country* will provide you with useful information and interesting recipes. We think you will be stimulated by the stories of the people involved in the fascinating Virginia wine industry. Most of all, we hope this book will encourage you to venture into the Virginia wine country to find out for yourself the Virginia wines you most enjoy.

Hilde and Allan Lee

Contents

Introduction

The wine country of Virginia has played a significant role in the history of our nation for over 350 years. The first permanent settlement in America was established here and many of the important battles of the Revolutionary and Civil Wars were fought here. It was also in the Virginia Wine Country where Thomas Jefferson tried so diligently to raise European type grapes. Although he was unsuccessful, Jefferson was a pioneer in developing America's appreciation of fine wines.

That same pioneering spirit and determination has carried down to the modern vintners of Virginia. They have had to learn grape growing and winemaking as they progressed – true on-the-job training. Since there was nobody around to guide themthey have had to be pioneers every step of the way. Many of the problems faced by Thomas Jefferson in his grape growing efforts were still problems in the 1960's and 1970's.

The backgrounds of the Virginia vintners are varied. There are airline pilots, farmers, investment bankers, nurserymen, engineers, civil service employees, college professors, and retired military – a cross section of rural and urban Virginians. Being a vintner is a second, even a third career. They have one thing in common - they love fine wine and want to produce it. In spite of all of the obstacles they have faced – climate, vine loss, crop loss, learning commercial wine making, and carving a place in the market – they have persevered to make world class wines in Virginia.

The reasons why these pioneers started wineries in Virginia were also varied. Most wanted a different lifestyle. Others had set a goal of eventually owning a vineyard and winery. For the professional farmers, raising grapes and making wine was an alternative to traditional crops. For many, winemaking had been a hobby that they turned into a commercial venture. For others, a vineyard was a recreational project which ultimately expanded to include a winery.

Growing grapes, making wine and operating a winery is not an eight hour-a-day, five day-a-week job. It takes long hours of hard work, in the summer heat and the winter cold, in damp wine cellars and in busy tasting rooms. The life of a vintner, particularly a Virginia vintner, is not an easy one. If the winery is small, it is family-operated. It takes the efforts of the entire family to make it succeed. There are many sacrifices, particularly by the vintners' wives. They not only help their husbands operate the winery and take care of the household, many work full-time outside the home as well.

On the weekends the winery and its tasting room become a joint activity for the whole family. A number of the vintners have full time jobs and tend the vineyards and winery on the weekends. Others devote full-time efforts to their vineyards and winery, The larger wineries employ managers, winemakers, and marketing directors to handle all of activities connected with growing grapes and making and selling wines.

Today, the Farm Winery is not only a way of life for the owners, it has become a part of the community. In the recent past, old time residents would have turned their noses up at a winery in their community. Today, many of the winery festivals are community social events, tourist attractions which benefit all the local businesspeople.

Thomas Jefferson was the nation's first connoisseur of wines. Through his own hospitality he promoted the concept that wine and food naturally go together. Today, wine is an integral part of the enjoyment of food. Winemakers take great delight in preparing and serving foods that complement their wines. The recipes of the wineries in this book are a sampling of some of dishes that do just that.As one would expect, the food styles of the Virginia wine families vary considerably. There are diverse backgrounds – French, Italian, German and Belgian - reflected in the recipes, which vary from ones that are simple to prepare to those that are more complicated and elegant.

Restaurant dining in Virginia is an important aspect of the wine country. Many of the restaurants located near wineries feature Virginia wines. Thus it is only fitting that these restaurants also be included in this book. Their stories, too, are interesting and varied.

The backgrounds of the restaurateurs range from long-time culinary professionals to those who have only recently opened a restaurant (often embarking on second or third careers. Many of these restaurants not only are known for their excellent cuisine, but are also located in historically significant buildings. It is the combination of history, atmosphere, good food, and wine which makes these establishments worthy places to visit and enjoy. You will find a wide range of restaurants described in the book; some are quite casual, while others contain the most elegant surroundings. Each restaurant has been selected for its local contribution to the *Virginia Wine Country*.

The recipes in this book range from appetizers to desserts, with a heavy focus on main dishes (most wines are selected to accompany the main course). Since Virginia is known for its seafood, many seafood recipes are included – fish, crab, shrimp, mussels and clams. Virginia ham, as old as the history of Virginia, also is prevalent in the entrée recipes. No book of recipes of Virginia would be complete without fried chicken, spoon bread, cornbread, and peanut soup. The recipes for these historic delicacies are from restaurants specializing in colonial dishes.

For the most part, the recipes in this book are as written by the vintner or restaurateur. Wine suggestions, where applicable, are those of the vintner or restaurateur. We hope the personal stories of Virginia vintners and restaurateurs will better acquaint you with the people who make up VIRGINIA WINE COUNTRY. Through these pages, we hope you will learn to enjoy Virginia wine and those who make it as much as we have.

A History of the Virginia Wine Industry

Colonial Times

The Thomas Jefferson Era

American Hybrids

Prohibition and 40 Years Beyond

The Capitol at Williamsburg

The settlers at Jamestown performed their first crush and made their first wine in 1609, within two years after they landed in America. The wine was made from wild native grapes, and their comments about the palatability of the wine were less than complimentary. Since that first attempt on the shores of the James River, wine growers in the eastern United States have suffered through 350 years of frustration from their attempts to grow and produce European types and styles of wine. Only in recent decades of the 20th century have vitacultural techniques developed to the point where European varieties of wine grapes, *vitis vinifera*, can be grown commercially in Virginia and other mid-Atlantic states.

However, this is getting ahead of the story. It's a story worth narrating; one involving a mixture of ignorance, determination, frustration, politics, and unquenchable entrepreneurial drive. It is a story that is still unfolding today.

The saga of winemaking in eastern United States is not confined to Virginia, although the Old Dominion has played a key role at various times. Its position between the northern states with their severe winters and shorter growing seasons and the hot, humid southern states has caused it to be a melting pot of approaches to grape growing and winemaking.

While Virginia ranks today among the leaders in development of vitacultural techniques on the Eastern Seaboard, winegrowing and winemaking all but disappeared in Virginia from around the turn of the century to the late 1970's. The recent renewal of winegrowing in Virginia resulted in part from advances in grape growing technology. It was spawned by a realization within the state in the 1970's that the state needed to diversify its agricultural base, particularly away from heavy reliance on tobacco and livestock.

COLONIAL TIMES

While the making of wine was not uppermost in the minds of the English settlers at Jamestown, it was considered a natural staple of life and expectations that it could be produced in America were justifiably high. The English were heavy consumers of wine by the end of the 16th century, and it had been the basis of controversy and treaties between England and several countries of Europe including France, Germany, and particularly Portugal. The Virginia Company, chartered by King James I to exploit the economic opportunities of the New World on the mid-Atlantic Coast, had looked forward to developing a wine industry and thereby reducing England's dependence on the European continent for wine. As the colony developed, settlers hoped wine growing would help make them become self-sufficient.

Reports by various explorers had touted the wine producing potential of America based on their enthusiasm over seeing the proliferation of native grapes. Early explorers recorded how they could smell the ripened grapes even before reaching shore and had found them floating in the ocean near shore where the waves had knocked them off the vines. It was assumed, therefore, that if native grapes could grow with such profusion in the wild, cultivated European grapes would perform at least as well. Captain John Smith, Lord Delaware and other officials of the Company wrote glowing reports from Jamestown back to the home office in London about the winegrowing potential of Virginia. They urged the London Company to diversify into wine.

There are a number of historical references to continued but unsuccessful efforts by the colonists in Virginia to produce drinkable wine. By 1611, vineyard specialists had been designated within the colony. By 1618, French winegrowers (called vignerons) had been sent over by the Company to accelerate the development of a wine industry. The colonists requested that slips and seeds of European vine stocks be sent over, as they had concluded wine from native grapes was close to unpalatable. Immigrants to America from throughout Europe started arriving with cuttings of vines from their homeland. None of these efforts were successful.

Legislative Solutions

In 1623, the Virginia House of Burgesses passed an act requiring each free man to set aside a quarter-acre for the planting of vines, herbs, roots, etc. The following year, this was made more specific by declaring that 4 mulberry trees and 20 vines were to be planted by the following February for every male in the family above the age of 20. (As it later turned out, the Virginia Company's attempts to develop a silk industry in the colony by cultivating silkworms on mulberry trees was no more successful than that of winegrowing.)

King James I criticized the Virginia Company for lack of progress in commercializing the colony. In 1621 the Company stated in one of their lists of accomplishments to the Crown that vignerons had planted vineyards, "In divers places of the colony ..... some of them containing ten thousand plants" (approximately 20 acres). Protestations of progress such as these were not sufficient, and in 1624 King James dissolved the Virginia Company, making Virginia a Crown Colony. The relatively massive planting of vines notwithstanding, little progress was made. Governor Francis West and elected members of the House of Burgesses wrote to London in 1628 that, " ...with respect to the planting of vines, they have great hope that it will prove a beneficial commodity; but the vignerons sent here either did not understand the business or concealed their skill; for they spent their time to little purpose."

In 1631, still trying to generate an adequate amount of decent wine, the General Assembly passed an act that put the blame on the French winegrowers for failure to produce commercial quantities of quality wine. The act stated,"Frenchmen, having failed in the culture of vines, are not permitted to plant any tobacco." The following year, the Assembly passed an act that required corn and tobacco farmers to plant 20 vines per person "upon penaltie to forfeite one barrell of corne for every one that shall make default, one half to be to him which shall make the information thereof and the other half to public use. And the commissioners for the monthly courts shall have full power to hear and determine this matter and to see that the said vines be weeded, tended and well preserved."

The frustration over the inability of the colony to produce sufficient wine was clearly shown by both the officials appointed by the Crown and the locally elected members of the House of Burgesses. This concern about wine in a time of incredible hardship and danger from disease and Indian massacre points up the importance of wine in the everyday eating and social habits of the English settlers. Of the 7500 immigrants that had arrived in Virginia by 1624 only 1100 had survived. Even with a growing influx of new settlers every year, by 1634 the population had only reached 5000.

Importance of Tobacco

While grape growing wasn't succeeding, tobacco production was expanding rapidly. Virginia proved ideal for the raising of a sweet, mild tobacco from the Caribbean. Introduced in 1612, tobacco production grew to 20,000 pounds by 1619. In 1627, production had risen to 500,000 pounds. Since the processing of the dried tobacco was done in England, one Virginian involved in raising tobacco kept three workers employed in England.

By the 1630's, the commercial success of the colony was almost entirely dependent on tobacco. It became the currency of exchange. Prices and even wages were quoted in pounds of tobacco. As soon as a colonist could obtain land, he planted tobacco. Skilled trades people left their trade to become tobacco farmers. The House of Burgesses finally passed a law in 1633 requiring gunsmiths, carpenters, joiners, brickmakers and other craftsmen to stick to their trades.

The General Assembly kept trying to diversify the economy. In 1657, they enacted a law specifying that, "For the better encouragement of the inhabitants for the making of staple commodities in this colony, ... what person or persons soever shall at any time hereafter make .... two tuns of wine (302 American gallons) raised out of a vineyard made in this colony shall be given him by this country for an encouragement ten thousand pounds of Virginia tobacco."As far as the record shows, no farmer was ever able to obtain such a reward.

The Williamsburg Experiment

One hundred years later, the colonists were still trying. The General Assembly in Williamsburg, in its continuing effort to create a wine industry, passed legislation in 1769 called "An Act for the Encouragement of the Making of Wine." This Act stated that because of the suitability of the soil and climate of York County for the production of "most delicious wine ..... it is certain that the introduction of so valuable an article would bring riches to the people and give a very favorable turn to the commerce of the mother country." A Board of Trustees was established and authorized to purchase up to 100 acres of land for the purpose of cultivating vines. A Mr. Andrew Estave, a French vineyardist, was appointed vitaculturist and winemaker. Authorization was given to the Trustees to purchase three Negro men slaves and two poor boys (the latter to be assigned as apprentices to the winemaker). Mr. Estave was to be given title to the land and the slaves if he could produce ten hogsheads of good commercial wine within six years.

Before this experiment could reach fruition, the Assembly ran out of patience and money. They rescinded the Act in 1776 and declared York County "unfit" for the production of wine. This is where the Virginia wine scene stood as Virginia declared independence from Great Britain and ceased to exist as a colony of Englishmen, with all of the heritage that implied. The fact that the Burgesses (of which Thomas Jefferson was a member) took such a strong stand on wine at a time when they were laying their future and their lives on the line must say something about how important they felt wine was to their well-being.

Underlying colonial officialdom's sense of futility and despair, progress *was* being made – or at least conclusions were being drawn. While Mr. Estave's efforts were considered a failure by the House of Burgesses in 1776, three years before that he had publicly switched his own allegiance for the future from viniferas to native American grapes. In the March 18, 1773 issue of the *Virginia Gazette*, Estave is quoted as saying, "It is my humble Opinion, that the native Vines of the Country can alone be cultivated with Success." Other knowledgeable vineyardists and plantation owners were also arriving at the same conclusion. However, it would be another 50 to 75 years before this conclusion would be generally recognized and American grapes would be cultivated on a commercial scale in the eastern United States.

The Vines Were The Problem

Why were the colonial planters meeting with such failures with European grape varieties after 150 years of trying? Why did they continue to keep trying when failure seemed inevitable?

Failure with the European varietals was due to the delicate nature of these exotic vines. The cold winters and hot, humid summers of the mid-Atlantic region of North America were simply not suitable for this species of grapes at that time in history. (A different conclusion is being developed today as will be discussed later).

At the time, few vinifera vines survived more than one or two winters. The problems included drought, black rot and mildew from the humid summers, root aphids (*phylloxera*), caterpillars, cold winter weather destruction of roots and stems, spring frost destruction of buds and leaves, and many others.

During the 1600's, the tendency was to blame the incompetence or laziness of the vineyardists. Later, as farmers gained experience, they tried to cope with the weather by planting in locations with favorable microclimates. They used dry cow dung for smudges when they anticipated frost. Attempts to combat vinifera-killing phylloxera included coating roots with "cow dung or animal grease". Cut worms were attacked with coatings of tar or lard on the roots. Attempts to repel caterpillars could involve the application of the blood of a goat or the lard of a bear. Mildew and rot were simply cut away. The "yellows" (leaves) were thought to result from bad fertilizer or overbearing, the cure for which was manure and pruning.

In spite of these seemingly insurmountable problems, farmers and plantation owners continued to experiment with European wine grapes. They kept trying because success would have meant large profits on this high-value agricultural product. The market was there, both in the colonies and especially in England. Further, as loyal citizens of England, grape growing was the patriotic thing to do. On the other hand the risks were obviously high. Only the wealthy could afford to experiment since it took six years to bring a vineyard into production, and failure was likely. Most farmers were limited to planting tobacco since it generated needed cash flow in one year.

Pressure From English Press

For 150 years, both private and public interests in England pushed Virginians and other colonists to develop a wine industry. One enthusiastic commentator in England published a pamphlet in the mid-1600's stating that, "God and nature have pointed them a soyle out with their own finger....[and to ignore such advantages would be]... an affront to Nature." A particularly persuasive writer named Edward Williams wrote in 1650 that growing grapes had the advantages of personal profit, pleasures of the cup, and patriotic duty. He wrote that vitaculture in America, "would be a staple which would enrich this country [England] to the envy of France and Spain, and furnish the Northern parts of Europe, and China ... with the Noblest Wine in the World and at no excessive prices."

These types of exhortations continued up to the Revolution. In 1775 the author of *The American Husbandry* made the plea that planters should grow grapes to free them from the relentless debt of tobacco. A Robert Bolling wrote in the *Virginia Gazette* in 1773 that the benefits to the Empire of grape growing were cheaper Madiera, greater flow of money to England, greater demand for English products in the colonies, better internal commerce in the colonies and improved subsistence for poor farmers. A French vitaculturist, apparently speaking for the interests of the Empire stated, "Why then do we hesitate where everything promises success?. ...in a word, honour, independence, wealth, stretch out their hands to us: shall we be wanting to ourselves?" In spite of all of this constant hammering, a commercial wine industry would not develop in the colonies until early in the 1800's – 25 years after the colonies became independent.

Colonial Drinking Customs

Since there was no wine industry during colonial times, what did people drink? Colonial Virginia was an agrarian economy and most people grew berries, apples and peaches. Consequently, they would ferment the juice of these fruits and make mobby (brandy) and cider. Farmers picked wild grapes and made wine for home consumption. Wine that was produced for sale required 25% brandy for purposes of preservation. They also made their own beer.

Since there were no supermarkets or liquor stores at the time, the only other sources of beverages were local distilleries and breweries, or the local inns and taverns. The latter usually served beer, ale and rum. The better establishments also served imported Port, Madiera and brandy. The absence of a domestic wine industry in those formative years probably set the tone of drinking habits in Virginia that still exist today.

The citizens of Virginia and the other colonies had to rely for the most part on England as their source of alcoholic beverages which included rum, Port, Madiera and other highly fortified spirits. The local wine was made from native American grapes, typically from the Scuppernong grape of the *vitis rotundifolia* (or Muscadine) species. This was the same grape that the original settlers used to make wine starting in 1609, and its palatability probably had not improved much in the interim (although wine from the Scuppernong continues to have an intense and loyal following in the Southeast). Only the gentry and the wealthy merchants could afford the fine wines of Europe.

Those who did attempt to make home wine from native grapes found it necessary to modify the taste with various flavorings, including myrtle and other berries, orange and lemon peel, grape and other wild blossoms. Honey and brandy (up to 3 gallons for every 10 gallons of juice) were added for sugar as well as flavoring and preservation.

Wine was used for medicinal purposes. It was used by itself to relax patients or to dilute the taste of the more unpalatable medicines of the times. Since decent wine had to be imported, it was expensive. More than one apothecary or plantation owner grew what grapes they could in order to make home wine and avoid the high cost of imported wine. Landon Carter wrote in 1764, "I never had so much sickness in my family as this year, and the expense in such times is very great in Wine to gruels, Wine to drinks, and Wine to Vomits and bitters." He reportedly used camomile dissolved in wine to calm hysterical females, and opium in wine to cure small pox. Many other remedies for various ailments involved the use of wine.

It was within this political, economic and social setting that Thomas Jefferson began to make his contribution to the development of the American wine industry, both within Virginia and throughout the colonies.

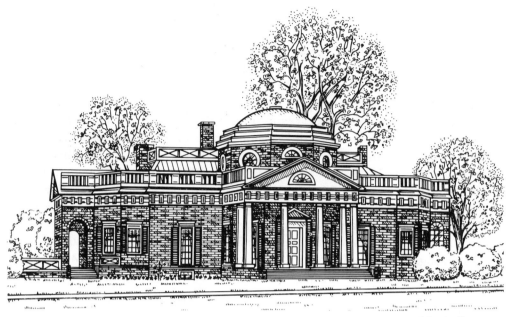

Monticello

THE THOMAS JEFFERSON ERA

There is no record that Thomas Jefferson ever produced palatable wine at Monticello during more than 30 years of experimentation. His contribution to the development of wine in Virginia and the nation is that he became the nation's first wine connoisseur. Jefferson's heritage to America's appreciation of wine has undoubtedly been more lasting than any technical triumph he might have made in the vineyard.

Jefferson first planted grapes at Monticello soon after moving there in 1770. The vine cuttings were obtained from George Wythe in Williamsburg. During the following 55 years, he continued to experiment with all types of crops in a continuing effort to determine which were best suited to Virginia's soil and climate. He was concerned about Virginia's overdependence on tobacco and believed that wine growing was one of the means farmers could use to diversify.

Philip Mazzei

In 1773, Philip Mazzei arrived in America for the purpose of forming a joint venture of plantation owners (including Washington, Jefferson and Madison) to raise grapes and, hopefully, olives and lemons. Soon after arriving, he visited Jefferson, who took to him immediately and gave him 2000 acres adjoining Monticello.

Mazzei believed the land was ideally suited to wine grapes and brought over additional vine slips and vignerons from Italy. He did have early success in making wine, although his vignerons refused to drink it and sold the wine locally. Unfortunately for the Virginia wine industry, but fortunately for the nation, this energetic and personable Italian became bitten by the Revolutionary fever and neglected his agricultural pursuits. In 1778, Jefferson and Patrick Henry arranged to send Mazzei to Italy to borrow money for support of the Virginia war effort. The vineyards deteriorated and ultimately were destroyed in 1780 by the horses of a Hessian general who had rented the property from Mazzei.

Jefferson continued to pursue his agricultural experiments, although intermittently during his career of public service which ended in 1809. He continued to grow grapes and encouraged others to do so, based on his belief that Mazzei was correct in his judgment that Virginia provided a suitable environment for winegrowing.

Wine in the White House

During his many years of public service, Jefferson served as wine advisor to four Presidents and to many of the other founding fathers. His appreciation of fine food and wine was further enhanced by his appointment as Ambassador to France during George Washington's administration. When Jefferson was later elected President, he became famous for his banquets and dinners at the White House which typically included unique European foods and fine wines from France, Germany, Italy and Austria.

Until Jefferson's time, very little table or sparkling wine was consumed in America – table wine being the relatively dry wine we enjoy with food today. In 1776, when the Declaration of Independence was signed, the first *vitis vinifera* vines (called the Mission Grape) were just being planted by the Spanish missionaries in California. It would be another one hundred years before wine from the European *vinifera* varietals would be produced in California in any quantity.

One of Jefferson's major contributions to the enjoyment of wine in America was the creation among our founding fathers and their peers of an appreciation of European wines – not merely French but also Italian, German, Austrian, Portuguese and Spanish. The leading figures of his time sought his advice on how to select, serve and enjoy fine European wine. At George Washington's request, Jefferson selected the first wines stocked at the White House.

During his 8 years in the White House (1801-1809), Jefferson hosted dinners four or five times each week. Several times a week he would invite 8-10 members of Congress from both parties. Invitations usually specified dinner at "half after three" with after-dinner conversation accompanied by wine going into the night. Generally, wine would be served after the meal. It was the custom in those days for each guest to make a toast of some sort. Jefferson deviated from this custom with the philosophy that, "You drink as you please, and converse at your ease." The conversation was apparently both easy and stimulating. As one frequent visitor reported about dinner with Jefferson,"an elegant mental treat." John Quincy Adams – no friend of

Jefferson at the time – commented, "You never can be an hour in this man's company without something of the marvelous."

During the Jefferson Presidency, White House food and wine bills were understandably high. In his first year as President, food costs totaled $6500 and wine $2400. At today's prices these would total approximately $150,000 and $55,000 respectively. In spite of this comparatively lavish spending on wine, Jefferson drank rather sparingly – usually one or possibly two glasses of wine after dinner. He did not touch harder spirits. Jefferson once commented that he attributed his long life to his love for vegetables and greens, and his preference for wine instead of liquor.

Political Position on Wine

Jefferson was an active and continuous importer of European wines. While Ambassador to France from 1785 to 1789, Thomas Jefferson visited each of the principal winegrowing regions of Europe and recorded his impressions. He studied the champagne making process at Epernay in detail. When purchasing wine, he preferred to deal directly with vineyard and winery owners throughout France, Germany and other European countries. His tastes were specific and knowledgeable.

While President, Jefferson did not hesitate to express his personal opinion on the state of the wine industry in the United States. In a letter dated 1808 to one of his wine colleagues in France, he commented that, "We could, in the United States, make as great a variety of wines as are made in Europe, not exactly of the same kinds, but doubtless as good. Yet I have ever observed to my countrymen, who think its introduction important, that a laborer cultivating wheat, rice, tobacco or cotton here will be able with the proceeds to purchase double the quantity of the wine he could make."

Jefferson had concluded that unlike the other crops, wine could not be grown and produced commercially in the United States in competition with France. He also had concluded that each country should concentrate on the production of those commodities that it was best suited to produce. He was an early proponent of free trade, having observed when in France, the damage high tariffs were doing to agricultural trade in Europe. He took a strong position within the government regarding the advantages of keeping tariffs low on European wine. Jefferson went so far as to develop a classification system for European wine for purposes of keeping imported wine as inexpensive as possible for his fellow countrymen.

By 1809, Jefferson became more hopeful that America could develop its own wine industry. He wrote to John Adlum, an American grape grower who Jefferson admired, "I think it would be well to push the culture of that grape [a native American hybrid called the Alexander] without losing our time and efforts in search of foreign vines which it will take centuries to adapt to our soil and climate." He was not as supportive of the Scuppernong, however, as in 1822 he commented to a prospective Scuppernong grower in South Carolina, "The Scuppernong of North Carolina will succeed here .... however, [it] is more desirable for domestic use than profitable as an occupation for market."

Jefferson pushed the concept that wine was a gentler and therefore healthier alcoholic beverage than the harder spirits. He often commented to his countrymen that, "In countries which use ardent spirits, drunkenness is the mortal vice; but in those which make wine for common use, you never see a drunkard." Another famous quotation of Jefferson is that, "No nation is drunken where wine is cheap and none sober where the dearness of wine substitutes ardent spirits as the common beverage ..."

As the Jefferson era came to a close, the country had made little progress in establishing a domestic wine industry. Signs of progress were evident, however. As mentioned earlier, Jefferson was excited about the the American hybrid called the Alexander. He also seems to have abandoned his concept – at least with respect to winegrowing -- that each country should produce only what it can do best. In 1811 he wrote to John Dortie:

> "...I am come over to your opinion that ... we must endeavor to make everything we want within ourselves, and have as little intercourse as possible with Europe in its present demoralized state. Wine being among the earliest luxuries in which we indulge ourselves, it is desirable it should be made here and we have every soil, aspect and climate of the best countries, and I have myself drunk wines made in this state and in Maryland, of the quality of the best Burgundy...."

Wines made from American hybrids had begun to show up, and Jefferson had recognized their worth.

AMERICAN HYBRIDS

By the time of the American Revolution, most experienced planters such as George Washington had given up trying to grow *vitis vinifera* grapes. We can look back today and wonder why it took them 200 years to arrive at that conclusion. However, it must be kept in mind that the benefits of success were high, and the alternative of drinking wine made from native grapes was abhorrent to the upper class of plantation owners. Further, the scientific approach to experimentation had not arrived as yet, and the ability to infer causation from often conflicting data was not well developed.

Fortunately, time and nature intervened to help relieve much of the frustration. The first truly palatable wine from native American-grown grapes began to emerge as the country entered the 1800's. Attempts to grow European *vitis vinifera* grapes over the previous 200 years had permitted nature to create hybrids by cross-pollination with the native grapes. This cross-pollination had produced varietals with a wide range of unique characteristics. In general, these hybrids exhibited the hardiness of the American parent, yet they also exhibited some of the finesse and complexity in flavor of the European parent. The most popular of these American hybrids were the Alexander (also called Cape of Good Hope),

Norton, Catawba, Isabella, Niagara, Concord, and Delaware – most of which are still being grown today.

While the difficulties associated with winegrowing in the eastern portion of North America has been mentioned before, it is worth repeating that the United States has two grape growing environments. One is the Mediterranean-like climate of California, with its mild winters and long dry summers. In this environment, the vinifera found a natural habitat. The other region, which is generally east of the Rocky Mountains, is termed a continental rather than maritime climate, with very cold winters and hot, humid summers coupled with frequent rain. The eastern United States lacks the moderating effect of the maritime climates in the winegrowing regions of Europe. In the more vigorous American climate, the delicate vinifera grapes find a hostile environment and become subject to insect attacks above and below ground, as well as mildew, rot and freezing.

The native grapes of the East, on the other hand have hardy roots – almost like tree trunks – accompanied by vigorous vines with thick skinned berries containing an abundance of seeds. These species of grapes have long since adapted themselves to the harsh clime in which they live and procreate. Unfortunately, Mother Nature had put her best efforts into procreation and little into those characteristics that would make their fruit enjoyable to man as a wine.

The *vitis labrusca* species is the most common base for American hybrids. Its varietal offspring vary in flavor, but generally have been described as having one of four distinct savors: foxy (wet dog); perfumy (floral); strawberry(cotton candy); and methyl anthranilate (bubble gum). Labrusca grapes generally have low sugar and high acid content. Water and sugar must frequently be added to wine from the native grapes of this species in order to make a palatable wine.

Era of the Amateur Viticulturist

The 1800's can be characterized as the era of the amateur viticulturist. During this period farmers, nurserymen, home gardeners and hobbyists vied for the honor of discovering a better wine hybrid. Generally, these hybrids were based on the *labrusca* and *riparia* species. Heated debates took place in various journals over the origins, quality and discoverers of hundreds of hybrids. Hybridizers used trial and error, coupled with intuition based on experience. This process more nearly paralleled that of an Easter egg hunt than scientific research. The tools and rigor of science were not applied to grapegrowing until the late 1800's.

In the early years, there were a number of attempts to classify American vitaculture. In 1773, Philip Mazzei reported counting over 200 varieties on his property near Monticello. John Adlum, Jefferson's friend, published *A Memoir on the Cultivation of the Vine in America* in 1823. The first definitive effort, however, was by C. S. Rafinesque in 1830 in a privately printed book entitled, *American Manual of The Grape Vine* . He defined fifteen distinct species in the Chesapeake Bay region. William Byrd, in his natural history of Virginia in the mid-1700's, classified Virginia's grapes into six categories.

Since 1900, much progress has been made to properly classify and establish the heritage of American grape varieties. One of the most pioneering efforts was published in 1909 by Thomas V. Munson entitled, *Foundation of American Grape Culture*. Munson, who resided in Denison, Texas, is considered one of the world's greatest hybridizers. He and a fellow breeder in Missouri named Hermann Jaeger shipped thousands of American root stocks to France during the phylloxera epidemic of 1860-80. In 1888, they received the French Legion of Honor Cross for "Merite Agricole" in recognition of their contribution. A more recent effort of classification, and one that is widely used today, was published by U. P. Hedrick in 1924 in his book entitled, *Manual of American Grape Growing*. Dr. Hedrick headed the New York State Agricultural Station in Geneva New York in the early 1900's.

The currently accepted classification of grape species that are grown in Virginia are:

Vitis Labrusca – the so-called fox grape, having a strong "wild" flavor; the species most common in Virginia and in the American hybrids tends to have low sugar and high acid content; wild flavor ameliorates somewhat with age.

Vitis Rotundifolia – grows primarily in the South, including southeastern Virginia; has a sweet taste and some foxy flavor; is characterized by the well-known Scuppernong variety; frequently also referred to as the Muscadine family; vines resistant to most diseases.

Vitis Aestivalis – grows in most states in the East, including Virginia; the American parent of the Norton hybrid; has high sugar content with good sugar-acid balance for wine.

Vitis Riparia – grows in northern half of United States, including Virginia; the American parent in many hybrids including a French-American hybrid called Baco Noir; most early ripening and winter-hardy of the native American species.

Vitis Vinifera – the species of Europe, originally from the Middle East; phenomenally successful in California and rapidly becoming practical in Virginia – particularly the Chardonnay, Riesling, and Cabernet Sauvignon varieties; a delicate species susceptible to insects, cold, humidity, and disease.

Commercialized American Hybrids

The Alexander is considered the first American-bred wine grape to receive widespread attention. It is a cross between the *vinifera* and the *labrusca* families and was discovered by James Alexander, gardener to the son of Governor William Penn of Pennsylvania around 1740. Extensive acreage began to appear around the year 1800. The Alexander was the hybrid Jefferson nominated as the replacement for attempts to grow European varietals, as mentioned earlier in his letter to John Adlum.

Around 1820, John Adlum discovered a hybrid which he called the Catawba in recognition of its origin near the Catawba River in North Carolina. He cultivated the vines on his farm, called The Vineyard, in what is now Rock Creek Park in Washington, D.C. After tasting a bottle of Catawba sent to him by Adlum, Jefferson wrote back, "...[the Catawba] is a truly fine wine, of high flavor, and, as you assure me, there is not a drop of brandy in it...." Wine from the Catawba continues to be popular in various parts of Virginia and other eastern states even today.

In the 1830's, a Dr. D. N. Norton of Richmond domesticated an American hybrid called the Norton Virginia (also called Cynthia). Many consider this red wine grape as one of the best of all of the American hybrids. The wine from this grape became famous as Virginia Claret and won awards on both sides of the Atlantic in the 1870's and 1880's. The production of wine from this grape in Virginia reached over 230,000 gallons (95,000 cases) by 1880, making Virginia a significant producer of American-made wine. The Norton was ideally suited for Virginia and very little grew elsewhere. Charlottesville became known as the "capital of the Virginia wine belt" since most of the vineyards were nearby.

The Norton grape had the advantage over previous hybrids of not having the foxy taste so overwhelming in native grapes and other American hybrids. The term foxy refers to the rather wild flavor common to the *vitis labrusca* family of grapes; many people relate the taste to the smell of a wet fox or dog. Extensive hybridizing has not completely removed this overwhelming characteristic.

The fever of hybridizing started to die down in America in the 1850's. By then, the eastern vintners had pretty well settled on the Delaware, Concord, and Catawba hybrid varietals. The Delaware was derived from a combination of *labrusca, aestivalis* and *vinifera* species. It was developed in New Jersey in 1849, but initially became famous for plantings around Delaware, Ohio for which it was named. The Concord, which is still grown in Virginia as a table grape,was developed in Massachusetts in 1854. It is a *labrusca* -based hybrid used now mainly for grape juice and jelly. The Catawba and the Delaware are still used for the cuvée of many fine eastern champagnes.

In the early 1900's, another famous wine appeared with a Virginia label, causing many people today to assume it was grown and produced in Virginia. This is the famous Virginia Dare label developed by Paul Garrett, produced initially in North Carolina and sold throughout the United States. The grape used in this wine was the Scuppernong which grows in North Carolina and other southeastern states but only in the southeastern corner of Virginia. It is a member of the Muscadine or *vitis rotundifolia* family of grapes. Garrett selected the name, not out of deference to the state of Virginia, but to avoid the regional connotation suggested by the Scuppernong grape. The name he chose refers to the first English child born in America.

Virginia Peaked in 1850's

Virginia reached its peak wine production in the 1850's, just prior to the Civil War. After that period, production started to fall off and vineyards were plowed under. This was in contrast to North Carolina, where Scuppernong wine production was focused, which doubled production from 1860 to 1900. While volume declined in Virginia, the quality of the wine remained high into the 1900's as Prohibition approached. Virginia Claret won several awards at the Paris Exposition of 1900. A typical vineyard in Virginia during the mid-to-late 1800's would have contained a mix of American hybrids such as Catawba, Delaware, Concord, and Norton.

There were a number of reasons for the drop-off in production during and after the Civil War. First, many of the battles of the Civil War were fought in and around Virginia vineyard lands. Consequently, vineyards were destroyed, pilfering occurred, field and winery hands became scarce, transporting the wine to market became almost impossible and many of the vineyard owners themselves went off to fight. Then, following the war, California wines began to flood the market. In 1860, California represented only 15% of total U.S. production, but by 1880 it was producing over 60%. Compounding this unfavorable trend, the southern states, counties and cities began to vote dry in the 1880's, further shrinking the market for Virginia wines. By the time Virginia went dry in 1914, there were few vineyards left within the state.

Ironically, the disastrous phylloxera epidemic in France and Europe during the 1870's that almost destroyed the European wine industry, did not affect Virginia. It neither destroyed Virginia vines nor stimulated the market for the wine. The irony is that the insect that caused the epidemic could well have come from the mid-Atlantic area through shipments of experimental American hybrid plants to England. As touched on earlier, native American vines with their hardy trunk-like roots are resistant to this root louse, and the European wine industry was saved by the expediency of grafting *vinifera* canes onto American root stock.

PROHIBITION AND 40 YEARS BEYOND

The Prohibition movement in Virginia started with the formation of the Anti-Saloon League of Virginia in 1901. This was followed two years later by the passage of the Mann Act by the Virginia legislature which severely limited the operation of saloons in places with fewer than 500 inhabitants. The Mann Act resulted in the immediate closing of 500 of Virginia's 2500 saloons. In 1914, the Virginia voters passed a referendum outlawing the sale of alcoholic beverages, statewide. Congress made Prohibition nationwide in 1919. While the Virginia legislation had permitted householders to purchase one quart of liquor, three gallons of beer, or one gallon of wine per month from outside the state, the federal legislation was more stringent and abolished all purchases.

By the time Virginia passed its legislation, grape growing in the state had declined to 300 acres, from a high of approximately 600 acres in 1860. During Prohibition, Virginia maintained approximately 300 acres of vineyards and produced 2000 tons of grapes each year – table grapes and grapes for home winemakers. Unfortunately, Virginia did not benefit from the binge in home winemaking during Prohibition, which resulted in almost a doubling of vineyard acreage nationwide, between 1919 and 1928.

Immediately following repeal of Prohibition, Captain Paul Garrett reintroduced his famous Virginia Dare wine. He tried to encourage Virginia farmers to plant the Norton grape and make Virginia Claret, famous back in the late 1800's. Unfortunately, the market for wine in the middle Atlantic and southern states had not developed yet, as many of the states and counties were still dry. Further, the "dries" in Congress were still powerful enough to prevent the government from using federal funds to finance farmers who wanted to plant wine grapes.

The effect of Prohibition on Virginia was to kill the Virginia wine industry for 50 years. By 1960, grape acreage in Virginia had declined to slightly over 15 acres – all table grapes. Only a few wineries reopened in Virginia after repeal and fewer still remained opened through World War II. The nucleus of expertise in winegrowing and wine making had essentially disappeared within the Virginia farm community by the turn of the century and did not return until 1970.

Modern Revitalization

French Hybrids

Introduction of Vinifera

Cooperative and Governmental Contributions

The Future

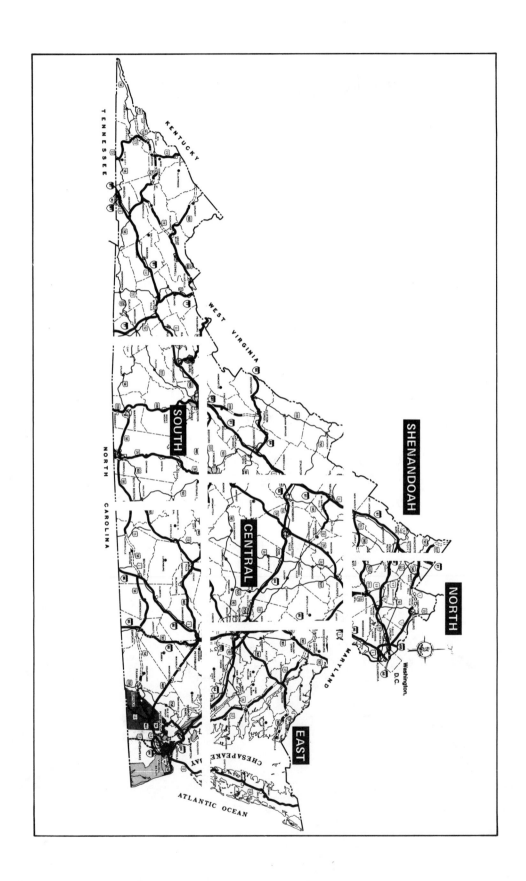

During the 1960's, Virginia began to experience a revival of its grape industry. After over 100 years of decline, acreage began to grow from a base of 16 acres in 1960 to 750 acres by the end of 1982. A recently completed survey by the state shows that Virginia vineyard acreage in 1987 has further grown to 1220 acres.

This amount of grape planting is hardly significant when compared to the 343,000 acres planted in California or the 39,000 acres in the next largest state, New York. It does, however, place Virginia in the top ten winegrowing states.

Annual production of wine in Virginia is approaching 300,000 gallons (125,000 cases) per year which exceeds the highest production previously attained in the mid-1800's. There are currently 34 wineries and 175 vineyard owners in Virginia, and these numbers are growing monthly.

What caused this renewal of activity in grape growing in the Old Dominion? A number of favorable trends coincided in the 1970's to make winemaking attractive again in Virginia. First, the demand for wine throughout the nation had risen substantially as the drier table wines became accepted as the "in" drink for moderate drinkers and the beverage to drink with food. Second, the growth in population of the Washington D.C. metropolitan area and the western movement of suburbia into Virginia created a built-in market for local wines. Third, the farm community began to look around for alternative crops as prices fell for livestock, tobacco, grain, and other farm products.

Coupled with the increase in demand for wine, was the development of a group of landowners who had come to appreciate fine wine – many as a result of sojourns to the European wine areas. This group included active military and civil government personnel, as well as farmers and business people. Generally, there was some type of farming on their property, such as raising cattle, corn, tobacco, grain, and fruit orchards. Others had started new activities such as tree farms and plant nurseries.

By the early 1970's, the feasibility of raising wine grapes in the middle Atlantic region was being publicized by pioneering growers. The climate in Virginia and Maryland has always been more suitable for wine grape growing than the cold winter states to the north and the hot summer states to the south. True winemakers are a hardy lot – and perhaps slightly masochistic. To these landowners, talk about growing wine grapes in Virginia was like giving a shot of adrenalin to a race horse. They were off and running.

The first of the new vineyards began appearing in the late 1960's, but real growth started in the early 1970's. In 1960, only 16 acres of commercial vineyards existed in Virginia. These consisted of American hybrids–mostly Concord table grapes. By 1970, plantings of American hybrids had risen to 30 acres (the increase was all in Concord). However, several of the modern pioneers had by then planted 9 acres of French hybrid wine grapes. By 1978, American hybrid acreage had doubled to 60 acres; however, the French hybrid had increased by a factor of 10 to 90 acres. The total acreage was still small by commercial standards, but the seed (or one might say, "cuttings") had been planted.

FRENCH HYBRIDS

What are the French hybrids? They are, like the American hybrids, crosses between *vitis vinifera* and American species except they were developed in France. While the term American hybrid refers to varietals developed through cross-pollination in the wilds of eastern United States, French hybrid refers to varieties systematically developed by French hybridizers in the late 1800's and early 1900's.

Backtracking one more step, hybridizing is an age old practice in agriculture and, in fact, is Mother Nature's way of allowing her offspring to accommodate to new environments. Random hybridizing in the wild can take centuries for a new variety to stabilize – as was the case with the American hybrids. Professional hybridizing takes at least 10 years, and can take up to 40 years, to achieve a commercially viable hybrid. Professional hybridizers consider themselves successful if they can achieve one new variety out of 1000 seedlings during that period.

Once a new hybrid has been developed, viticulturists (vineyard specialists) work with cuttings rather than seeds or seedlings. The cuttings assure maintenance of the selected hybrid, while seeds can become further hybridized by stray pollen from other species or varieties.

Another approach used by viticulturists to achieve the desired results in the vineyard is the grafting of one varietal onto the roots of another. During the crisis of the phylloxera epidemic in Europe, which started in the mid-1860's, this was the method used to save the European wine industry. Vinifera cuttings were drafted onto American varietal root stocks which are much hardier and resist most insects and diseases. This continues to be the practice today for the majority of vines growing in Europe, as well as in the United States.

As the phylloxera crisis began to wane in Europe by 1890, private French hybridizers began to develop varieties called direct producers (producteurs directs). The purpose of this effort was to develop varieties that combined the hardy character of the American vine with the European vinifera flavor characteristics without the need for grafting. Also, it had been found that many of the American root stocks could not tolerate, as could the vinifera, the high pH caused by lime in the French soil. Finally, such hybrids would also reduce the cost of fungicide spraying in the vineyards. In selecting American root stock for one of the parents, these hybridizers avoided using a *vitis labrusca* variety because of the unwelcomed foxy flavor it contributes to the offspring. In general, they preferred to use the *vitis riparia* species.

There were a number of these individual hybridizers working in France around the turn of the century. Some of those whose names are associated with French hybrids grown in Virginia today are Francois Baco, Georges

Couderc, Albert Seibel, Bertille Seyve, J. L. Vidal, and Victor Villard. Seyve married the daughter of Victor Villard in 1919, and produced a number of hybrids under the name Seyve-Villard.

These hybrids did surprisingly well in France. By 1929, there were 500,000 acres planted and by 1958, almost 1 million acres, or one third of the total vineyard acreage in France. In the 1950's, the French government took steps to curtail the use of hybrids because the hybrid farmers in the north were making bulk wine in competition with major producers of bulk wine in southern France and Algeria. Still today, however, hybrid acreage in France is comparable to the total acreage of vinifera planted in the United States, including California.

The French hybrids began to find their way to North America at the turn of the century, but during the following 40 years acquisitions were small and mainly for experimental purposes. It wasn't until the end of World War II that French hybrids began to be planted commercially for winemaking in America.

During the War, the few North American experimenters who knew of these varietals – mainly in New York and Ontario – were unable to obtain vines. But when they again became available in 1945, several members of the group started commercial plantings of French hybrids. Enough research had been done by then to convince this small band of pioneers that these vines were capable of making excellent wine. The best known of this group today are Adhemar de Chaunac, George Hostetter, Charles Fournier, and Philip Wagner who were all winemakers or nurserymen. Lesser known members of the group, but equally important, were a number of researchers at the Geneva Research Station in New York, and the Ontario research station at Vineland.

Vineyards and wineries of French hybrids began to spring up throughout the East. Federal law requiring a two year quarantine of all cuttings brought from France slowed expansion somewhat. However, there was no restriction on cuttings from Canada, so they were acquired from the nursery at Brights Wines Ltd., in Ontario, until sufficient cuttings could be obtained from Geneva and other U.S. agricultural stations. Phillip Wagner, who had started a nursery in Maryland in the early 1940's, became a major supplier of French hybrid cuttings.

As mentioned, the first plantings of French Hybrids in the Old Dominion did not occur until the 1960's. One of the earliest planters was Charles Raney, of Farfelu Vineyard, near Flint Hill in Northern Virginia. In 1966, he planted an experimental vineyard of French hybrids. Mr. Raney was, and still is, a United Airlines pilot who planted and cared for his vineyards between flights. His efforts and those of other pioneers, brought additional growers into the picture in the early 1970's.

Winegrowers in the 1970's continued to emphasize French hybrids – the vinifera explosion came soon after. Until the early 1980's, both the federal Department of Agriculture at their Beltsville, Maryland facility, and the state agricultural agency, Virginia Polytechnic Institute (VPI) at Blacksburg, Virginia, cautioned Virginia farmers against planting vinifera grapes. As is the nature of public agencies, they have an obligation to be conservative and minimize the economic risk for those who ask their advice.

The limitation of making wine from French hybrids in Virginia is that while they yield good wine, the urban buying public in the mid-Atlantic region has already developed a more sophisticated taste for European and California vinifera wines. It cannot be ignored that French hybrid varietals are used in France for blending their everyday table wines. On the other hand, it also cannot be ignored that in Virginia, these hybrids were instrumental in getting the Virginia wine industry on its feet.

In those early years, the market for Virginia-made wine was primarily with local wine enthusiasts. This mainly rural constituency grew up on the sweeter wines made from the Scuppernong grape of the South or the native *vitis labrusca* grapes of the mid-Atlantic region. The drier and more delicate wines depended on an acquired taste.

INTRODUCTION OF VINIFERA

One of the most noticeable pioneering achievements of the early 1970's was carried out at the Meredyth Vineyard, near Middletown, by Archie Smith, Jr. In 1972, he decided to start a vineyard and winery on his farm. Initially, he concentrated on French hybrids but started to plant vinifera varietals in 1974. Archie Jr. and his son, Archie III, have succeeded to the point where they are producing 18,000 cases of wine per year – 60% French hybrid and 40% vinifera. In terms of total production, Meredyth is currently third in size behind Prince Michel and Ingleside, both of which are producing 20,000 cases per year.

A second early pioneer was Elizabeth Furness. At the age of 75, Mrs. Furness decided to plant a vinifera vineyard of Semillon in 1973; the first commercial vinifera vineyard planted in Virginia since colonial times. Her decision to plant vinifera was made in spite of advice from agricultural specialists to the contrary. Piedmont Vineyards and Winery continues as one of the leading wineries in Virginia and the principal producer of Semillon.

This was the situation with respect to the growing of vinifera grapes in Virginia in 1976 when the Italian wine entrepreneur, Gianni Zonin, sent his trained agronomist, Gabriele Rausse, to the Charlottesville area to grow vinifera grapes and make wine in the European style. Zonin had purchased the 830 acre Barboursville Plantation – the estate of John Barbour who was Governor of Virginia (1812-1814) and a close friend of Thomas Jefferson. In spite of seemingly insurmountable technical, political, and cultural difficulties, Rausse succeeded. Today, Barboursville is one of the leading vineyards and wineries in Virginia, specializing in European style wines from European grapes.

The shift from growing predominantly French hybrid grapes to the vinifera happened even faster than the shift from American to French hybrids. As the following table shows, American hybrids lost out to the French hybrids around 1974, while the French hybrids lost out to the viniferas around 1980. Currently, over 65% of the 1220 acres of vineyards in Virginia are planted in vinifera.

GRAPE TYPE				ACRES OF VINEYARDS			
	1960	1970	1973	1976	1979	1982	1987 *
American Hybrid	16	30	30	47	57	75	85
French Hybrid		9	27	107	161	244	330
Vinifera			3	15	68	437	805
TOTAL ACREAGE	16	39	60	69	286	756	1220

NOTE *: The 1987 acreage estimates were compiled through a somewhat different process than were the 1960-1982 data, and are somewhat more conservative. The 1987 statistics were prepared jointly by VPI and the Winchester Fruit Research Laboratory, while the earlier data was prepared by the state Agricultural Statistics Service in Richmond.

Among the vinifera varietals, Chardonnay, Riesling, and Cabernet Sauvignon have proven to be the most successful in Virginia, with Chardonnay being by far the most popular. Of the French hybrids, Seyval Blanc and Vidal Blanc are in demand. The table below shows estimates of the current percentage of the total 1220 acres for each of the principal grapes grown in Virginia. Of the total, approximately 92% are used for wine and the remaining 8% are sold as table grapes. All of the Concord and most of the other American hybrids grown in Virginia are sold as table grapes.

AMERICAN HYBRID Varietal Percent		FRENCH HYBRID Varietal Percent		VINIFERA Varietal Percent	
Concord	4.1	Seyval	6.2	Chardonnay	29.1
		Vidal	4.6	Whte R'sling	13.9
		Villard Blanc	2.1	Cab. Sauvignon	11.1
		Chancellor	1.6	Merlot	3.3
		Marechal Foch	1.4	Pinot Noir	2.0
		Chambourcin	1.4	Gewurztram'r	1.2
All Other	2.9	All Other	8.7	All Other	5.3
TOTAL	7.0%		2 7.1%		65.9%

Clearly, Chardonnay and White Riesling have taken over the lead in Virginia, with Cabernet Sauvignon not far behind. The six most popular French hybrids constitute less one fifth of the total plantings. Merlot – an important vinifera grape from the Bourdeaux region of France and one that is generally thought of as very difficult to grow commercially in Virginia -- is in sixth place. Pinot Noir, the red wine of Burgundy, is another grape that is proving very difficult to grow in Virginia, but has strong market pull. The market is clearly pulling the growers and vintners toward the Bordeaux and Burgundian grape varietals.

COOPERATIVE AND GOVERNMENTAL CONTRIBUTIONS

An important force in spearheading the early development of vinifera wine, both in Virginia and throughout the East, was the creation of the Vinifera Wine Growers Association (VWGA). This association, head-quartered in The Plains,Virginia, was founded in October of 1973. Its purpose was (and still is) to encourage premium winegrowing among farmers and home vineyardists throughout the East. During the 1970's, with the federal and state advisers cautioning against growing vinifera grapes, the Association's journal and seminar programs were among the few means growers had to exchange information about their vinifera grape growing experiences in the eastern United States.

One of the founders of the VWGA, and its first President, was R. de-Treville Lawrence, Sr. Mr. Lawrence had an active career in the State Department for many years. In 1967 he had planted a small, successful vinifera vineyard on his family farm, Highbury, near The Plains.

During the 1970's, the Association promoted the argument that vinifera grapes could be grown in the East, counter to anti-vinifera publicity from the federal and state agricultural specialists. It also lobbied strongly, although unsuccessfully, to urge the USDA (United States Department of Agriculture) to re-establish its vitacultural research program which had been abolished during Prohibition. The Association was one of the early promoters in the 1970's of farm winery legislation in Virginia.

The State of Virginia, since the late 1970's, has played an active and visionary role in the development of the industry. In 1980, the state legislature established a Farm Winery Law – one of the most progressive in the country. For a winery to qualify as a farm winery, at least 51% of its wine must be produced from grapes grown on land owned or leased by the winery. This law simplified licensing procedures, reduced license fees, and allowed wineries to sell wine at both the retail and wholesale levels without additional licenses.

Following passage of the law, the state began to promote Virginia wine and grape growing. The services of both the USDA and VPI were made available to farmers regarding soil, climate and other technical matters. In 1983, Governor Robb declared the first Virginia Farm Winery Week. In 1984, the legislature set aside $190,000 to create a Wine Marketing Program in the Virginia Department of Agriculture and positions for both a state enologist and vitaculturist. In 1985, the legislature allocated $140,000 for a new Virginia Winegrowers Advisory Board, to be used for research and marketing programs. In 1986, the state initiated a vine certification program to improve the availability of virus free vines.

Bruce Zoecklein was appointed state enologist on the faculty of Virginia Polytechnic Institute at Blacksburg in 1985. Dr. Tony K. Wolf also joined the faculty of VPI as state vitaculturist at about the same time. He is located at the state Fruit Research Laboratory in Winchester. The overall objectives of the enology program are to help decrease wine productions costs and to increase the palatability of Virginia wines. The objective of the vitaculture program is to improve both the winter hardiness of vinifera grapes and the summer vineyard practices used in Virginia.

Currently, the principal negative aspect of Virginia state policies toward its fledgling wine industry is the continuation of the $1.40 per gallon state wine tax. This tax had been removed on wine grown and produced in Virginia by the Farm Wine Act in 1980, but the elimination was voided as the result of Supreme Court action on a similar discriminatory tax in Hawaii. The tax is the third highest in the country and compares with only 1 cent per gallon in California.

The Virginia wine industry has three active membership associations to represent and further its interests. The oldest of these is the Virginia Wineries Association which was founded in 1978. Until 1982, it represented both growers and winemakers. In 1983, the Virginia Vineyard Association was formed to represent interests of the growers, while the Wineries Association confined itself to winery interests. Both groups sponsor newsletters, seminars, short courses and other educational activities. They also work with each other and with state officials to further the development of the industry. The third association is the Jeffersonian Wine Grape Growers Association which was founded in 1981 and represents a broad constituency who are interested in providing general support to the industry. The activities of the Association focus on wine education, and include such activities as a newsletter, seminars and the annual Monticello Wine Festival.

Felicia Warburg Rogan, founder and owner of Oakencroft Vineyards, was instrumental in creating the Jeffersonian Grape Growers Association, and continues as its president. Mrs. Rogan has been an active promoter of the Virginia wine industry. She serves on the Virginia Wine Advisory Board and was instrumental in obtaining federal approval of the Monticello viticultural area designation for the Charlottesville region. Recently Mrs. Rogan was invited to address the Academy of Science and Letters in Dijon, France on the two hundreth anniversary of Jefferson's trip through Burgundy.

The industry has succeeded in obtaining vitacultural area designations for 5 regions of the state. These are Monticello, Rocky Knob, Shenandoah Valley, North Fork of the Roanoke and Northern Neck George Washington Birthplace. Several other such designations are pending with the federal government. Vintners are allowed to use the vitacultural area designation on their wine labels if over 85% of the grapes used in the wine are from that area. Thus the localized nature of the wine industry is taking shape in Virginia.

Virginia vintners are also active in providing educational and recreational events to promote Virginia wines. Almost all wineries have at least one special event during the year, such as a family day, barrel tasting, or a festival. The major annual industry-wide events scheduled during the year are:

Virginia Wine Weekend - The Homestead: Second week of April
Virginia Wineries Assoc. Festival - Culpeper: Mid-July
Middleburg Wine Festival - Northern Va.: Mid-August
Virginia Wine Festival - Middleburg area: End of August
Monticello Wine Festival - Charlottesville: Early October

Clearly, the Virginia wine industry has come a long way in the past ten years, both technically and in the overall structure of the industry. Even over the last two years, there has been noticeable improvement in the quality of both the grapes and the wine. As so often happens when rapid change takes place, the public recognition that world class wines are being produced in Virginia is slow in coming – but it is coming.

THE FUTURE

The vintners of Virginia are now producing premium vinifera wine and are competing with wines from both California and Europe. This achievement has only been reached in the past several years. Why has it taken so long? How far can it advance in the future?

In answer to the first question, one must keep in mind that until ten years ago, there virtually was no Virginia wine industry. Second, when it did start to develop, there were no experts to guide the way. In fact, many of the "experts" were discouraging the pioneers at every step. Third, the major market these pioneers hoped to serve had already become one of the most sophisticated in North America. Virginia vintners face world class competition from Europe to the east and California to the west. It is truly an accomplishment that the Virginia wine industry has been able to survive at all.

The know-how associated with growing grapes and making wine in Virginia from either French hybrid or vinifera grapes started in the 1970's. The California wine industry is also a modern upstart, but they do have a 40 year lead on Virginia. The history of the French wine industry goes all the way back to the occupation of France by the Romans at the time of Christ. Vineyards have been cultivated in Bordeaux since 50 AD and in Burgundy since 150 AD. Thus, the Virginia wine industry has a considerable amount of catching up to do. However, the quality of Virginia wine will continue to improve for many years, and very likely at a faster pace than elsewhere.

Before looking at the future, it is helpful to take a look at the present status of the industry. This look can be structured into three aspects: the still-existing technical barriers to making top quality wine in Virginia; the nature of the market for Virginia wine; and the economics of winemaking in Virginia.

The Current Technology

From the standpoint of the technology of actually making wine, there appear to be few real barriers to the producing of fine wine in Virginia. The winemaking skills are readily available. The best of equipment is in place or can be acquired. The management skills needed to put it all together either exist, or are rapidly developing. As Bruce Zoecklein, the state enologist has stated, "The technical capabilities of the current group of vintners is vastly improved over those of merely two years ago. Winemaking skills are no longer a major issue in Virginia. We now need to optimize on the styles of wine best suited for the Virginia market and to optimize the product of the vineyard in support of those styles."

Until several years ago, Virginia winemakers were self-taught. The industry was built on the abilities of such outstanding pioneers as Archie Smith III at Meredyth, Bob Harper at Naked Mountain, and Dirgham Salahi of Oasis. They and their peers learned how to grow grapes and make wine commercially as they went along. Most of the early pioneers had been home winemakers before turning commercial, so they knew the style of wine they wanted to make. However, they soon learned that commercial winemaking creates many challenges not faced by the home winemaker.

During the past few years, there has been an infusion of formally educated winemakers with experience in Europe, California, and elsewhere on the East Coast. Jacques Recht at Ingleside is the Dean of this group of winemakers, but the group includes, among others, Joachim Hollerith and Al Kinne at Prince Michel and Rapidan, respectively, Shep Rouse at Montdomaine and Steve Reeder at the Virginia Cooperative.

Jacques Recht's experience goes back 25 years in France and Belgium as a winemaker and consultant in Bourdeaux and Algeria. He was also a teacher of wine technology at the Institute of Fermentation Science in Brussels. Adriano Rossi at Barboursville came to America in 1982 with many years of experience in Italy as a winemaker – in fact, he is from a family with many generations of winemakers in his heritage.

Winemaking is one of the few remaining arts that can be practiced commercially in this modern age. The challenge and creativity is not in the chemistry of winemaking. That can, and must, be learned. Creativity is needed in the treating and blending of the varietal wines to achieve the optimum from what is available. The nuances of flavor in a given varietal wine differ from region to region, vineyard to vineyard, and year to year. Both the winemaker and those who appreciate fine wine, therefore, must first become comfortable with the nuances of Virginia varietal wines before these wines can be judged fairly against the competition.

For example, Chardonnay wine grown and produced in Virginia has inherently different flavor characteristics than Chardonnay from France or California. It has already become recognized that Virginia Chardonnay is lighter, more delicate and has a slightly higher acidity than those from

California. Therefore, the Virginia Chardonnay is much better suited for accompanying fish and shellfish than are those from California.

The techniques used to make wine in Virginia are not the limiting factor. Future progress of the Virginia wine industry will be determined, not in the winery, but in the vineyard. The vineyard problems faced by the colonial grape growers have been solved, or at least ameliorated to the point of being manageable. The most critical question today is not, "whether vinifera," but rather, "which vinifera," and, "where vinifera."

While the focus in this discussion is on wine produced from *vitis vinifera* varieties of grapes, this is not meant to slight the French hybrids. Several of these hybrids are doing well in Virginia, particularly Seyval Blanc and Vidal Blanc. Two of the red French hybrids, Chambourcin and Chancellor, also seem to be accepted, although to a lesser extent. The primary role for these grapes, however, appears likely to be in blended wines and, in the case of the reds, in blush wines similar to the popular White Zinfindel produced in California.

Meredyth Vineyards is the largest producer of French hybrid wine in Virginia. Mountain Cove Vineyards (La Abra) produces only French hybrid wines, while a number of others such as Burnley Vineyards, Oakencroft Vineyards, Stonewall Vineyards and Shenandoah Vineyards, feature both French hybrids and vinifera. A unique hybrid wine made by Chateau Morrisette is a blend of several American hybrids made into a dessert wine.

French hybrids will continue to be planted, grown and produced in Virginia because they do provide vintners with insurance against damage to vinifera vines and crops in years of adverse weather. Until the technology of grape growing in Virginia reaches the point where vinifera grapes can be grown with minimum risk of vine or crop damage, many vineyardists will hedge their investment with at least some portion of hybrid production.

Climate is probably the single most important concern to Virginia winegrowers. Much has been learned in recent years about cultivating grapes in the cold winters and humid summers of the East. Vineyardists have learned to plant on gentle hillsides, whenever practical, to avoid the frost that can be prevalent in the lowlands from November into April. Pruning is delayed until early spring to minimize damage from spring frost.

Severe winters are the most serious problem faced by Virginia farmers. At temperatures around 5° Fahrenheit, damage can start occurring to the above-ground trunk and canes of the vine. If the temperature drops to around -25° F for any length of time, vine damage can be massive. More than one Virginia vintner has experienced substantial losses in his vineyard due to such winter temperatures. Further research is needed, therefore, into methods of protecting the vines against winter cold or increasing their hardiness to resist it. Dr. Tony Wolf at the Fruit Research Laboratory has been funded by the Virginia Winegrowers Advisory Board to undertake a major research program to address these problems.

Developing and maintaining more healthy vines is one of the most important means of combating winter conditions. A step in this direction is provided by the state vine certification program, started in 1986. This program is designed to provide winegrowers with vines that are certifiably free of viruses and other diseases. The program involves all aspects of the Virginia wine industry. It is administered by the Virginia Vitacultural Technical Advisory Committee in cooperation with VPI and the Virginia Wine Advisory Board. Both the Committee and the Board are composed of leading growers, scientists and public citizens from throughout the wine industry of Virginia.

Summer weather can be almost as damaging to the grape crop as winter weather can be to the vines. To lessen the effects of summer humidity, vintners select vineyard sites that provide air flow in the summer. Vines are trained on trellises above the ground to keep air moving through the vineyards. Grapes ripen best if they are allowed to cool down through the night, so vineyard sites exhibiting cool evenings are preferred. Also, steep hillsides are avoided to minimize erosion from summer rains.

In general, vineyard sites are preferred that have mezzo-climates where extremes of temperature are minimized. (The term micro-climate, used frequently to define the climate at vineyard sites, more correctly refers to variations of climate within a specific vineyard.) Fortunately, Virginia is blessed with many sites favorable for growing wine grapes.

For example, several winegrowers are finding that the climate on the Eastern Shore and the Northern Neck of Virginia is more favorable for growing vinifera than that in the Piedmont and mountain regions of the state. This results from the neutralizing effect on both winter and summer temperatures of the two large bodies of water – the Atlantic Ocean and the Chesapeake Bay and its major tributaries. Spring frosts are almost nonexistent there. The trade-off, of course, is the increased potential for damage from hurricanes and the higher humidity in the Tidewater region.

Other growers have found that at certain elevations and locations in the foothills of the Blue Ridge Mountains, there are temperate zones (due to falling cold air and rising warm air) that are suitable for winegrowing. Vineyards located in these temperate zones have the additional advantage of benefiting from lower humidity in the summer at these higher elevations.

Climatic conditions in Virginia during the ripening season can also present problems to the vintner. Excessive summer rain, particularly at harvest, can make the grapes "watery" and degrade the flavor of the ultimate wine. Heavy rain near harvest can even split open the grapes and cause extensive spoilage if not picked quickly. Conversely, excessive heat at the time of harvest can make it difficult to get the grapes into the winery before they start to oxidize. At least one vintner, Prince Michel, uses a mechanical harvester so that the grapes can be picked at night when it is cooler. The harvester also helps overcome the perennial shortage of labor in Virginia at harvest time.

The relatively short growing season in Virginia can, in cooler years and in cooler locations, make it difficult to ripen the grapes beyond 20° Brix (percent sugar by weight). This is a marginal level to achieve adequate alcohol in the final wine. When this happens, the vineyard manager can only delay picking for a matter of days in the hope that the grapes will ripen further. Consequently, it must be corrected by the winemaker who is permitted to add sugar to the must (unfermented grape juice after crushing) before fermentation. This is called chaptalising and is an accepted practice throughout Europe and in the eastern United States.

Another area of concern in Virginia – in fact, wherever grapes are grown – is that of the suitability of the soil. However, in America this element of grape growing is not given the importance that it is in France. Wine grapes are adaptable to a wide range of soil conditions, although they prefer deep sandy loam. Deep plow trenching can alleviate many of the problems associated with the red Virginia clay, thus allowing the vines to follow their instinct of deep rooting. Land with shallow soil is avoided. The sandy loam of eastern Virginia may provide one of the more favorable soils in Virginia.

These brief paragraphs, which provide only a sampling of concerns faced by vineyard managers, may sound overwhelming. They are, however, typical of the problems faced by vineyardists throughout the world where winters are cold and summers are hot and humid. The problems that are particularly associated with growing vinifera grapes have become manageable in comparable climes in Europe through experience – and they will be in Virginia.

As matters now stand, the climatic difficulties associated with growing European grape varietals in Virginia have become more economic than technical issues. It is more a question of how many vines a vintner can afford to lose in winter, or how much of the crop can he afford to lose during the growing season – questions that farmers must deal with, whatever the crop. Continued research sponsored by the state of Virginia will no doubt reduce these losses.

The techniques for growing the three most popular grapes in Virginia – Chardonnay, Riesling and Cabernet Sauvignon -- are becoming fairly well established. It does appear likely, however, that Riesling is better suited to the shorter and cooler growing seasons of the more northerly states, such as New York. At present, the feasibility of growing other vinifera varietals in Virginia such as Merlot, Gewurztraminer, Pinot Noir or Sauvignon Blanc is also less clear. Certain of these grape varietals are overly susceptible to bunch rot due to the smallness and closeness of the grapes on the vine. Others are less able to withstand winter cold, while still others tend to blossom too early in the spring or ripen too early in the fall.

There is an old adage in the wine industry that, "You can make bad wine out of good grapes, but you cannot make good wine out of even mediocre grapes." During the next decade significant improvements can be expected in the basic flavor content of the grapes used to make Virginia wine. These will come about as vintners learn more about the selection of grapes and vineyard sites and the techniques of grape farming. These improvements will be supported by agricultural extension services and continuing research provided by the state of Virginia.

The Market for Virginia Wine

Now that Virginia vintners are making award winning wines, how wide a market will they be able to serve? For an industry that is only ten years old there is no way to predict the answer. For the foreseeable future, however, growth is almost assured. Currently, the Virginia wineries are able to sell all of the wine they can make – essentially all of it is being sold within the state of Virginia. Yet wine sales in Virginia and metropolitan Washington are approximately 15 million gallons each year, while state vintners are currently producing close to 300,000 gallons, or equivalent to only 2% of the total.

Probably at least two thirds of the wine sold by the farm wineries in Virginia is sold at the winery, while another 15% is sold through the state owned liquor stores. The remainder is sold through wholesalers and directly to restaurants or local stores. The latter is permitted under the state Farm Winery Law of 1980. A small portion of Virginia-grown wine is being sold out-of-state – primarily in the District of Columbia and neighboring states. The liquor stores are an important outlet for the small-to-medium size wineries, since these stores carry only wines produced in Virginia.

In terms of sheer volume of wine, the main competition is from bulk wines produced in California, or *vin ordinaire* imported from Europe. Yet Virginia wineries, with an annual output of 300,000 gallons, cannot compete with Gallo, Sebastiani, and other generic wine producers who measure their output in millions of gallons. These large wineries distribute nationwide, spend millions on advertising and promotion and are able to stock the wine shelves of major supermarket chains in Virginia and throughout the country.

Fortunately, the industry has almost universally set its sights on making and selling premium wine, rather than attempting to compete merely on price with generic wines. Unfortunately, however, the complaint is still heard that Virginia wines are over priced. This is certainly true when compared to prices of bulk varietal wines, but not true when compared to premium wines from either California or France. At $6-8, a bottle of Virginia wine is an excellent value when compared to out-of-state wines of similar quality. A $7 bottle of Virginia Chardonnay is certainly a better buy than a $12 -15 bottle of over priced California Chardonnay.

The Virginia wine industry is still basically a cottage industry. The average vineyard size is less than seven acres and the average annual winery output is only 9000 gallons (3500 cases). The production of the largest wineries is only 20,000 cases. The smallest of the farm wineries is less than 200 cases – little more than home winemaking.

Balanced against these physical limitations of the current industry is one vital ingredient that will undoubtedly bring ultimate success. Virginia wineries are next door neighbors to the Washington D.C. metropolitan wine market of over 4 million people. Further, it has been estimated that there are over 25 million people living within a one day drive of the Virginia wine country.

Retailers and restaurants within the District of Columbia sell 6.7 gallons of wine per capita; the highest rate of wine consumption in the country. That is almost three times the national average of 2.4 gallons per capita, and even 40% higher than California. Virginia, in contrast, is not a heavy wine drinking state, consuming only 1.9 gallons per capita – considerably below the national average.

Large Versus Small Winery

There are two alternative strategies being used by Virginia vintners to tap the middle Atlantic market. One approach is to keep the winery small enough to permit the vintner (and his or her family) to personally sell the winery output, either through the tasting room or directly to restaurants and local stores in the area. The other approach is to grow large enough to enter the wholesale distribution network used by nationally distributed wineries.

The economics of these two approaches is necessarily different, as is the winemaking philosophy. The larger wineries tend to be more capital intensive and able to attract more highly trained specialists. However, because of the large investment in wine inventories, they are less able to experiment with their wines. The smaller wineries have the advantages of the boutique. They can offer unusual and experimental wines, and they can focus on the preferences of their narrower range of clientele. Size is no measure of quality in the wine business, however; both the large and the small can make excellent wine and they can make poor wine.

The Small Vintner

The smaller, do- it-yourself winery is attractive to many vintners from a business standpoint because it avoids the payment of markups to the "middlemen"– the wholesalers and distributors. If the vintner sells most of his or her winery output through the tasting room, the retailer's markup is also saved. By keeping small, the vintner is able to continue to do his own hands-on winemaking.

Many Virginia vintners had made wine as a hobby in their garage or basement before going commercial and particularly enjoy this aspect of the business. Staying small permits them to experiment and place their own signature on what can be very interesting wines. The do-it-yourself approach does, however, limit the vintner's annual production to less than 10,000 cases, or a gross income of less than $400,000. This limits the vintner's ability to generate capital. On the other hand, it also reduces the investment required for the more sophisticated and automated winemaking facilities and equipment.

The small "family" winery in Virginia is a way of life. The family home, winery and tasting room are all part of a close knit operation where personal and business activities are almost indistinguishable. Essentially doing business out of their homes, the vintners treat their clientele almost as house guests. While closely tying personal and business life has its drawbacks, it does create the very atmosphere that true wine lovers enjoy and, therefore, makes an important contribution to wine sales. Since all of these vintners are close to centers of urban population and reside in the most beautiful parts of Virginia, they will very likely continue to be an important part of the Virginia wine scene.

Several vintners, particularly in the more rural southern part of Virginia, make a special effort to design the style of their wines to suit tastes in the local community. For example, Arthur Hodges, owner of Chateau Naturel near Rocky Mount, makes several interesting rather sweet wines from Labrusca varieties. He also produces French hybrid and blackberry wines. Similarly, Al Weed of La Abra Vineyards in Lovingston has developed a following in Nelson County and the surrounding area for his French hybrid wines. He also makes a much-in-demand peach wine from fruit provided by local farmers.

Other examples of vintners who cater to the wine preferences of local residents include Howard Bryan at Stonewall Vineyards and Tom O'Grady of Rose Bower. Howard makes, among other wines, one called Pyment from Vidal Blanc spiced with honey, cloves, and citrus. Tom makes a range of off-dry wines, one of which is a sweet Port-like blend of Cabernet and Chancellor, called LeBateau Rouge.

Undoubtedly, the most unusual small winery in Virginia is Fruit of the Bloom Farm Winery near Salem, Virginia, owned by Jim and Barbara Guthrie. Jim produces fruit, berry, herb and blossom wines and has a loyal following in the area around Salem and Roanoke. Since colonial days, farmers have made wine from whatever was handy and Jim is merely continuing that pioneering tradition.

The sugar content of many of these local wines tends to be higher than most of today's popular table wines – in the 2.5 to 3.5% range. This is generally achieved by fermenting the wine dry or semi-dry, then adding back a portion of the unfermented grape juice, called "sweet reserve" ("dosage" in French and "sussreserve" in German), to achieve the desired sweetness. Throughout the centuries, sugar has been used to help stablilize wine for storage. There is a sizable market even today for these sweet table wines (distinguished from fortified dessert wines which contain over 14% alcohol). In fact, many vintners in Virginia follow the adage, "Wine drinkers talk dry, but buy sweet." This adage is becoming less of a truism in our modern calorie-conscious age, but the market is there and the small vintners are best suited to serve it.

The Large Vintner

While many vintners prefer to remain small, others have a burning desire to grow larger. Growth in volume of at least a few vineyards provides direction to the industry. For those vineyards who commit to growth, however, it requires a shift to reliance on established distribution channels. This means that the principal point of sale moves out of the winery and onto the store shelf. Selling becomes more impersonal with reliance on competitive tastings, advertising and promotion of retailers and restaurants.

Becoming large also implies a commitment to raise major amounts of capital since, as a winery grows, the need for capital rises faster than increases in capacity. Also, as a winery becomes larger, cost control becomes critical – in part because the gross margin is being reduced by the discounts given to the middlemen and, in part, because the cost of invested capital increases.

The relatively sudden emergence of the larger Virginia wineries has resulted in an identity crisis for Virginia wine in the marketplace. Most retailers in the urban areas, and particularly in Washington, D.C., still consider Virginia wines a "novelty." Compounding this problem is that many distributors are conveying this impression to the restaurants in Virginia; consequently, only a few restaurants carry more than a token selection of Virginia wines on the their wine lists. One of the reasons for including restaurants in this book is to identify some of the restaurants that do feature Virginia wines.

While the industry is currently selling essentially all of its output, this will not always be the situation. As wineries become larger, they will have to compete head-to-head with the best and almost-best wines of the world. In this competitive age, offering world class wines requires world class marketing techniques and effort. The capabilities and resources necessary to become a major competitor in the metropolitan Washington market do not appear feasible for the Virginia wine industry for a number of years to come – the promotional expenditures needed are just too great, given the size of the Virginia wine industry.

The leading vintners of Virginia are well aware of this marketing challenge. The larger wineries such as Meredyth, Prince Michel, Ingleside and Oasis have already moved into the metropolitan Washington market.

It is surprising, however, that the industry has not established Virginia wines in the more outstanding restaurants and hotels throughout the state. While individual wineries have done this with local restaurants, the industry, state-wide, has not yet made much progress with the major restaurants of Virginia.

Currently, few restaurants in Virginia can provide knowledgeable advice to diners about local wines. An unstructured sampling (by the authors) of excellent restaurants throughout Virginia showed that all too frequently restaurants will carry a number of French wines, a selection of California wines and, at best, one or two Virginia wines. Seldom can one run across a wine list that reflects an appreciation of the truly fine wines available in Virginia.

In conversations on the subject with owners and managers of major restaurants, it is clear that they want to help. Yet they need to be convinced that Virginia wine can be sold in competition with other fine wines – that it is no longer merely a novelty.

Few restaurant operators in Virginia appear to be knowledgeable about wine in general – particularly how it can complement food. They need education on what constitutes a good food wine, since Virginia wines do make excellent matches with food. Virginia wines tend to be more delicate and have slightly better acidity than wines produced in the Mediterranean-like climate of California. This natural affinity between Virginia wine and food needs to be exploited if the industry is to continue to develop. A Virginia restaurant that relies on a California wine consultant to develop its wine list is not likely to have a very wide or good selection of Virginia wines.

The Economics of Producing Wine in Virginia

The attractiveness of the lifestyle of winemaking can frequently outweigh the economic base of winemaking as a business. The joy of living and raising one's children in the country, on one's own land, and being engaged in a partnership with nature to make one of man's most enjoyable products, can mean total fulfillment to the true winemaker. To a small minority, however, it can mean being at the mercy of nature's darker side, toiling daily for unending hours, being one step ahead of bankruptcy and worrying about whether and where the output of the winery can be sold.

While this book is not intended as an economic textbook on becoming a vintner, it is helpful to have some sense of the economic aspects of the business. Without such a knowledge, one does not gain a full understanding and appreciation of those engaged in winemaking.

The following table summarizes some of the physical and financial characteristics of a typical vineyard-winery combination in Virginia. It should be kept in mind that these ratios and values probably do not exist at any specific winery. Each individual vineyard-winery combination operates uniquely, with different mixes of grape varieties, vineyard and winery practices and new versus old facilities and equipment. However, the general relationships are indicative of the typical vintners situation. The ranges given are meant to be typical and do not represent the extremes. For example, the "500-800 per acre" range shown below does not cover the 1200 vines per acre used at Prince Michel.

Starting with the vine and the vineyard, some of the key physical characteristics are:

Buds per vine after pruning	50-80
Grape cluster per vine after thinning	50-100
Frost free days required to maturity	150-180
Pounds of harvested grapes per vine	10-20
Quarts of wine per vine	3-4
Number of vines per acre	500-800
Tons of harvested grapes per acre	2-5
Gallons of wine per ton of grapes	140-160
Gallons of wine per acre	400-600
Grape acres required for 10,000 gallon winery	18-24
Number of gallons of wine per bottled case	2.4
Cases of wine per acre of vineyard	165-250

As shown, winemaking requires tens of thousands of individual buds producing millions of grape clustersrto produce a few thousand gallons of wine. A 10,000 gallon winery requires approximately 70 tons of grapes. In converting these grapes to wine, care must be taken not to allow the individual grapes to spoil or be prematurely crushed. The process of bringing the grapes to the fermenting tank is as fascinating and exacting a task as the making of wine itself.

Using the characteristics listed above, it is possible to estimate the general magnitude of the investment typically needed to start up and operate a 10,000 gallon (4200 case) winery, accompanied by 20 acres of vineyard.

Cost of winery and equipment @ $15-25/gal	$150,000-$250,000
Cost of land @ $3000- 5000/acre	$60,000- $100,000
Cost of planted vineyard @ $10-15,000/acre	$200,000- $300,000
Total Investment First Three Years	**$410,000- $650,000**
Time required for vineyard to be productive	3 to 4 years
Time to recover investment: Vineyard	6 to 8 years
Winery	8 to 10 years
Maximum negative cash flow (year 4 or 5)	$500,000-$600,000
Gross Income (yr 6) - 50,000 btls/year @ $4.75	$275,000
(Assumes 50% winery @ $7 & 50% whlsl @ $3.50)	
Operating costs (yr 6) - $15-$20/gallon	$150,000-$250,000
Net Income (before tax)	$125,000-$25,000
Price per ton of grapes:	
Chardonnay and Cabernet Sauvignon	$1000-$1200
Riesling	$700- $800
American Hybrid	$150-$300
French Hybrids	$350-$550

Keep in mind that these estimates are merely approximations of the costs and income likely to be experienced by a vintner.

The net income shown needs to be viewed with four caveats in mind:

1. The vintner and his or her family derives income for their services out of Net Income, not out of Production Costs; if these services were hired from the outside, costs could easily increase by $75,000.

2. The production costs include only a modest allowance for lost vines or crops due to unusual weather – a 10% loss could easily increase costs by $20,000, including the cost of grapes acquired to make up the deficiency.

3. Operating costs assume only a modest amount of interest on borrowed capital. If the vintner had been required to borrow 60% of his maximum negative cash flow, or $300,000, his annual interest payments would have further reduced his Net Income in the order of $25,000.

4. Should the vintner be able to sell only 25% of the winery output through the tasting room instead of the 50% assumed above, his Net Income would be reduced by an additional $25,000.

Thus, financially, the lot of a Virginia vintner is not a secure one. While the mid-range of the estimated Net Income would provide the vintner and family with a comfortable income, the uncertainties could easily put them in a loss position. As a consequence, most of the smallest vintners maintain a steady job elsewhere, at least until they retire or their vineyard and winery operations become well established. The 8 to 10 year payback period subjects the vintner to considerable financial risk over a long period of time.

New Market Innovations

In spite of these financial uncertainties, the vintners continue to expand and to experiment with new styles of wines – at least in Virginia. For example, nouveau style wines are being made by Rose Bower, Meredyth, and Ingleside. This style of wine is made by placing whole bunches of grapes into the fermenter and allowing the grapes to ferment from the inside out. The result is a much fruitier and fresher wine. It is the process used in the Beaujolais region of France to produce its very distinctive wines.

Another recent development in Virginia that warrants watching is the reestablishment of Virginia's sparkling wine (champagne) industry. The original manufacture of champagne in Virginia was started by Paul Garrett near Norfolk, in 1904. In modern times, Ingleside and Oasis are now making champagne and by the original French method called "methode champagnoise." Other wineries are also in the process of developing their own champagne production.

Champagne making may prove to be well suited to Virginia. For champagne, the grapes are picked slightly on the "green" side with a sugar level of only $16\text{-}18^\circ$ Brix, rather than the normal $20\text{-}23^\circ$ Brix for still wine. This early picking keeps the acidity higher than it is for still wine.

When Virginia's climate occasionally causes too short a growing season for proper ripening of wine grapes, champagne grapes could still be harvested. An important advantage of Virginia's climate is that it permits the growing of a range of both vinifera and hybrid grape varietals from which champagne could be made. These advantages, plus the rapid growth of sparkling wine sales, might cause sparkling wine to provide a considerable boost to the growth of Virginia's wine industry. New York state has become famous for its bottle-fermented champagne based on a cuvée blend of Catawba, Delaware and French hybrids. Virginia could easily do likewise with its greater flexibility in the varietals it can grow successfully.

Another development worth watching in Virginia is the wider acceptance of blended wines. Federal regulations require that for a wine to have a varietal label, it must contain at least 75% of the varietal grape. Unlike France, the United States wine drinking public has been educated to consider varietal wines of higher quality than blended wines. This educational program was developed by the California wine industry to take advantage of the recognizable and pronounced varietal characteristics of California varietal wines. Eastern wine drinking preferences, however, are more evenly divided between the blended wines from France and the California styles.

While the metropolitan New York area predominantly prefers European wines (65% versus 45% domestic), the Washington-Baltimore metropolitan areas prefer domestic wines in a ratio of 75% domestic to 25% imported. The mid-Atlantic urban region, therefore, clearly is more open to American produced wine than is the other major Atlantic Coast market.

The Virginia wine industry, therefore, can offer both styles as long as they do not become blends of the "bottom of the barrel." There are a number of excellent proprietary blends currently being offered by Virginia wineries. Several combine both hybrid and vinifera varieties to produce a delicate and complex wine. It is likely that these offerings will increase as Virginia winemakers experiment with various combinations.

Examples of interesting Virginia blended wines on the market today involving both hybrids and vinifera include:

Accomack Vineyards – Old Dominion White (Seyval Blanc plus Chardonnay).
Ingleside Plantation – Chesapeake White (Seyval Blanc plus Chardonnay).
Ingleside Plantation – Chesapeake Claret (Chancellor plus Cabernet Sauvignon).
Rose Bower Vineyard & Winery – Hampton Forest Claret (Chancellor and Cabernet Sauvignon).
Stonewall Vineyards – CLARET (Chambourcin plus Merlot).

The Virginia wine industry will undoubtedly continue to grow. The market opportunities are too large to ignore. While there is likely to be considerable fallout over time, others will step in to keep the industry growing. Ultimately, the industry will settle out at some currently undetermined level of production. It is not unrealistic to predict, however, that the Virginia wine industry could provide up to 10% of the combined Virginia and metropolitan Washington market. This would bring about a growth of the Virginia wine industry up to five to ten times its current size. Beyond that point, the industry would need to market and distribute nationally, requiring financial resources that appear beyond the capacity of individual wineries. The industry is likely, therefore, to realize its destiny primarily in Virginia, plus the District of Columbia and neighboring states.

While this forecast of the future may seem conservative to some, it is a giant step into the future for this fledgling industry, and one that requires imagination, perseverance and astute marketing. Achieving this goal will keep Virginia in the top ten winegrowing states. By specializing in the wine preferences of the mid-Atlantic states, Virginia is likely to fulfill a special niche in the eastern wine market. Nationwide, the wine industry is moving toward local markets and local preferences – a role for which the Virginia wine industry is well suited. The market clearly favors the vinifera varietals and that is where the growth will occur. However, Virginia's unique climate provides its wine industry with the ability to grow a range of both vinifera and French hybrid grapes. This, in turn, will enable Virginia vintners to develop a variety of unique wines.

The Northern Region

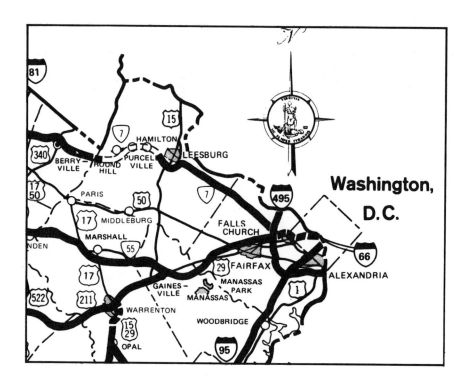

WINERIES:

Farfelu Vineyard

Linden Vineyards

Loudoun Valley Vineyards

Meredyth Vineyards

Naked Mountain Vineyard

Oasis Vineyard

Piedmont Vineyards & Winery

Willowcroft Farm Vineyards

RESTAURANTS:

Ashby Inn

Jordan's

Little River Inn

Red Fox Inn

Windsor House

FARFELU VINEYARD Charles Raney and his family first planted a few grape vines on their property in 1966. Over the next few years they experimented with more than 40 different grape varieties.

The Raney vineyard was one of the first in Virginia to grow vinifera and French hybrid grapes. Consequently, there was a lot to learn about the climatic hardiness, productivity and quality of wine from these grapes. Farfelu was also one of the first Virginia wineries to receive a commercial license as a farm winery and produced its first wines in 1975.

Charles Raney's interest in grape growing and wine began with several visits to the wine countries of Europe while he was in the Navy. After leaving the service he became a pilot for United Airlines, but could not dismiss the thought of planting a vineyard and operating a winery.

After reading a number of books on the subject and consulting with several Northeastern viticulturists, Charles decided to plant an experimental vineyard on his farm property near Flint Hill. The vineyards were planted on the hillside where an apple orchard had once flourished. A decade after the planting, Charles converted the barn into a winery and the first Farfelu wines were released in 1976. "Since then we have made some good and some mediocre wines," he says.

Charles Raney has recently assessed his operation and consulted with various experts in the field. They have advised him to tear out some of his vines and plant other varieties better suited to his climate and terrain. To date Charles has taken out most of the French hybrids in his 7 acre vineyard and planted Chardonnay and Cabernet Sauvignon.

For the past two years no wine has been made at Farfelu. However, Charles plans to add new equipment and be back in operation in the fall of 1988. He will limit production to two varietals -- Chardonnay and Cabernet Sauvignon -- and possibly one red blend. He also plans to add oak cooperage for aging of the wines.

Charles feels that running a vineyard and a winery cannot be done successfully on a part-time basis. He plans to retire from his commercial flying job on January 1, 1988 and devote full time to being a vintner. "I love the growing of the grapes and the development of the wine; it's more than technical, it's an art," Charles Raney commented.

Virginia Raney, who is administrative assistant to columnist James Kilpatrick likes to prepare dishes using Virginia seafood.

TOURS
➡

FARFELU VINEYARD, *Highway 647 Flint Hill, Va. 22627 703-364-2930*
Directions: *4 miles east of Flint Hill, 13 miles west of Marshall on Route 647*
Visitation: *By appointment*
Principals: *Charles J. Raney*
Wines Produced: *Chardonnay, Chancellor*
1987 Production: *Unknown*

BAKED SCALLOPS

Serve with Chardonnay

This easy to prepare scallop dish needs no watching. The crumbs form a nice crust as the seafood bakes. Virginia Raney suggests the use of fresh bread crumbs instead of prepackaged ones.

2 lbs. scallops, rinsed and patted dry	1/2 cup heavy cream
Salt and pepper to taste	1/2 cup fresh white bread crumbs
2 tablespoons lemon juice	2 tablespoons melted butter
1/4 cup dry white wine	

Place scallops in a large mixing bowl. Using your hands, gently toss the scallops with the salt, pepper, lemon juice and wine. Transfer mixture to a 12 x 16 buttered baking dish. Sprinkle cream over mixture. Sprinkle top with bread crumbs and drizzle melted butter over the crumbs. Bake in preheated 400 degree oven 12 to 14 minutes. Crumbs should be slightly golden. *Serves: 8*

LINDEN VINEYARDS is a true farm operation in every sense of the word. Not only is it a vineyard and a winery, but it is also a pick-your-own-fruit operation. Jim and Peggy Law, a young couple who in partnership with Jim's parents own Linden Vineyards, have always wanted to farm on a small scale, producing a variety of agricultural products.

Jim Law is a native of Ohio and graduated from Miami University there. He has spent time in the Peace Corps in Africa helping to improve fruit production. On his return to the United States he apprenticed himself to a winery in Ohio for two years in order to learn winemaking. In 1981 he came to Virginia and began working at Tri-Mountain Winery. Jim also acted as a consultant to several other wineries, drawing on his experiences in wine-making and fruit growing.

Peggy Law grew up in a suburban environment in Connecticut, graduating from Hobart and William Smith College with majors in English and Biology. She came to Virginia to work at the National Zoological Park's Conservation and Research Center, helping to manage the zoo's bird collection. At the end of her one year assignment Peggy decided to stay in the rural area where she was living. She next accepted a job at a local bookstore and used her spare time to read about farming and gardening. The more she read, the more interested she became. Peggy decided that the best way to learn was by doing. She left the bookstore and took a job in a local vineyard – Tri-Mountain Winery -- where she learned how to prune and take care of the vines.

While at Tri Mountain she met Jim, who was the winemaker and vineyard manager. A year later they were married and decided to find their own land and develop a farm. They spent two years looking for property and finally purchased land close to Linden and next door to the log cabin they were renting. The land consists of 76 acres on a rolling hillside. It had been timbered over 20 years ago and allowed to grow wild. The first task for the Laws was to clear the land so that they could plant their crops. They tried to retain the natural attributes of the property and disrupt its beauty as little as possible.

Peggy and Jim both have an interest in fruit crops. Consequently, they decided to diversify their plantings and produce not only wine, but also edible fruits – particularly apples. In addition to wine grapes, they now have plantings of table grapes, blueberries and an apple orchard.

The apple orchard contains all dwarf trees to facilitate a pick-your-own operation. The Laws have chosen to specialize in old time varieties such as "Black Amish," Newtown Pippin," (an Albemarle County variety) and "Esopus Spitzenburg," (a favorite of Thomas Jefferson). All of the dwarf trees are trellised to permit better ripening of the fruit and also to facilitate picking. It is one of the first trellised orchards in Virginia.

At present the Laws have 7 acres planted in wine grapes at Linden Vineyards – Chardonnay, Cabernet Sauvignon, Cabernet Franc, Vidal and Seyval. Each of the five varieties are in their own separate section of the vineyard. The elevation of the vineyard is 1200 to 1400 feet. Jim Law chose the specific location of the vineyard for several reasons. At that elevation the vineyard is in a special thermal zone of warmer winter air, pushed up by the falling cold air. This inversion of air gives frost protection, particularly helpful in the spring when the danger of spring frost occurs. At over 1000 feet in elevation, there is later ripening of the grapes and a longer growing period which results in more flavor in the fruit.

An Eastern exposure of the vineyard helps to dry out the morning dews, thereby reducing the potential for bunch rot and fungus. The vineyard also has well drained volcanic soil. Periodically, Jim and Peggy have grape leaf analysis done to determine what extra nutrients, if any, should be added to the soil for wine grape production. They work closely with both the state viticulturist and enologist. "Proper canopy management," Jim says," is essential for good grape growing." He is experimenting with various methods of trellising and canopy management.

The winery, which was started in the spring of 1987, will be completed for the fall crush. Not only will it have the winery equipment, but also a large tasting room, and a separate room for seminars, since both Jim and Peggy are involved in the teaching of agricultural practices. Also scheduled for completion in the near future is a large log cabin that will be the Laws residence. It is an original cabin that the Laws purchased, then dismantled, and is being reassembled adjacent to the vineyard.

Linden Vineyards is the first in Virginia to use a de-juicing tank. This custom made de-juicing tank permits a gentle, cool extraction of juice from the berries. By this method the subtle aromas and fruit flavors of the grapes are retained. Jim says, "Proper temperature control during crushing and pressing is most important in winemaking."

As winemaker for the Linden Vineyards winery, Jim Law can now put his favorite techniques into operation. The Chardonnay is fermented in both French oak and stainless steel and then further aged for several months in French oak to soften the wine. The Seyval grapes are picked while the acid is still high to give a crispness to the finished wine. The Seyval juice is fermented cold and aged in stainless steel.

For the Linden Cabernet Sauvignon, Jim will blend a small portion of Cabernet Franc with the Cabernet Sauvignon to achieve complexity. Whole berries are added to the fermenting wine to increase varietal aromas. The wines are aged in small American oak casks before blending.

Vidal is blended with Riesling, creating a balance that does not require aging and produces a young and fresh wine. The wine is 80% Vidal and 20 % Riesling. Since the Laws do not grow any Riesling they purchase it from growers in Northern Virginia.

Jim and Peggy Law want their winery to remain small – 6 to 7 thousand cases per year. They want to stay totally involved in their agricultural enterprise encompassing not only wine, but other fruit related products. Also, through their seminars and other educational activities, they want to help other growers solve some of the growing problems they are encountering. The Laws are pioneers of the 1980's.

The recipes that follow were developed by Jim Law's mother, Nancy Law, to complement Linden Vineyards wines.

TOURS
➤

Linden Vineyards, *Route 1, Box 96 Linden, VA 22642   703-364-1997*
Directions: *Route 55 to Linden, right at Post Office, take Route 638 over wooden railroad tracks, 2.2 miles to Linden Vineyards, sign on the right*
Visitation: *11 a.m. to 5 p.m. Tuesday through Sunday beginning April 1988. Fall of 1987 by appointment only*
Principals: *The Law Family : Jim, Peggy, Nancy, Dick and Bob.*
Wines Produced: *Chardonnay, Cabernet Sauvignon, Seyval, Vidal/Riesling*
1987 Production: *1400 cases*

CHICKEN VIDAL

Serve with Vidal/Riesling

This recipe was developed to include some of the table grape varieties grown on the farm at Linden Vineyards. It also features fresh shiitake mushrooms. Both items are available in most gourmet markets and some supermarkets.

4 chicken breasts, skinned and boned	1 cup Vidal/Riesling
Salt and pepper, to taste	1 tablespoon fresh, chopped tarragon, or
Flour	1 teaspoon dried tarragon
2 tablespoons vegetable oil	1 cup chicken broth
1 tablespoon unsalted butter or margarine	2 teaspoons cornstarch
1 cup thinly sliced shiitake mushrooms	3/4 cup red seedless grapes: Canadice,
2 tablespoons finely chopped shallots	Suffolk Red or Tokay

Sprinkle chicken breasts with salt and pepper. Dredge with flour and shake off the excess. Heat 1 tablespoon of oil and add the butter in a skillet over medium high heat. When hot, but not brown, add chicken pieces. Cook on 1 side about 4 minutes. Turn and cook other side until golden brown, 2 to 4 minutes. Lower heat to medium. Cover and cook about 5 minutes until tender.

Transfer pieces to warm platter and keep warm. Add the mushrooms to the skillet and sauté briefly, about 2 minutes. Add them to the chicken and keep warm. Add the remaining oil to the skillet, heat and add the shallots. Sauté briefly until soft. Add 3/4 cup of the wine to the skillet along with the tarragon. Reduce liquid over high heat to half of the volume. Pour in stock and again reduce by half. Mix cornstarch with remaining 1/4 cup wine. Reduce heat to low and stir in the cornstarch mixture. Blend to thicken sauce. Add grapes and cook for 2 minutes. Adjust salt and pepper to taste. Pour sauce over chicken and mushrooms and serve. *Serves: 4*

NAVARIN OF LAMB

Serve with Cabernet Sauvignon

"Navarin" is the French word for a stew with main ingredients of mutton, onions and potatoes. According to the French, in rare cases the term may be applied to lamb. In today's usage, however, the term is used for lamb. Navarin Printanier denotes a lamb stew cooked with spring vegetables – small spring carrots, baby turnips, tiny new potatoes and juicy young peas. The techniques used in preparing this stew are different from the ordinary ones, but well worth the effort. Snow peas and rice are an excellent accompaniment to this entree.

3 lbs. lamb, cut into 1 inch cubes	1/4 cup rice or sherry vinegar
3 tablespoons vegetable oil	2 tablespoons red currant jelly
1 tablespoon sugar	2 tablespoons tomato paste
1/2 teaspoon salt	3 medium carrots, cut in 1 x 1/4 inch
1/4 teaspoon pepper	lengths
3 tablespoons flour	1/4 cup chopped fresh parsley
1 medium onion, sliced	1 teaspoon dried rosemary
2 cloves garlic, chopped fine	1 teaspoon dried thyme
2 cups beef stock, or 1 14 1/2 oz. can	1 bay leaf
beef broth	20 to 24 white pearl onions
1 cup Cabernet Sauvignon	1/2 lb. fresh mushrooms, sliced
	1 tablespoon butter

Preheat oven to 450 degrees.

Divide lamb cubes into four batches. Heat oil in heavy skillet over medium high heat. Brown each batch of lamb a few minutes on all sides. After each batch of lamb browns, place it in a dutch oven. When all of the lamb has browned, set the skillet aside. Sprinkle lamb with sugar and mix well. Place dutch oven on medium high heat for 3 to 4 minutes, stirring meat well to caramelize the sugar and to obtain a rich, brown appearance.

Add salt, pepper and flour and stir to mix. Place dutch oven in preheated 450 degree oven for 2 to 3 minutes to further brown the meat. This creates a nice brown crust. Remove dutch oven and lower oven temperature to 325 degrees.

Place skillet back on medium high heat, and add onion and garlic and sauté until onion is limp. Add stock, wine, vinegar, jelly and tomato paste. Stir, scraping up all particles and incorporating them in the sauce. Bring to a boil and cook over medium heat about 5 minutes.

Add carrots, parsley, rosemary, thyme and bay leaf to the meat and mix well. Pour sauce over the meat mixture. Stir well and bring to simmer on top of stove. Cover and bake in 325 degree oven for 1 1/2 hours or until meat is tender.

In the meantime prepare the white onions: cut a shallow X in the root end of each onion. Bring 2 quarts of lightly salted water to a boil and drop the onions into the water. Cook them over medium heat for about 10 minutes, until they are tender, but firm. Drain the water, transfer onions to a small bowl and cover with cold water for 10 minutes. Drain, peel the onions and set them aside.

Saute sliced mushrooms in 1 tablespoon of butter for a few minutes. Set them aside.

When meat is tender add onions and mushrooms, stir to mix well. Remove bay leaf. Replace meat in oven for about 10 more minutes to warm the mushrooms and onions which were added. Thicken gravy if necessary and serve. *Serves: 6*

LOUDOUN VALLEY VINEYARDS Grape growing is not a new venture to Hubert Tucker. He is a well seasoned professional who has grown grapes in two states on the Eastern seaboard – first in New York and now in Virginia.

In 1963, Hubert Tucker and his father purchased 60 acres in the Finger Lakes region of New York state. Hubert, who is an engineer with a masters degree in physics, was working in New York state in the aeronautical laboratory at Cornell University.The two men decided to grow grapes on the property and planted 30 acres of French hybrids plus some vinifera. In order to better acquaint himself with this new venture, Hubert took viticulture and enology courses at Cornell University. Although the vineyard flourished, Hubert's father decided to move to Missouri when he retired. They sold the property and Hubert moved to Virginia where he accepted a position as an aeronautical engineer with the FAA. He is now in charge of acquiring new communication equipment for airports throughout the country.

In 1978, Hubert and his wife Dolores purchased a farm near Waterford, a charming old colonial town in northern Virginia. The climate and the area were well suited to the growing of vinifera grapes.With his knowledge of viticulture, Hubert decided to fill a niche in the grape growing enterprises of Virginia. There was a need for a nursery to produce certified vinifera root stock, so Hubert started a nursery operation.

The nursery is known as Schloss Tucker-Ellis Nursery and has been a very successful venture. It now ships grafted vinifera and root stock to 20 states. Ed Ross, who has an agricultural background, is the full time nursery and vineyard manager.

After long and careful climate and soil studies, the Tuckers decided to plant their own vineyards and start a winery. Charles Ellis, the retired chief financial officer of RCA and a neighbor of the Tuckers, became interested in the vineyard project, so the two men decided to form a partnership. They planted the vineyard on parts of both properties.

In 1983, 4 acres were planted, and the next year 21 more acres were added. All of the vines are vinifera – Chardonnay, Riesling and Cabernet Sauvignon. Shortly another 4 acres of Riesling and Pinot Noir will be added. On the combined property of 90 acres there is more suitable land for vineyard expansion.

Hubert Tucker likes to work with small plots and experimental clones. He is working with different clones of Chardonnay and is trying to determine the best trellising system for this varietal. "Vinifera requires excellent management techniques. It is a known fact that 5 to 10 percent of the vines have to be replaced every year due to weather damage," says Hubert.

In choosing the nursery stock for his own vineyard, Hubert has matched less vigorous root stock with more vigorous vine cuttings. In this manner, Hubert Tucker feels that some of the climatic problems could be solved.

Dolores Tucker is very much a part of the entire operation. She is the administrative manager of the nursery and will also take on the administrative work of the winery. In addition, she also takes care of the two Tucker children. Dolores, who worked for the federal government, was involved with the design and creation of traveling exhibits promoting the bicentennial.

The winery has been built, the tasting room and visitor's center is almost completed, and the license has been granted for the operation of the winery. The Tuckers and Charles Ellis are ready to start on a new joint venture.

Rowan LaCompte, the stained glass artist who designed the massive stained glass windows for the Washington National Cathedral, has accepted the commission to design the Loudon Valley Vineyards wine label.

The fall of 1987 will inaugurate the first crush of Loudoun Valley Vineyards. "The first releases will be a barrel fermented and French oak aged Chardonnay and a Riesling," said Hubert who is the winemaker.

All of the grapes used for the Loudoun Valley Vineyards wines will be estate grown. There will be more acreage of grapes planted and the winery will eventually go to 5000 cases per year. "We do not want to grow so big that we cannot keep control of the winemaking," say the Tuckers.

Dolores Tucker loves to cook and particularly likes to use fresh ingredients from their vegetable and herb garden. In the winter months the herbs grow in a greenhouse attached to the lovely kitchen.

TOURS ➡

Loudoun Valley Vineyards, *R D #1, Box 340 Waterford, VA 22190 703-882-3375*
Directions: *From Leesburg take Route 7 to Route 9 west, about 4 miles to Route 698 on right, on Route 698 first driveway on left*
Visitation: *By appointment in fall of 1987 and until April of 1988; then 10 a.m. to 4 p.m. daily*
Principals: *Hubert Tucker and Charles Ellis*
Wines Produced: *Chardonnay, Riesling, Cabernet Sauvignon*
1987 Production: *400 cases*

FRESH TOMATO SAUCE

Serve with Sauvignon Blanc

When accompanied by a green salad and some crusty French bread this is a wonderful summer meal.

2 lbs. fresh, ripe plum tomatoes	1 medium yellow onion, peeled and
1/4 lb. butter	cut in half
Salt to taste	1/4 teaspoon sugar

Wash tomatoes, cut in half and cook over medium heat in a covered stockpot for 10 minutes. Remove from heat and puree the tomatoes in a food processor. Put the tomato mixture in a saucepan. Add the butter, onion, sugar and salt. Cook very slowly, uncovered for 45 minutes. Remove the onion. Serve sauce over spaghetti or linguine. *Serves: 4*

FETTUCCINE ALFREDO BARCHELLA

Serve with Pinot Grigio

This is a very simple way to prepare the classic dish Fettuccine Alfredo.

1/4 lb. butter, softened	3/4 cup heavy cream
2 teaspoons finely chopped fresh parsley	1/2 cup freshly grated Parmesan cheese
1/2 lb. fettuccine	

Cream butter in a bowl, add chopped parsley. Set aside. Cook fettuccine in salted water until al dente. While the fettuccine is cooking, heat a casserole dish in a 250 degree oven. At the same time slowly heat the cream, being careful not to allow it to come to a boil. Drain the fettuccine.

Remove preheated casserole from oven. Place half of the creamed butter in the bottom of the casserole dish, add the drained fettuccine and the remainder of the butter and the Parmesan cheese. Slowly add the cream and toss gently. Top with freshly grated ground pepper and serve immediately. *Serves: 2 or 4 as a first course*

TARRAGON CHICKEN

Serve with Chardonnay

Tarragon adds a slightly anise-like flavor and is most often used with chicken or fish. It is believed to have come to America in the early 19th century.

4 whole chicken breasts, skinned	6 tablespoons butter
1 1/2 tablespoons tarragon	1/2 cup dry white wine

Sprinkle tarragon over the chicken. Place in a baking dish. In a small saucepan melt the butter and add wine. Remove from heat and gently pour over the chicken, trying not to remove the tarragon from the top of chicken. Bake in a preheated 350 degree oven for 1 to 1 1/4 hours. Baste occasionally if desired. Serve over rice. *Serves: 4*

MEREDYTH VINEYARDS Archie Smith, Jr., owner of Meredyth Vineyards, is one of the founders of the modern Virginia wine industry. His hard work and that of his family (wife Dody, son Archie III and daughter Susan) have paid off over the years. Meredyth has probably won more medals for its wines than any other winery in the state. At the 1987 Virginia Wine Competition at the Homestead, Meredyth took five medals – three silver and two bronze.

Archie Smith was the founder and first president of the Virginia Wineries Association. It was in this capacity that Archie, a pioneer in grape growing in the state, helped draft the 1980 Virginia Farm Winery Law. It encouraged grape growing in the state and set down the regulations for farm wineries. In addition, the law provided for strong state technical support and marketing aids. It is one of the most progressive pieces of wine legislation in the country.

It all started for the Smith family when they decided in the early 1970's that their family cattle farm of 215 acres was no longer a profit making operation. The raising of corn was not much better. Archie started looking for something else to grow. He wanted to produce the entire product and control every step of the process. That way he would also know the profit situation. Furthermore, he most definitely did not want to leave the farm.

His roots were there. Archie's mother was born in 1886, a half mile down the road. Even though the family moved away and Archie was born in New Orleans, his mother never forgot they were Virginians. Every summer she brought her son home for a visit. After graduation from high school, Archie became a pre-med student at the University of Virginia. His studies were interrupted by service in the Marine Corps where he was a dive bomber pilot. Archie saw action at Guadalcanal, and later crashed in Okinawa while on a test flight.

Back home with a disability pension, Archie wanted a place to settle down. He moved his family to Virginia in 1952 and purchased the farm next door to where his mother was born. The farm was named Sterling and later the vineyard was named Meredyth after Archie's maternal grandmother."It sounded better than Smith," he said.

In 1972, after doing a great deal of research on grape growing and winemaking and visiting wineries in New York state, Archie Smith decided to try grape growing as the alternative to cattle and corn farming. The climate, he concluded, was similar to France.

Archie planted 5 acres of French hybrids. He felt that since there was virtually no experience in growing wine grapes in Virginia, he would plant the varieties that would better withstand the cold winters. Records showed that the French hybrids fared better than the more delicate vinifera. The first plantings did well and in the following years of 1973 and 1974 he planted more grapes, adding some vinifera the last year. Today there are 56 acres of grape vines – 60 % in French hybrids and 40% in vinifera -- on the rolling hills of the Smith farm south of Middleburg. There are plans to plant 10 more acres.

Since this was the first large vineyard in Virginia, Archie spent many sleepless nights that first year as he watched the vines grow, worried about frost, and wondered if he was using the right trellis system, pruning techniques, fertilization and watering. It was all new and each year still is another new experience for the Smith family in their grape growing and winemaking. Each vintage is different although the routines of grape growing have become the same.

What is done in the vineyard through the growing season affects the harvest. "Pruning is an important activity in the success of winemaking," is Archie Smith's philosophy. Spring pruning in the Meredyth vineyards, for instance, dictates the number of buds that the vines will produce. The pruning work actually proceeds through the summer as the shoots are thinned out to control the size of the crop. "It limits the vines and limits the strain on the vines," commented Archie Smith.

Grass is planted between the vine rows to protect the vines. It is kept short during dry periods, but is allowed to grow in moist periods to absorb some of the moisture and nutrients. The Smiths constantly monitor the grapes for acid and sugar content to determine the right picking time. Harvest begins in mid-August and usually stretches into mid-October depending upon the variety of grape. The De Chaunac, a red grape which hangs in loose clusters, is the last to be harvested.

By 1975, there was enough of a harvest to make wine and start the winery. The stable, which had once housed horses, was converted into the winery. The building was designed by Robert Smith, the youngest son who is an architect and works in Washington, D. C. Meredyth vineyards was one of the first two commercial wineries in Virginia.

Archie Smith started out as the winemaker. He was well suited to the job and loved the constant testing and research involved. His biology and chemistry background from his pre-med school days were a great help. He also induced Archie III, the eldest son, who was a lecturer in philosophy at Oxford University, to commute to Virginia to help in the winemaking. Archie III was a member of a prestigious wine tasting panel at Oxford and had coached wine-tasting competitions. Five years later, in 1980, Archie III gave up his teaching career and became the full time winemaker at Meredyth. "I felt more needed here than in the academic world, and the pioneering aspect appealed to me," he commented.

Archie Smith III is a very innovative winemaker. He uses some of the same varietals to produce different types of wines. For instance, at present Archie III is one of the few making a true nouveau wine by the maceration carbonique technique in Virginia. This French technique requires hand harvesting of the grapes into small lug boxes to prevent any breaking of the skins. The grapes, whole clusters with the stems, are put into a large wooden vat. Carbon dioxide is added and the vat is tightly sealed. Fermentation takes place inside of the grape skins – it works from the inside out, bursting the skins in the process. After about seven to ten days, the fermentation is complete and the grapes are lightly pressed. The wine is then stored in wooden casks to age for a few weeks and is released around the middle of November. Archie III does this process with two French hybrids – Marechal Foch and Villard Noir. The two wines are blended together before bottling.

The other Meredyth Vineyards' red wines are fermented in open top tanks for anywhere from 3 to 10 days. The cap, composed of skins and pulp, is punched down periodically to extract color and flavor. The pulp is then pressed and the remaining wine goes into large 750 gallon redwood or oak tanks for settling. The wine is racked every two to three weeks and then goes into small wooden barrels for 12 to 18 months of aging.

The Meredyth Chardonnay grapes are pressed, the juice is cold stabilized, and then fermented in large wooden uprights. After fermentation, the wine is aged for one month in new wooden barrels.

Meredyth wines are becoming known all over the East Coast. The Smiths believe in a strong retail program and rely on a good distribution system. Meredyth wines are sold in ten eastern states and the District of Columbia. The Meredyth Seyval Blanc has been served at White House dinners.

A strong hospitality program is also a part of Meredyth's promotional activities. There are festivals, lobster dinners and special events at the winery. Quite often one of the 15 wines Archie III has produced will be released for a special event.

All of the Smith family is heavily involved in the winery. Archie, Jr. does the administrative work and oversees the operation. Dody, a former real estate agent, is in charge of accounting. Archie III is the winemaker. Robert, the architect, aids in any remodeling or enlarging of the winery.

There is more to this story of Archie Smith, a pioneer in the Virginia wine industry. It is more than experimentation with grape growing in unknown soils and climates. He is doing his part to save a way of life – the agricultural life -- which he feels is too quickly disappearing from the American countryside.

John Feist, who does catering for Meredyth vineyards, often prepares special foods to serve with the Meredyth wines at the many hospitality events.

TOURS
➡

Meredyth Vineyards, *P. O. Box 347 Middleburg, VA 22117 703-687-6277*
Directions: *From the blinking light on Route 50 in the center of Middleburg, take Madison Street south for 2 1/2 miles, right on Route 628 for 1 1/2 miles to entrance of winery on the right*
Visitation: *Daily 10 a.m. to 4 p.m., except Thanksgiving, Christmas, New Year's Day and Easter.*
Principals: *Mr. and Mrs. Archie Smith, Jr., Archie Smith III*
Wines Produced: *Seyval Blanc, Chardonnay, Villard Blanc, Riesling, Aurora Blanc, Rougeon Rose, De Chaunac, Cabernet Sauvignon, Marechal Foch, Villard Noir*
1987 Production: *18,000 cases*

CHEVRE CHEESE LOAF

Serve with Chardonnay

The mixture of rosemary, goat cheese and cream cheese provides a pleasant spicy hors d'oeuvre to serve with a full bodied wine. Serve the sliced cheese loaf with French bread, sun-dried tomatoes and wine.

1 tablespoon fresh rosemary, chopped	1/2 cup heavy cream
2 lbs. cream cheese, softened	6 oz. sesame bread sticks
1 lb. Virginia goat cheese, softened	6 tablespoons unsalted butter, melted
6 eggs	

In a large bowl combine the rosemary, cream cheese and goat cheese. You may use a food processor. Mix in the eggs and cream.

In a food processor pulverize the bread sticks. Remove from processor bowl and put into a mixing bowl. Add melted butter and blend well to combine. Take this crust mixture and press into bottom and around sides of a 5 lb. loaf pan or two 9x5 inch loaf pans. Fill pan or pans with the cheese mixture and place in a water bath in preheated 350 degree oven. (For water bath take a large cake pan or roaster and fill with 1/2 inch of water. Place cheese pans in the water, and then place both pans in the oven.) Bake for 2 to 2 1/2 hours, or until a toothpick inserted in the center comes out clean. Let cool and remove from pan. *Makes: a 5 pound loaf and serves 30.*

NAKED MOUNTAIN VINEYARD Chardonnay is the classic of the white burgundies and in recent years has become "the wine" to drink at cocktail parties as well as with food. According to James Conaway, wine critic of the *Washington Post*, one of the best Chardonnays made in Virginia is the one produced by Bob Harper of Naked Mountain Vineyard.

Bob Harper and his wife Phoebe have not always been vintners. Until the mid 1970's Bob was a direct sales representative for Texaco and Phoebe still works for the Federal government in northern Virginia as a computer systems analyst.

In 1972, the Harpers purchased a sloping hillside property of 42 acres near Markham, Virginia, about 50 minutes from Washington, D.C. Bob had always had an interest in agriculture, as did Phoebe since her major in college was agricultural economics. His long interest in wines and his hobby of home winemaking led him to plant a vineyard on his property.

By 1975, Bob had built a house for their residence and cleared the land for a 5 acre vineyard to be planted the next year. He wanted to grow only vinifera and decided to plant Chardonnay, Riesling and Sauvignon Blanc. Bob also grows some Cabernet Sauvignon, Cabernet Franc and Merlot.

The Harper's vineyard is one of the few in Virginia growing Sauvignon Blanc and Merlot. Although both of these varieties of grapes are subject to frost kill, Sauvignon Blanc fares better than Merlot. It usually sends off 4 to 5 new shoots each year, thus keeping the vine alive and producing. Bob leaves more than the usual amount of buds on the vines and does not trim excessively. This results in a crop of 7 to 8 tons of Sauvignon Blanc grapes per acre. He uses a spread trellis system to enable the vine to grow up and out. The result is Sauvignon Blanc grapes which ripen to 22 degrees Brix (sugar). Bob uses the same method of trellising for his Chardonnay which he picks at 23 degree Brix, and produces 2 1/2 to 3 tons per acre.

The Naked Mountain Vineyards are planted on the slopes of hills where there is a tendency for erosion. Bob Harper has devised a system to alleviate some of this problem. At the foot of each row he throws up little mounds of dirt which force the vine roots to develop in that area and result in the roots holding the soil. Since the soil is fairly shallow – only 6 inches deep -- it takes longer to establish a root system. However, once the roots are established the plants remain healthy.

Naked Mountain Vineyard is in a thermal inversion area. Located between 800 and 1000 feet elevation, it profits from the winter phenomenon of warm air rising and cold air falling. Thus, the vineyard has frost protection. The soil has also proved to be excellent for a vineyard. Although it has a clay base it has good mineral content.

For years Bob and Phoebe sold their grapes to other wineries. However, by 1981 Bob's hobby of winemaking became professional. He built a winery – literally doing most of the work himself. The building houses the winery equipment and has a spacious tasting room on the second floor surrounded by a lovely deck, suitable for outdoor entertaining. In order to supply the winery, the Harpers lease an additional 7 acre vineyard on a neighboring farm.

Bob Harper believes in traditional methods of winemaking. Naked Mountain's Chardonnay is cold-fermented. The fermentation is stopped at 17% sugar, and the wine is transferred to French oak barrels to finish fermentation and aging on the lees (on the yeasts). This takes about 4 months, during which time the wine is stirred once a week. Bob has also devised a mechanical stirrer consisting of an electric drill with fans attached to a rotating rod.

Naked Mountain's Claret is in the traditional European style, although it could be classified as a Cabernet Sauvignon. The wine consists of 93% Cabernet Sauvignon and the remainder Cabernet Franc and Merlot. Bob Harper, however, chose to call it a Claret in honor of one of the famous wines of Virginia.

Catamount Hollow is a second label for the Harpers. It is the old English name for mountain lion. At the present time it is a white table wine blending white vinifera grapes from the vineyard.

The Naked Mountain Vineyard label features a red shouldered hawk to pay tribute to that species which annually stops on the nearby Blue Ridge Mountains on its north-south migrations.

Bob and Phoebe Harper turned a love of wine making into a truly professional operation. By expanding vineyard acreage, it is their aim in the near future to increase their production to 5000 cases per year.

Bob and Phoebe Harper both like to cook and have taken numerous cooking classes together. One of their favorites was a French cooking class taught by a graduate of Cordon Bleu. Their teacher was particularly influential in the Harper's interest in preparing soups. Phoebe says that most of the soups she prepares are hearty enough to become the main part of a meal when accompanied by a green salad and some warm bread.

TOURS
➡

Naked Mountain Vineyard, *P. O. Box 131 Markham, VA 22643   703-364-1609*
Directions: *From Markham on I-66 take exit 4, go north on Route 688 for 1 1/2 miles, winery is on right side of road*
Visitation: *January and February:Saturday, Sunday and holidays, 11 a.m to 5 p.m. March through December: Wednesday through Sunday and holidays, 11 a.m. to 5 p.m.*
Principals: *Phoebe and Bob Harper*
Wines Produced: *Chardonnay, Sauvignon Blanc, Riesling, Claret, Catamount Hollow White*
1987 Production: *2,500 cases*

BROCCOLI SOUP

Serve with Chardonnay

The broccoli soup may be served hot or cold. It also freezes well.

1 bunch of broccoli	Bouquet Garni made with 1 bay leaf and
1 medium size potato, peeled and cubed	1/4 teaspoon each of thyme, tarragon,
1/2 cup chopped onion	rosemary and chervil, several sprigs
3 cups chicken broth	of fresh parsley
1 1/2 cups half and half	Salt and pepper to taste
1 teaspoon curry powder	Served hot, chopped parsley for garnish
	Served cold, chopped chive for garnish

Remove thick stem pieces from broccoli and peel. Cut broccoli into 1-inch pieces. Place in medium size sauce pan with potato, onion, chicken broth and Bouquet Garni. Cover, bring to a slow boil and then simmer gently for about 20 minutes.

Remove Bouquet Garni and put soup mixture into a blender. Blend until smooth. Cool soup to lukewarm and add half and half. Then stir in the curry powder, and salt and pepper to taste. Heat to serve or serve ice cold garnished accordingly. *Serves: 6*

BEEF BOURGUIGNON

Serve with Claret or Cabernet Sauvignon

This recipe can be multiplied several times. Bob and Phoebe Harper have prepared it for 65 people for a ski weekend. They made several batches and froze them. If after freezing the sauce seems too thick add a little more red wine. Serve over medium size flat noodles.

1 1/2 cups lean salt pork, diced	1/2 teaspoon thyme
3 tablespoons lard	1 bay leaf crumbled
12 small white onions peeled	4 sprigs parsley
2 cups fresh mushrooms, sliced	1/2 teaspoon salt
2 pounds beef shank, cut into small	1/4 teaspoon pepper
cubes with fat removed	1 1/2 cups dry red wine
Salt and pepper to taste	2 1/2 cups beef broth
2 to 4 tablespoons flour	Chopped parsley for Garnish

Place salt pork in a small saucepan and cover with cold water. Bring to a slow boil and simmer for 10 minutes. Drain, rinse in cold water and pat pieces of pork dry.

Place half of the lard in a heavy frying pan over medium heat and add onions and salt pork. Sauté until pork is yellow. Remove onion and salt pork and drain on paper towels. In the same lard, adding more if necessary, sauté mushrooms until tender. Remove mushrooms, drain and set aside for later use.

Sprinkle meat with salt and pepper and coat with flour. Sauté in same lard until meat is brown on all sides. Put meat into an oven proof casserole. Add spices, salt and pepper, wine and beef stock. Cover and cook in a preheated 350 degree oven for 2 hours. Add onions, mushrooms and salt pork. Check seasonings and adjust if necessary. Return covered casserole to oven and cook for another 1/2 hour. The sauce will have reduced by half. Thicken gravy if desired. Serve hot, over noodles, garnished with parsley. *Serves 4*

Oasis Vineyard

Chardonnay
Virginia
1985

Table Wine
Grown, produced and bottled by
Oasis Vineyard, Hume, Virginia. Net Contents 750 M.L.

OASIS VINEYARD For most of the Virginia vintners growing grapes and making wine is a second career. This is true for Dirgham Salahi of Oasis Vineyard near Hume, Virginia.

Dirgham Salahi was born in Jerusalem and came to the United States in 1955. He did his undergraduate work at Louisiana State University and received a Master's Degree in Geology from George Washington University in Washington, D. C. Dirgham worked as a geologist for the American Geology Institute in Washington and as a geological consultant until he became a full time vintner in 1981.

Wanting to get away from the pressures of city life Dirgham and his Belgian-born wife, Corinne, purchased property near Hume in the mid 1970's. They built a French provincial style home and in 1977 planted 15 acres of French hybrid grapes as a hobby. Dirgham and Corinne have an appreciation and interest in wine. For many years Dirgham was a home winemaker in the basement of their home, and won many medals in amateur winemaking competitions.

That same year the Salahis planted 25 more acres of grapes – this time vinifera. Dirgham's geology training indicated that the soil on his property was well suited for wine grape growing. There was the right amount of acid in the soil to produce fine quality grapes with distinctive flavor components. The vineyards are planted on sloping hills which ensure natural drainage.

Dirgham Salahi found some grapes easier to grow than others. First of all he had to learn about the location of the frost pockets in his vineyards which are at 600 to 800 feet elevation. The growing season in the Oasis vineyards is about two weeks later than most of the state and not susceptible to the killing May frosts.

Sauvignon Blanc is difficult to grow, but is an award winning wine for Oasis. Dirgham produces one of the few Sauvignon Blanc wines produced in Virginia.

Sixty more acres were planted in the spring of 1987. These are all vinifera – Cabernet Sauvignon, Merlot, Cabernet Franc, Chardonnay, Sauvignon Blanc and Gewurztraminer. The Cabernet Franc and some Merlot will be used to blend with Cabernet Sauvignon in a traditional Bordeaux style.

By 1980, this hobby of growing grapes was starting to get out of hand. The vines that had been planted in 1977 were producing, and Dirgham could not possibly use all of the grapes in his home winemaking. He and Corinne tried giving the excess grapes away until they realized the grapes were of superior quality. Since he was already an amateur winemaker of some renown, Dirgham decided to make wine commercially.

The Salahis obtained a farm winery license and Drigham made 2,000 gallons of wine in a converted garage. Included in the first vintage was the 1980 Sauvignon Blanc that won a silver medal and best of its class in the

1981 Wineries Unlimited Competition. With that encouragement, the Salahis decided to build a full scale winery in 1981. They spent a year designing the structure after visiting numerous wineries in California and abroad.

The winery, which has one of the largest capacities in Virginia (100,000 gallons), is built partially underground for natural cooling. There are stainless steel tanks and also epoxy lined concrete tanks – the only ones of this kind in Virginia. Dirgham had the concrete tanks shipped from Italy. He uses a portable heat exchanger to maintain the proper temperature of the juice in these epoxy lined tanks. "These are more efficient and less expensive than the popular refrigerated jacketed stainless steel tanks," said Salahi. Another plus for these tanks is that they can be used for either white or red wine and they are easy to clean.

Three types of oak cask – Nevers, American and Yugoslavian   are used to age the Oasis wines. Dirgham believes that aging wine in oak is like a chef using herbs and spices in cooking. He uses the different types of oak to achieve different styles for his wines. Some of the wines are aged in stainless steel to capture only their fruitiness and not add additional flavor components. The Chardonnay is aged in new oak for about two months, while the Cabernet Sauvignon receives about 18 months of oak aging.

Oasis produces about 1600 cases of Champagne each year. This is made by the méthode champenoise developed in the Champagne region of France. The grapes are picked at 18 to 19 degrees Brix – a lower sugar content than for still wines. Oasis uses Chardonnay and Pinot Noir in its Champagne. The two wines are fermented separately, and at the end of the fermentation period they are blended together in about a 80% Chardonnay to 20% Pinot Noir ratio. This may vary slightly according to the vintage.

After the cuvée – as the still wine for Champagne making is called – has been blended, sugar and yeast are added for the secondary fermentation. This is what creates the bubbles in the Champagne. The Champagne bottles are carefully filled, and a pop bottle cap is used to close the bottle.

The secondary fermentation takes about 90 days during which time the bottles are laid on their sides in boxes. The wine continues to age in this position for at least another 15 to 18 months. After the aging, the yeast particles which are still in the wine must be removed. The bottles are put into a rack, called a "riddling rack," neck down so that the yeast particles, which have accumulated along one side of the bottle, can be forced down into the neck. The bottles are turned periodically so that the yeast sediments can flow downward. This procedure is called riddling. When all of the yeast has settled in the neck of the bottle, the neck is dipped into a special solution which freezes the neck of the bottle. The plug with the sediment of yeast is removed or "discorged."

The amount of liquid that escaped from the bottle during discorging is then replaced with what is called a dosage. Since the Champagne is very dry at this point, some sugar, still wine and/or brandy is usually added. Oasis makes an Extra Dry and a Brut style of Champagne. At the 1987 Virginia Wine Competition at the Homestead both Champagnes won medals – the Extra Dry a silver and the Brut a bronze.

Although much of Oasis' wine is sold at the winery, it is very visible in the marketplace. Many restaurants in Washington, D.C. feature Oasis wines on their wine list.

Dirgham and Corinne Salahi are a team. He makes the wine and she is in charge of hospitality, promotion and sales. There are frequent festivals and other patron involvement activities held at the winery.

With the recent planting of 60 additional acres of grapes, the Salahis will continue their already established tradition of premium winemaking. The winery has the capacity, and Dirgham and Corinne are doing their part to make Virginia an important wine producing state.

Corinne Salahi is an excellent cook. She combines European recipes with local Virginia ingredients and accompanies her dishes with Oasis wines.

TOURS
➡

Oasis Vineyard, *Route 1, Hume, VA 22639 703-635-7627*
Directions: *From Washington. D.C. west on I-66 to Marshal (second exit), take Route 647 from Marshall, right on Route 635 for 10 miles to the winery. From Front Royal take Route 522 south towards Flint Hill for 7 miles, then left on Route 635 for 1 mile.*
Visitation: *All year, 10 a.m. to 4 p.m. (except Christmas, New Year's Day & Thanksgiving)*
Principals: *Dirgham Salahi*
Wines Produced: *Chablis, Sauvignon Blanc, Chardonnay, Seyval Blanc, Riesling, Gewurztraminer, Rose, Chelois, Merlot, Cabernet Sauvignon, Champagne*
1978 Production: *10,000 cases*

MUSSEL SOUP

Serve with Sauvignon Blanc

Mussels, bivalved mollusks, are abundant along the shores of Virginia. Since their shells are thin, there is more food in a pound of them than in oysters or clams. This soup, originally a Belgian recipe, served with a green salad and French bread is a most pleasing meal.

4 lbs. Mussels	1 1/2 cups chopped carrots
4 bottles clam juice	1 cup chopped celery
1 1/2 cups dry white wine	1 1/2 teaspoons fennel seeds
1 bunch parsley, chopped	1/2 teaspoon thyme
8 cloves garlic, pressed	1 cup heavy cream
1/2 cup butter	1 tablespoon orzo
2 cups chopped onions	Salt and pepper to taste

Scrub mussels and remove the beards.

In a large saucepan bring wine, 1 bottle of clam juice, parsley and garlic to a boil. Add mussels and steam for 5 minutes, or until shells open. Remove mussels from broth and take the meat out of the shells. Save some of the shells for garnish. Strain the broth and save it.

In another large saucepan or stock pot, melt the butter over medium high heat and sauté onions, carrots and celery until tender. Add rest of clam juice, fennel and thyme. Simmer for 15 minutes. With a slotted spoon remove vegetabless and purée them. Add the vegetables back to pan along with the reserved broth. Just before serving add cream, mussels and orzo. Cook for 1 minute. Season with salt and pepper to taste. Serve garnished with some of the shells. *Serves: 6 to 8*

VEAL STRIPS IN WINE AND CREAM

Serve with Chardonnay

This recipe is similar to a Stroganoff, but with the veal it is much more delicate.

1 1/2 lbs. veal scallops	1/3 cup dry white wine
5 tablespoons butter	1 cup heavy cream
3 tablespoons vegetable oil	Salt and pepper
1 tablespoon minced shallots	

Cut veal scallops into strips 2 x 1/4 inches.

In a large skillet over medium high heat, melt 2 tablespoons butter with the oil. Add veal and sauté until lightly browned. Do this in 2 batches adding 2 more tablespoons butter as necessary. Remove all veal from the skillet.

Add remaining tablespoon butter and sauté shallots. Add wine and bring to a boil. Then add cream and juice from the veal. Reduce liquid by half. Season with salt and pepper. Return veal to sauce and heat through. Serve with noodles or rice. *Serves: 4*

PEARS IN RED WINE

Serve with Chelois

The Bosc pear, like most varieties grown in the United States, was developed from European pears. Poaching pears in wine gives a different flavor dimension to the pear. Serve with a piece of plain cake or a cookie.

6 Bosc pears	1/2 cup sugar
Juice of 1/2 lemon	1 cinnamon stick
2 cups water	1 large piece lemon rind
2 cups red wine	2 tablespoons cognac

Peel and core pears. Add lemon juice to water and immerse the pears in the water so that they will not discolor.

In a saucepan combine the wine, sugar, cinnamon and lemon rind. Bring to a boil over medium heat. Add pears and simmer for 15 minutes, turning pears 2 or 3 times. Remove pears.

Boil liquid until it becomes the consistency of syrup and is reduced by half. Remove cinnamon and lemon rind. Add cognac. Pour syrup over pears and chill for at least 2 hours before serving. *Serves: 6*

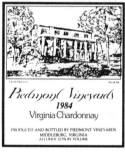

Piedmont Vineyards
1984
Virginia Chardonnay

PRODUCED AND BOTTLED BY PIEDMONT VINEYARDS
MIDDLEBURG, VIRGINIA
ALCOHOL 12.5% BY VOLUME

PIEDMONT VINEYARDS & WINERY Elizabeth Furness had always been a woman of vision – a woman who had goals and knew how to accomplish these goals. In 1973 at the age of 75 she planted the first vinifera vineyard in Virginia since colonial times.

As far back as 1928, when she first caught a glimpse of a stately, but rather dilapidated manor house, Mrs. Furness vowed that someday she would own this property and restore it to its original splendor. Fourteen years later, in 1942, she and her husband, Thomas Furness, purchased Waverly – as the house was called – and its surrounding 500 acres.

Waverly had neither electricity, nor plumbing and needed repairs. The house constructed in 1730, is of Greek Revival architecture, and the Furnesses wanted to preserve the historical significance of Waverly. David Adler, the architect, was hired to undertake the restoration. However, since it was wartime renovation of the home had to wait. It was not until 1946 that the job was completed, and the Furnesses were able to move into Waverly from their home in Lake Forest, Illinois. The property became a working dairy.

The Furnesses quickly became part of the Middleburg community. Mrs. Furness was an accomplished horsewoman and hosted many hunt breakfasts at the magnificently restored estate. She also became active in functions and projects geared to the preservation of other historical properties in northern Virginia. Through her efforts Waverly has become a registered Virginia Historical Landmark.

In the late 1960's, Elizabeth Furness realized – as had many other dairy farmers at the time -- that dairy operations were becoming an unprofitable business. Although she was getting on in years, she did not want to see her beloved property subdivided. Mrs. Furness believed in the preservation of the land. Since the state of Virginia and the Federal government had established favorable tax bases for agricultural land use, Mrs. Furness decided to utilize part of her property for a vineyard. Eventually she also wanted to establish a winery in order to totally produce a farm product.

When Mrs. Furness planted her vineyard, and at the age of 75 she did in fact plant many of the vines, the Department of Agriculture did not know whether growing vinifera would be a viable project. Five acres each were planted in Chardonnay and Semillon and another five were planted with Seyval Blanc, a French hybrid . The vines, including the vinifera, flourished.

The property proved to have good growing conditions for grapes. The Little River, which flows through the area, provides a constant air flow. This is particularly important in the humid periods of late summer, as it prevents bunch rot of the grape clusters.

In 1976 to complete her agricultural project, Mrs. Furness converted the old dairy barn into a winery. Piedmont Winery, in 1977, was the first to sell Virginia wine outside of the state. For this accomplishment Mrs. Furness was honored by the Governor of Virginia.

Elizabeth Furness died in 1985 at the age of 87, having realized her dream of a vinifera winery. Today the winery is administered by Elizabeth Worrall, Mrs. Furness' daughter. She and her husband William, a retired Army colonel, live at Waverly.

Charitable social functions are still being held at Waverly. However, now they are usually formal dinners held in the winery, instead of the hunt breakfasts of former days.

More grapes were planted over the years. Today there are 30 acres of vineyards, with 20 acres in Chardonnay. Semillon and Seyval Blanc are also grown.

Curt Sherrer, a graduate enologist from the University of California at Davis, is the winemaker at Piedmont Winery. He is currently producing three white varietal wines and two white blended wines. "However, we are doing a little experimenting with some reds," he said. Curt harvests the grapes on sugar, usually at 22 to 23 degrees Brix. "That way we harvest on taste and can add acid if needed," Curt explained. The wines are made in the French style.

Almost half of the production is Chardonnay. Curt ferments half of the Piedmont Chardonnay in French oak and puts it through secondary malolactic fermentation. He then blends this Chardonnay with the half that was fermented and aged in stainless steel.

The Semillon is also aged in French oak after fermentation in stainless steel. For a more subtle taste, however, the Semillon is aged in larger – 130 gallon – French oak casks. In October of 1986, the 1984 Piedmont Virginia Semillon won a silver medal in London in the International Wine and Spirits Competition. The award was presented to Elizabeth Worrall in the House of Commons.

The Piedmont Hunt Country White is 90% Seyval Blanc and 10% Chardonnay. It has been aged in oak barrels for six months.

Piedmont Vineyards will release its first methode champenoise Champagne in December, 1987. It is 100 % Chardonnay, made in a Brut style and aged for almost two years.

Elizabeth Worrall, with Curt Sherrer's assistance, plans to expand the winery to 6000 cases per year. They will also plant Cabernet Sauvignon and Cabernet Franc. In addition some acreage of Sauvignon Blanc will be planted. This will be used for blending with the Semillon.

A pen and ink sketch of Waverly by Lloyd Kelley graces the 1984 Piedmont Vineyards Semillon label. His still-life and landscape paintings also adorn other vintages of the Piedmont Semillon. A well-known East Coast artist, Lloyd Kelley resides in Middleburg. Elizabeth Worrall who believes in the melding of fine wine and fine art will continue the tradition of artistic labels for the Semillon. Each year she will select a different artist's work for the label – very much in the tradition of the Rothschild labels. Mrs. Furness would have been delighted with this combination since she was an art and wine lover and had studied in France.

As the first grower and producer of vinifera wine in Virginia in modern times, Elizabeth Furness helped establish the Virginia wine industry. She helped create a product derived from her farm, Waverly, which was so dear to her heart. Her daughter, Elizabeth Worrrall is carrying on that tradition.

Elizabeth Worrall is as much at home in the winery as in the kitchen. She is a gourmet cook and likes to prepare recipes which complement Piedmont's wines.

TOURS
➡

Piedmont Vineyards & Winery, *P.O. Box 286 Middleburg, VA 22117*
Directions: *3 miles south of Middleburg on Route 626, turn left at the winery sign and follow signs to the winery*
Visitation: *Tuesday through Sunday, 10 a.m. to 4 p.m. Same hours on major Monday holidays.*
Principals: *Elizabeth Worrall*
Wines Produced: *Chardonnay, Semillon, Seyval Blanc, Hunt Country White, Little River White*
1987 Production: *4000 cases*

TOMATOES A LA REINE

Serve with Semillon

As the name implies, this dish is fit for a queen. It is excellent as a first course or may be served as a summer luncheon entree.

3 tablespoons butter
3 tablespoons finely chopped onions
3 tablespoons finely chopped carrots
1/8 teaspoon garlic powder
2/3 cup Semillon

2/3 cup water
1/2 teaspoon Bouquet Garni seasoning
4 zucchini, sliced, unpeeled
10 tomatoes, peeled, seeded and drained

In a medium size sauce pan over medium heat melt butter and add onions and carrots. Saute until limp, then add garlic, wine, water and seasoning. Cook over low heat for about 15 minutes until liquid is reduced by one half. Add zucchini and simmer until tender. If mixture is too dry add a little more wine.

Chill mixture and stuff tomatoes with it. Serve on a bed of lettuce with mayonnaise, if desired. *Serves: 10*

BEEF BIRDS IN WHITE WINE

Serve with Chardonnay

Red meat is usually cooked with red wine. However, a full bodied Chardonnay is used here to achieve a lighter meal. The same wine is also served with the entrée. Serve with rice and a green vegetable

12 1/4 inch slices of beef sirloin, about
    5 x 3 in size
1 small onion, chopped
1 stalk celery, diced
1 teaspoon butter
1 1/2 cups toasted bread crumbs
1/8 teaspoon marjoram

1 cup finely chopped parsley
3 tablespoons grated Parmesan cheese
Salt and pepper to taste
1/4 cup flour
2 tablespoons butter
3/4 cup Chardonnay

Place the beef slices between two sheets of wax paper and pound them very thin. In a small skillet melt 1 teaspoon of butter. Add onion and celery and cook until they are transparent. In a bowl combine bread crumbs, marjoram, parsley, Parmesan cheese, salt and pepper. Add the onion mixture and combine to blend.

Divide the filling among the beef slices, roll them up and tie them with a string. Dredge the beef birds with flour. In a large skillet melt 2 tablespoons butter over medium high heat. Lower heat, add beef birds and brown them on all sides. Add the wine and cover the pan. Cook over low heat until meat is tender, about 30 minutes. Carefully remove the strings and serve. *Serves: 4*

Author's note: The beef birds may also be cooked in a preheated 325 degree oven for 25 to 30 minutes.

Virginia

GHARDONNAY
1984

VINTED and BOTTLED BY
WILLOWCROFT
FARM VINEYARDS
Leesburg, Virginia
BW-VA-61
Alcohol 11.5% by Volume

WILLOWCROFT FARM VINEYARDS When Lew and Cindy Parker purchased their farm south of Leesburg, the main farm activity was the 4-H animal projects of their daughters. Lew, however, was looking for an economic agricultural activity for the property.

Located high on Mt. Gilead, the farm has beautiful views of Loudon County and the Blue Ridge Mountains. The area at one time was a popular resort. People came by train in the 20's and 30's to partake of the mineral springs abundant near Mt. Gilead.

Willowcroft Farm dates from the early 1800's. The house was originally a log cabin which has had many additions over the years. Today it is a comfortable white farm house. The old barn, built shortly after the Civil War, is partially underground and has an ideal temperature for a winery.

Lew Parker, an engineering graduate of Lehigh University with an MBA from Wharton, is vice president of Hazelton Laboratories. He is in charge of the company's biotechnology division and divides his time between company headquarters in northern Virginia and a branch in Kansas City. However, he does have time for winemaking with lots of help from his wife Cindy and a full-time employee, Dave Collins. Dave is a graduate of horticulture and manages the vineyards and the farm.

In the spring of 1980 they planted 40 vines. All were planted in the wrong place with the wrong exposure. All but three died the next year. This did not discourage Lew and Cindy and the next year they tried again.

Today there are 3 acres with 1800 vines producing a variety of vinifera grapes – Chardonnay, Riesling and Cabernet Sauvignon. The Parkers are planting another acre of grapes and are leasing an additional 2 acres.

With the first full crop of grapes in 1984 Lew decided to convert the old barn into a winery. He was fortunate in being able to purchase some used dairy equipment which was convertible to winemaking. The decline of the dairy industry in Virginia has been a boon to many winemakers by providing usable stainless steel equipment.

Lew Parker's association with biotechnology proved to be a great aid in his winemaking. Lew recalled, "We won several medals with our first wines, particularly the Chardonnay and the Riesling."

Lew believes that temperature control during fermentation is an extremely important aspect of winemaking. Generally the white wines are fermented in cool temperatures (50 to 55 degrees) so that the fermentation process is a slow one. In this way the best characteristics of the fruit are extracted. On the other hand, the Cabernet Sauvignon is fermented at a higher temperature to obtain better color extraction from the skins.

Lew Parker gives his Chardonnay some oak aging in American oak. The Seyval Blanc, made from purchased grapes, is also aged in American oak, but for a shorter time.

Fifteen percent Chambourcin is blended into the Willowcroft Cabernet Sauvignon. The Parkers feel that this addition helps to smooth out the wine. The Cabernet Sauvignon spends about a year in oak before bottling.

This year Lew and Cindy are adding a Cabernet Blush to their wine repertoire. The Parkers intend to keep their winery operation small and emphasize quality rather than quantity.

Cindy Parker is an accomplished gourmet cook and enjoys experimenting with food to serve with Willowcroft wines – from soup to desserts.

TOURS
➡

Willowcroft Farm Vineyards, *Route 2, Box 174 A Leesburg, VA 22075*
703-777-8161
Directions: *South of Leesburg on Route 15, turn right on Route 704, immediately left on Route 797(dirt road), 3.1 miles to winery sign*
Visitation: *By appointment*
Principals: *Lew and Cindy Parker*
Wines Produced: *Chardonnay, Riesling, Seyval Blanc, Cabernet Sauvignon, Cabernet Blanc*
1987 Production: *1100 cases*

POTAGE CRECY

Serve with Seyval Blanc

This carrot soup may be served as a first course or as a luncheon dish accompanied by a salad and French bread. The addition of tomato paste to the soup is a good flavor complement for the carrots.

2 tablespoons butter	2 tablespoons white raw rice
3/4 cup finely chopped onions	Salt and white pepper to taste
3 cups finely chopped carrots	1/2 cup heavy cream
1 quart chicken stock	1 tablespoon soft butter
2 teaspoons tomato paste	8 to 12 carrot curls

In a heavy 4 quart saucepan, melt the butter over moderate heat. Stir in the onions and cook, stirring occasionally for five minutes or until the onions are soft but not browned. Add the carrots, chicken stock, tomato paste, rice and simmer uncovered for 30 minutes. Purée the soup in a blender or food processor. Season with salt and pepper to taste. Stir in the cream.

Before serving, return the soup to low heat and bring it to a simmer. Remove from heat and stir in the tablespoon of soft butter. Ladle the soup into individual soup bowls and garnish with one or two carrot curls. *Serves: 4 to 6*

SICILIAN SAUSAGE SOUP

Serve with Cabernet Sauvignon, french bread and a tossed salad.

Cindy Parker likes to prepare this hearty soup with an Italian accent at crush time. Since sausage is used in the preparation, the soup has a pleasing blend of spices which complement the zucchini and the orzo – tiny rice shaped pasta..

1/2 lb. bulk pork sausage	1/2 cup orzo
1 large onion, chopped	1/4 teaspoon salt
1 can (2 lb. 3 oz.) Italian tomatoes	1/8 teaspoon pepper
3 1/2 cups chicken broth	1 can (15 oz.) zucchini in tomato sauce
1 teaspoon leaf basil, crumbled	

In a large saucepan cook sausage over medium heat, breaking it up with a wooden spoon until all color has disappeared. Add tomatoes, chicken broth and basil. Bring to a boil and stir in orzo and salt and pepper. Lower heat and simmer, partially covered, for 20 minutes or until orzo is tender. Add canned zucchini and heat through. Serve in soup bowls. *Serves: 4*

BAKED FISH WITH SPINACH STUFFING

Serve with Chardonnay or Seyval Blanc

Florentine is a cooking method which uses spinach as a base and is used with fish. The fish may be set on a base of spinach and baked, or as in this case stuffed with a spinach mixture and then baked.

4 tablespoons butter	1 4 lb. dressed fish – trout, turbot,
1/3 cup chopped shallots	pollack or cod
1 10 oz. package frozen spinach	6 tablespoons butter
2 cups bread crumbs	1 cup dry white wine
4 tablespoons heavy cream	Salt and pepper to taste
1 teaspoon lemon juice	Parmesan cheese
Salt and pepper to taste	

Melt 4 tablespoons butter in medium size saucepan and cook onions until soft, but not brown. Add spinach and cook to evaporate moisture. Transfer to a large mixing bowl, add bread crumbs, cream, lemon juice and salt and pepper.

Preheat oven to 400 degrees. Stuff the fish cavity with the spinach mixture. Close opening with roasting pins and lace firmly with string. Place fish in oven proof dish, uncovered. Pour in wine and place 6 butter pats on top. Sprinkle with salt and pepper and Parmesan cheese. Bake for 40 to 50 minutes or until fish is done. Garnish with watercress and lemon slices when serving. *Serves: 4*

SPAGHETTI PIE

Serve with Cabernet Sauvignon

Pasta forms the crust in this unusual pie reminiscent of a pizza. The use of sausage meat eliminates the need for spices in this dish. The pizza may be prepared, however, with ground beef with the addition of Italian herbs.

6 oz. spaghetti
2 eggs, beaten
1/4 cup grated Parmesan cheese
2 tablespoons butter
1/2 cup chopped green pepper
1/3 cup chopped onion

1 cup sour cream
1 lb. sausage
1 6 oz. can tomato paste
1 cup water
4 oz. mozzarella cheese, cut into strips

Break spaghetti in half and cook in boiling salted water until al dente. Drain. While still warm, combine spaghetti with eggs and Parmesan cheese. Put mixture into a well-greased 10 inch pie plate. With the back of a spoon press it up and around the sides to make a "crust."

Melt butter in skillet and sauté green pepper and onion until the onion is transparent. Add sour cream and spoon over spaghetti. Cook sausage in another skillet, crumbling the meat. Drain off fat. Add tomato paste and water. Mix well. Simmer 10 minutes. Spoon over the sour cream. Bake in preheated 350 degree oven for 25 minutes. Remove pie from oven and place strips of mozzarella cheese on top in spoke wheel fashion. Return to oven to melt the cheese. *Serves: 6*

CHOCOLATE MOUSSE CAKE

Serve with Riesling

There is no flour in this cake because it is really a chocolate mousse that when baked turns into a rich, fudgy cake. If the cake is baked the day before and chilled thoroughly it will be easier to unmold and slice.

6 eggs
1/2 cup sugar
16 oz. semisweet chocolate
1/4 cup strong brewed coffee
1/4 cup Grand Marnier or dark rum

2 teaspoons vanilla extract
3 cups heavy cream
2 tablespoons sugar
1 tablespoon Grand Marnier or dark rum
Shaved chocolate

Put the eggs and sugar into a bowl and begin to beat on high speed. Continue beating for at least 5 minutes or until the mixture is thick and creamy.

Put the chocolate in the top of a double boiler. Add coffee and Grand Marnier or rum and melt until smooth. Remove from heat. Add vanilla and set aside.

Whip 1 cup of the cream until thick and stiff. Fold the chocolate into the beaten egg mixture and then gently fold in the whipped cream. Make sure the batter is well mixed and then pour it into a 9 inch springform pan.

Set the springform pan into a larger pan and fill the larger pan with about 2 inches of hot water. Bake the cake in a preheated 350 degree oven for 1 hour until the center of the cake seems firm to the touch.

When cake is done, remove it from the oven and carefully lift it out of the water bath. Set it on a rack to cool completely. Cover and chill at least 8 hours or overnight.

To serve the cake, whip the other 2 cups of cream with the 2 tablespoons of sugar and 1 tablespoon Grand Marnier or rum. Whip until thick and stiff. Remove the cake from the refrigerator. Run a knife around the side, and gently release the sides of the springform pan. Invert the cake onto a serving platter and carefully lift off the bottom. Frost top and sides of cake with whipped cream. Decorate with shaved chocolate. Surround the cake with fresh fruit, if desired. *Serves: 8 to 10*

THE ASHBY INN   Paris, Virginia, once called Pun'kinville, is a small village two blocks long in the Northern Virginia Hunt Country. It is a tranquil community of about 60 residents with two streets each two blocks long. The village changed its name to Paris soon after the Revolutionary War in honor of the Marquis de Lafayette who had come for a visit.

Across the street from the present Ashby Inn lies the site of the Ashby Tavern frequented by George Washington during his early days as a surveyor, when he did considerable work in the area. The Ashby Tavern was also a coach stop between Winchester and Washington. During the Civil War, the little town of Paris changed hands a number of times and General J.E.B. Stuart and Mosby's Raiders spent time there.

The three story Ashby Inn, which has six guests rooms, is a converted residence. The original building dates back to 1829 and the additions predate the Civil War. In the early 1980's, John and Roma Sherman purchased the old building with the intention of remodeling it and opening a country inn. Great care was taken to preserve the early architectural proportions of the building. The Ashby Inn is the only business in the little town of Paris.

The original kitchen, located on the first floor of the four story house, is the gathering place in the late afternoon for local horse breeders, trainers and riders; and guests of the inn. The walnut beams and stone fireplace have been meticulously preserved in what is today known as the Tap Room. On the second flour of the inn are two dining rooms and an enclosed porch, also used for dining.

Although the dining facilities of the inn have been open for only two years, the cuisine of the Ashby Inn has gained a fine reputation. It has been the aim of both John and Roma Sherman, who had never operated a restaurant before, to offer first rate food at moderate prices. Roma is English and has a love for cooking. It is due to her influence that many English items are featured on the menu. John, on the other hand, also likes to cook and has added some of his favorites to the menu. He prefers country fare such as venison and duck and these are also featured on The Ashby Inn menu.

The menu at the Ashby Inn varies according to the season. The Shermans grow a good part of their own vegetables and herbs, and feature such items as asparagus and fresh raspberries when they are in season. Soft-shelled crabs from the Eastern Shore are also presented when available.

The combination of English and country American cuisine is working well at this country inn located in a peaceful setting along the eastern slope of the Blue Ridge Mountains.

DINING →

The Ashby Inn, *Route 1, Box 2 A Paris, VA 22130 703-592-3900*
Directions: *Route 50 west of Middleburg and Upperville take Route 759 into Paris. Route 50 becomes a four lane highway just before Paris.*
Principals: *John and Roma Sherman*
Meal Times: *Breakfast for overnight guests only; May through October, Saturday Lunch: 12:30 p.m. to 3:30 p.m. Sunday Brunch: 12:30 p.m. to 3:30 p.m. Wednesday through Saturday (year around) Dinner: 6:30 p.m.. to 9 p.m.*

SAUSAGE AND GREENS SOUP

This sausage and greens soup is influenced by Roma's English heritage. The English love hearty soups and this is no exception. The use of kale or turnip greens give this basic bean soup an extra dimension.

1 cup dried white (Navy) beans	1 cup finely diced leeks
8 cups cold water	4 cups cleaned trimmed and coarsely
1/4 lb. prosciutto, or ham	chopped kale or turnip greens
8 cups beef veal or chicken stock	1/4 teaspoon freshly ground pepper
2 smoked ham hocks	6 oz. chorizos or 6 oz. length of kielbasa
1/8 lb. salt pork, cut into small cubes	1 lb. potatoes, peeled and cut into
1/2 cup chopped onion	1/2 inch cubes

The night before cooking soup, put the beans and cold water into a bowl and let the beans soak overnight. Cut the prosciutto into 1/4 inch cubes. Drain the beans and put into a stock pot along with the stock and ham hocks.

In a skillet, heat the salt pork on medium high heat. When the pork has rendered some fat, add the onions, leeks and cubed prosciutto or ham. Sauté until the onions are soft. Drain excess fat, and add mixture to beans in the pot. Add the kale and bring soup to a boil; cover and cook gently for 40 minutes to 1 hour until the beans are almost done or al dente. Skim off and discard any fat from the surface.

Add the chorizos and the potatoes. Bring to a boil and let simmer about 15 to 20 minutes or until potatoes are tender. Remove the chorizos and cut them into 1/2 inch rounds. Return the sausage to the soup and heat through. Serve with French bread and a green salad. *Serves: 6 to 8*

Author's note: There are two ways of soaking beans – the overnight method and the quick method. Quick method: Put water and beans in a pot and bring to a boil. Cover pot and cook for 2 minutes. Remove from heat and let stand for 1 hour. Then cook according to the recipe directions.

JORDAN'S From the front the restaurant looks like many of the other 18th century houses on Loudoun Street in Leesburg. It was just the place Kim and Peggy Jordan had been seeking. They had been looking for a house in a small town near Washington that could be turned into a restaurant.

Kim Jordan is a graduate of the prestigious Culinary Institute of America and has worked as the Chef de Cuisine in such well known Washington Restaurants as Le Maison Blanche, Vincent and Restaurant Nora. It had always been Kim and Peggy's dream to own a small restaurant of their own. "We even planned it before Kim went to the Culinary Academy," Peggy recalled.

The Jordans wanted their two small children to grow up in the country in a more relaxed atmosphere. They spent almost every free day looking for a suitable location for their restaurant. Whenever they found a likely place, it turned out that the owners were not willing to remodel for restaurant facilities.

Luckily when they found their present location, much to their delight it was owned by an architectural firm that was willing to make the necessary changes. The firm, Ballinger-LaRock not only did the remodeling, but they also designed the restaurant. The firm retains an office above Jordan's.

The outside of the building does not look like a restaurant, except for the side which has the entrance and a glass facade. The inside is very subtly designed with sophisticated soft-colored decor that suggests comfort and leisure dining. The grey and beige color scheme is broken with the use of arches and soft indirect lighting.

The food is every bit as sophisticated as the decor. The cuisine is not trendy, but classic. Since Kim Jordan uses only fresh ingredients, the menu changes almost daily. Many items are cooked to order, guaranteeing freshness. Sauces are Kimberley's forte and are subtle enough not to be overpowering. Desserts are all made in house and are also very special. Kim particularly likes to work with chocolate and there is always either a white or dark chocolate dessert on the menu.

In spite of its popularity, Jordan's refuses to extend its hours. Kim and Peggy have two small children and want to care for them personally. Peggy acts as hostess most of the evenings and is in charge of the wine list. Wines of a local Virginia winery, Willowcroft, are featured, along with California and French selections.

Jordan's, *107 Loudoun Street S.W. Leesburg, VA 22075 703-777-1471*
Directions: *Jordan's is located in the center of town on Loudoun Street, just up the street from the Loudoun Museum*
Principals: *Kim and Peggy Jordan*
Meal Times: *Tuesday through Thursday, Dinner: 6 p.m. to 9 p.m.*
Friday and Saturday, Dinner: 6 p.m. to 9:30 p.m.
Reservations: *advised*

BRAISED SALMON WITH VEGETABLES

Most of the salmon in the East comes from the Pacific Northwest, Nova Scotia or Norway. With modern air transportation, fresh salmon is available almost anywhere. However, it is still a great delicacy and is served in the finest restaurants. The use of tomato and black olives gives this salmon entrée an unusual flavor combination.

2 tablespoons extra virgin olive oil	1 cup tomato, peeled, de-seeded and diced
1/2 teaspoon diced garlic	8 oil cured black olives, sliced
Pinch of cracked pepper	1 1/2 cups dry white wine
2 8 oz. salmon filets (thick, if possible)	Salt and pepper to taste
1/4 cup chopped onion	1/4 cup roasted pine nuts
1/4 cup chopped celery	

Heat oil in a heavy pan with deep sides and a tight fitting lid. Add garlic and red pepper and saute briefly. Add salmon. Cover the two pieces of salmon with the onion, celery, tomato and olives, dividing the ingredients evenly between the two. Add the wine.

Bring to a simmer and cover. Cook until salmon is just barely done, but cooked through, about 10 to 11 minutes. Remove salmon to two warm plates and keep warm. Quickly reduce sauce until full flavored but not thick. Spoon around the salmon filets and sprinkle the pine nuts over the fish. *Serves: 2*

CALVES LIVER WITH BALSAMIC VINEGAR AND SHALLOTS

Balsamic vinegar, popular in Italy, has a dark rich color and a somewhat pungent sweet taste. It is basically made from grapes and aged in a series of barrels. This simple preparation of calves liver is enhanced by the use of Balsamic vinegar which also lightens the richness of the dish. This preparation of calves liver is a very popular entreé at Jordan's.

8 oz. calves liver, thinly sliced	1/3 cup Balsamic vinegar
Flour	1/3 cup brown sauce
4 to 5 tablespoons clarified butter	Salt and pepper, to taste
3 tablespoons chopped shallots	1 1/2 tablespoons soft butter

Dredge the liver in flour. Quickly saute the liver in a skillet over medium high heat in 3 tablespoons of hot clarified butter. Remove liver when medium rare. Add 1 more tablespoon clarified butter to the skillet, and when very hot add shallots and saute until transparent.

Deglaze the pan with the vinegar, reduce to half and add brown sauce. Season with salt and pepper. Remove from heat and swirl in the softened butter. Spoon over individual servings of liver and serve. *Serves: 2*

Author's note: Melted butter has a milky sediment that settles in the pan and scorches easily. Since this dish is prepared over high heat, clarified butter is recommended. To clarify butter, heat it in a small pan until a froth rises. Spoon off the froth and pour off the clear oil (butter).

LITTLE RIVER INN In colonial days an establishment such as the Little River Inn might be known as an ordinary or a stagecoach stop. Today the Little River Inn is a journey into the past for the guests who stay there.

The village of Aldie was established by an act of the Virginia Legislature around a grist mill on the banks of the Little River in 1810. The mill and the land around the mill was owned by Charles Mercer who had inherited it from his grandfather. The land of 30 acres was divided by Mercer into town lots. He chose the name Aldie for the town in honor of his ancestral home in Scotland. Today the village looks very much as it did in colonial days. Most of the houses date back 150 to 200 years and are strung along the original road – now state route 50. The stone bridge, which is the entrance to the town from the east, dates from 1815. There are about 70 residents in the town and 1500 in the surrounding area.

The grist mill remained in operation until 1971. A few years ago the structure was given to the Virginia Outdoors Foundation by the Douglas family who had operated the mill since 1835. There is now a tremendous project underway to restore the mill and make it an operating entity. Tucker Withers, one of the local residents and the owner of the Little River Inn, is active in this project. One of the contributors to the project is the Vinifera Wine Growers Association, headquartered nearby in The Plains, Virginia.

In the late 1970's a pleasant young man, Tucker Withers, moved to Aldie from Bethesda, Maryland. He had deep roots in the town. His great aunt had lived in the house which is the center of the Little River Inn. When Tucker took up residence in Aldie, he also established a business – Stone Bridge Antiques. Located on one side of the old stone bridge, the business has not only become a landmark in Aldie, but has given Tucker the opportunity to pursue one of the great loves of his life – the antique business.

In early 1982 when the last tenants left his great aunt's house, which he had previously purchased, he decided to turn the property into an inn. Tucker and his partner, Monica Lee, stripped the many coats of paint from the original woodwork and restored and repaired the house. Each room is comfortably furnished with pieces representative of the mid 1850's.

Tucker wanted the type of atmosphere that existed in colonial days. He provided two sitting or common rooms where his guests could gather at day's end, compare notes on their individual sightseeing or discuss their respective homes over a pint of ale or a glass of wine. Both are complimentary and available in the refrigerator in the kitchen. A large table in the dining room next to the kitchen is the setting for breakfast each morning. Many times Tucker comes over from "up the street" to prepare breakfast for his guests. He always has a helpful hint as to where the best vineyards are and the best places to dine in the evening. All of the guests become an extended family, so to speak.

Tucker, recently married now, has a family of his own. His wife, Mary Ann who teaches in the county school system, and his infant son are both welcome additions to the town of Aldie.

In recent years, Tucker has purchased two small cottages, one on each side of the original house and has added them to the Inn's complex. He has also been busy renovating other houses in Aldie; one of which is to be a restaurant and scheduled to open in the spring of 1988.

Even though Tucker is expanding his operations, he will never lose sight of providing a relaxing and comfortable atmosphere for his guests. He will always try and provide colonial hospitality – out of the ordinary these days, but reminiscent of the days when Inns such as the Little River Inn were an *Ordinary*.

These breakfast recipes of Tucker Withers are typical of those served to the overnight guests at the Little River Inn. They would also be the star of any Sunday brunch.

DINING
➡

Little River Inn, *P. O. Box 116 Aldie, VA 22001 703-327-6742*
Directions: *Route 50, 35 miles west of Washington, D. C.*
Meal Times: *Until spring 1988: Breakfast only 7 a.m. to 9:30 a.m.*
After spring 1988, full dinner service in new restaurant, call for information.
Principals: *Tucker Withers and Monica Lee*

DUTCH APPLE BABY

This recipe takes about as long to prepare as it takes to drink that first cup of coffee in the morning.

3 large eggs
3/4 cup milk
3/4 cup flour

1/2 teaspoon salt, optional
2 to 3 tablespoons butter
Fruit Filling*

Preheat oven to 450 degrees.

Blend eggs, milk and flour at high speed in blender for 30 seconds. Scrape sides down with rubber spatula, cover and blend again. Place batter in freezer while skillet is heating. Place 2 to 3 tablespoons butter in a 10 inch heavy iron cast skillet and place in preheated 450 degree oven until butter sizzles and skillet is hot. Pour batter into skillet. Bake 15 minutes. Open oven and pierce center of puffed pancake with fork several times so that center deflates. Remove skillet from oven; carefully lift pancake from skillet and place on heated plate. Fill center with prepared fruit.* Sprinkle with confectioners sugar, cut into wedges and serve.

Apple Filling*

4 tablespoons butter
1/4 cup sugar
1 tablespoon chopped pecans
1/4 cup raisins

3 to 4 apples, cored and sliced
1 teaspoon cinnamon
Small amount of apple juice, optional

While pancake bakes, prepare fruit filling. In saucepan, over medium-low heat, cook all ingredients until apples are softened and moist. Add small amount of apple juice if mixture seems dry. *Serves: 4 to 6*

BAKED FRENCH TOAST

This dish is prepared the night before so that the bread will soak up as much moisture as possible. All that is necessary the next morning is to put the dish in the oven and bake.

1 cup packed brown sugar, light or dark
1/2 cup butter (1 stick)
2 tablespoons corn syrup, light or dark
5 eggs

1 loaf of French bread, sliced into 3/4 to
    1 inch slices
1 and 1/2 cups milk
1 teaspoon vanilla extract

Prepare either one 13x9 inch or two 8x8 inch baking dishes by spraying them with non-stick spray (PAM). Use refrigerator to cool ovenware casserole. In a saucepan, over medium low heat, mix sugar, butter and corn syrup. Cook until mixture is melted and blended, being careful not to let it caramelize. Slice French bread. Estimate 2 slices per serving or more for the hearty eater. Pour butter mixture into prepared pan or pans. Arrange bread slices flat in butter-sugar mixture.

In a blender mix the eggs, milk and vanilla. Pour this mixture over the bread slices, not missing any areas. Use all of the egg milk mixture, the excess will be absorbed by the bread slices. Cover baking dish and refrigerate overnight.

The next morning, uncover dishes and bake in 350 degree oven for 30 minutes. Serve directly from baking dish. Butter and syrup are not needed. *Serves: 4 to 6*

POST OFFICE BOX 385
MIDDLEBURG, VIRGINIA 22117

THE RED FOX TAVERN AND INN

The Red Fox Tavern is Virginia's oldest inn, dating from 1728. It was an early stagecoach stop known as Chinn's Ordinary. The original stone structure was built by Joseph Chinn in 1728 on the edge of a vast estate owned by Thomas, the sixth Lord of Fairfax and Baron of Cameron. Thomas was an eccentric bachelor who preferred rugged life in a log cabin on the Shenandoah to his social and political responsibilities in London.

Chinn's Ordinary was a popular stopping place about midway between the fashionable town of Alexandria and the frontier town of Winchester. In 1748 Lord Fairfax contracted with surveyors to do a plat plan of his landholdings around Chinn's Ordinary – the area which is now around Middleburg. One of the surveyors who not only worked on that project, but did much of the surveying of the lands between Middleburg and Winchester was young George Washington.

In the late 1700's Chinn's Ordinary and Chinn's Crossroads, as the little settlement around the inn became known, were sold to the newly chartered town of Middleburg. Fifty acres were included in this sale for the price of $2.50 per acre. Chinn's Ordinary continued to be the center of the community for social, and political activities. Middleburg was fast becoming the young nation's foremost area for fox hunting, thoroughbred breeding and horse racing. The town still retains that reputation. In 1812, after extensive renovations, Chinn's Ordinary was enlarged to 35 rooms and an extensive wine cellar was added. The name of the inn was changed to The Beveridge House.

Fierce fighting took place around The Beveridge House during the Civil War. Battle strategies were planned at dinner meetings at the inn by General Jeb Stuart and Colonel John Mosby who met there often. The Beveridge house also served as a Confederate hospital, utilizing the guest rooms for the wounded. The pine bar of the tavern became the operating table. Many evenings while the wounded were being cared for downstairs, battle strategies for the next day were being planned upstairs in the dining room.

In 1887, The Beveridge House became the Middleburg Inn. It continued to offer accommodations and food. In 1937 the name was again changed to the present Red Fox Inn. Turner Reuter, along with his mother and sister, acquired the property in 1976. They completely refurbished the inn with 18th century traditional furnishings but with 20th century comforts. Over the past few years satellite buildings have been acquired to enlarge the guest accommodations. The Stray Fox, one block away from The Red Fox was a residence built before the Civil War. It too was an inn in the early 1800's by the name of the Stray Shot. A misfired cannon ball had struck its foundation, hence the name. The Stray Fox's stable boarded the change of horses that were used on the daily Alexandria-Winchester stagecoach run. The stable was rebuilt in 1983 and today houses the Red Fox Fine Art Gallery.

The smokehouse, built in the early 1700's and a part of the early Chinn community, is one of the oldest structures in Middleburg. Today it serves as a specialty leather and tack shop. The McConnell House constructed in 1940 as the office and residence of the local doctor has also been acquired by the Red Fox establishment. The house known by the local residents as the "Pill Box" has added five more guest suites to the Inn.

There are seven cozy dining rooms at The Red Fox Inn. Marcel Van Eeckhaut is the Executive Chef. The cuisine is international but also emphasizes traditional Virginia specialties. Fresh ingredients are used, and all of the baking and desserts are made in house. The wine list proudly supports local vineyards which "carry on the tradition of the early Virginia vintner, Thomas Jefferson."

DINING
➡

The Red Fox Tavern and Inn, *2 East Washington Street P. O. Box 385 Middleburg, VA 22117 703-687-6301*
Directions*: On Route 50 in the center of Middleburg*
Principals*: Turner Reuter*
Meal Times*: Breakfast: 8 a.m. to 10 a.m. Lunch: 11:30 a.m. to 2:30 p.m. Dinner: 6:00 p.m. to 9:00 p.m. (closed Sunday evening) Lunch and Dinner reservations advised*

BLACK BEAN AND SAUSAGE SOUP

Beans and corn were the colonists first vegetables. They were taught bean cultivation by the Indians who had learned that they could be cultivated in poorer soil than was necessary to grow corn. The Indians also taught the early settlers to dry beans and store them for later use. Since beans are high in protein they made a good substitute for meat in colonial days. Dried beans also became a substitute for money and were used for barter with the Indians.

The black bean, which is known to have been used in Mexico over seven thousand years ago, is used throughout the Caribbean and has become a favorite in soups throughout the South. This soup recipe is a variation of the black bean soup which has been popular in the South for many years.

1 1/4 cups black beans
1 cup chopped carrots
1 cup chopped onions
1 cup chopped celery
2 cloves garlic, minced
4 tablespoons butter
Salt and pepper to taste

1/8 cup fresh chopped thyme
1/8 cup fresh chopped basil
1/8 cup fresh chopped marjoram
3/4 cup red wine
1 1/4 lb. Italian sausage, cut in
    1/2-inch slices
8 cups chicken stock

Soak beans overnight in water. The next day drain beans and place in a stock pot.

Melt butter in a medium size sauce pan over medium high heat and sauté vegetables, garlic and spices until the vegetables are limp. Add red wine to deglaze pan and cook to reduce liquid by two thirds. In a skillet sauté sausage pieces until lightly browned. *Serves: 6*

Add vegetable mixture, sausages and chicken stock to the stock pot. Bring slowly to a boil, cover and simmer until beans are tender, 1 1/2 to 2 hours. Serve in soup bowls.

Author's note: If fresh herbs are not available, substitute 1/2 teaspoon dried thyme, basil and marjoram. Beans may be precooked, the same day as the soup is being prepared. In a saucepan, simply cover the beans with water. Bring to a boil and cook for 2 minutes. Remove from heat and let stand for 1 hour. Drain beans and proceed with the recipe.

RASPBERRY CHAMPAGNE SORBET

Sorbet was originally an iced drink served in Turkey. In modern times it is served either before the meat course as a palate cleanser or as a dessert. If served as palate cleansers, sorbets are often served in goblets or glasses.

8 cups fresh raspberries	Juice of 1 lemon
2 cups extra fine sugar	Mint leaves for garnish
1 bottle Champagne	

Crush berries slightly and sprinkle with 1 cup of sugar. Let sit overnight in the refrigerator. The next day drain the juice and set the pulp aside in a separate bowl. Put pulp through a strainer to eliminate the raspberry seeds. Add the rest of the sugar to the pulp and stir well to blend. Add Champagne to the juice, and then add the lemon juice. Mix in the pulp. Pour entire mixture into a stainless steel bowl and place in freezer. Stir about once every hour until frozen. Serve garnished with mint leaves. *Serves: 10 to 12 as a dessert, makes 3 quarts.*

WINDSOR HOUSE RESTAURANT AND COUNTRY INN

WINDSOR HOUSE RESTAURANT AND COUNTRY INN The old stone building in the center of Middleburg, Virginia, which today is known as the Windsor House, is one of the landmarks of this small town in the Northern Virginia Hunt Country. Completely restored, this brick edifice with its black shutters and wrought iron fencework was built in 1824.

The stately house was a residence and an inn and started operations in 1829. During the Civil War the Colonial Inn, as it was called in those days, continued operation under the ownership of Catherine Broun and her husband. At that time it was not an easy task to operate an inn with the Civil War raging all about the premises.

In the early 1980's Jacqueline Watson and her husband David Welch started looking for an old house to remodel and possibly convert into a country inn. They fell in love with the old Broun house and were able to purchase it. The Welchs sold their house in Washington, took their savings plus a bank loan, and proceeded with the renovations.

David Welch had been an engineer and Jacqueline was Director of Social Events for the American Institute of Architects in Washington, D.C. Jacqueline was accustomed to supervising dinners and receptions for up to 2000 people. Running an inn and a restaurant would not be unusual for this energetic lady.

Most of the interior remodeling was done by David and Jacqueline. They kept the structure and atmosphere of this old Federalist style residence. Architectural details were carefully researched and special moldings and woodwork were custom made.

The third floor of the building was completed first, and served as living quarters for the couple. The first stage of the plan was to open the Windsor House as a restaurant and then open up guest rooms. There are three dining rooms, each with a fireplace. They all have a very comfortable and pleasant atmosphere. It was David and Jacqueline's intention to have their diners feel as if they were dining in someone's home. The restaurant opened in early 1982. Unfortunately in the spring of 1983, David died of a heart attack.

Jacqueline Watson did not give up on their dream. With great perseverance she went on to build the Windsor House into one of the prime restaurants in northern Virginia. In the spring of 1987 two lovely guest suites were opened for overnight accommodations.

A novel part of the Windsor House decor is the use of unicorns – sculptured, painted, china, pewter, crystal and tapestry. They are everywhere. "Queen Elizabeth of the House of Windsor has the lion and the unicorn on her crest," said Jacqueline Watson. In honor of this historical fact she choose the unicorn as a symbol of her English type establishment.

The original plan was to serve English cuisine, as the name Windsor House would suggest. Jacqueline soon found that the food selection of this cuisine was too limiting. The menu has been expanded and the cuisine could be classified as classic American. However, traditional English items, such as roast beef and Yorkshire pudding, meat pies, and Scottish trifle have remained on the menu. These were also some of the items on menus in colonial Virginia.

The menu changes frequently since all fresh ingredients are used in preparation of meals. In order to present an ever-changing menu, the selections are hand written daily on ceramic tablets and placed at each table.

Robert Mayer is the Chef de Cuisine at the Windsor House. He had originally planned to be a doctor, but his love for cooking took precedence. Robert has studied extensively in France with such renowned chefs as Marcel Kereval and Jean-Claude Guillisou. Prior to coming to the Windsor House, Mayer worked at the Hawks Cay resort in Florida and The Harvest in Boston. He works very closely with Jacqueline Watson to coordinate food and menu ideas. "We pretty much think alike," says Jacqueline.

An extensive Virginia wine list is featured at Windsor House, along with California and French selections.

DINING
➡

Windsor House Restaurant and Country Inn, *Middleburg, Virginia 22117*
703-687-6800
Directions: *Corner of Route 50 and Madison Street in center of Middleburg*
Principals: *Jacqueline Watson*
Meal Times: *Weekdays, except Wednesday Lunch: 11:30 a.m. to 2:30 p.m. Dinner 6 p.m. to 9:30 p.m. Sundays, Brunch 11 a.m. to 2 p.m. Dinner 5 p.m. to 9 p.m. Reservations advised*

CRAB SOUP

Crab is one of the most popular seafood items in Virginia. This elegant soup is a glorious beginning to any meal.

1 1/2 lbs. tomatoes	1/4 cup Madeira or dry sherry
6 scallions, finely chopped	1 cup whipping cream
1 cup chicken broth	1/2 teaspoon salt
1 cup clam broth	Black pepper, to taste
2 teaspoons tomato paste	1 lb. fresh crabmeat
2 tablespoons flour	

Cut the tomatoes into wedges and place in saucepan with the scallions, chicken broth, clam broth and tomato paste. Simmer partially covered for 20 minutes. Transfer the mixture to a food processor. Add flour and process until soup is smooth. Strain to remove the tomato seeds and skins. Return soup to saucepan.

Stir in Madeira or sherry and cream. Season with salt and pepper and simmer for 5 minutes. Add the crabmeat and continue cooking until hot. *Serves: 6*

SOUFFLEED BANANA RUM PANCAKE

The batter must be made just before cooking, since its lightness depends on the addition of egg whites at the last minute. Use only large eggs, since the proportions of this recipe depends on that. This could also be made in a large flat oven proof, pyrex skillet. Remove the handle and then it can go under the broiler. In that way more than one serving can be prepared at one time.

1 1/2 cups half and half	6 large egg yolks, reserve egg whites
1 cup flour	1/4 cup dark rum
1/2 teaspoon salt	1/4 cup sweet butter, melted

In a large bowl combine half and half, flour and salt. Add egg yolks one at a time. Then add the rum and butter. Set aside. For each pancake:

3 teaspoons egg whites	1/2 cup of the above batter
Pinch of cream of tartar	1 large banana
Pinch of Salt	1/4 teaspoon sugar
1/2 teaspoon sugar	Buttered rum sauce

Beat egg whites to soft peaks with cream of tartar and salt, add sugar and beat until stiff peaks form. Fold egg whites into batter, then spread into a hot 8 inch skillet, evening out the batter with a spatula. Cook 3 minutes while slicing banana. Place banana slices decoratively on top of batter and sprinkle with 1/4 teaspoon of sugar. Place under broiler for 1 to 2 minutes to puff golden. Serve with buttered rum sauce. *Serves: 6*

Author's note: For a quick hot buttered rum sauce combine 1 cup sugar, 1/2 cup butter, 1/2 cup light cream and 1/3 cup rum. Cook over medium heat until sugar is dissolved and the mixture is hot.

Central Region

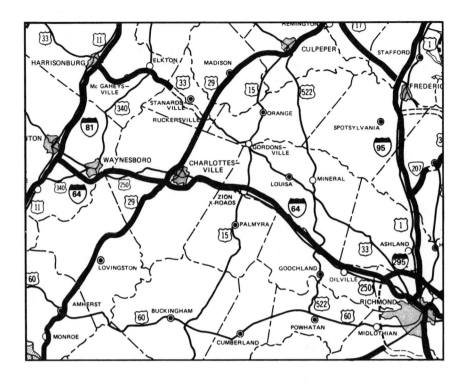

WINERIES:

Autumn Hill Vineyards

Bacchanal Vineyards

Barboursville Vineyards

Blenheim Wine Cellars

Burnley Vineyards

Chermont Winery

Dominion Wine Cellars (Virginia Winery Cooperative)

La Abra Farm & Winery (Mountain Cove Vineyards)

Misty Mountain Vineyard

Montdomaine Cellars

Oakencroft Vineyard & Winery

Prince Michel Vineyards

Rapidan River Vineyards

Simeon Vineyards

RESTAURANTS:

The Bavarian Chef

The Boar's Head Inn (The Old Mill Dining Room)

The Book Gallery & Restaurant

Michie Tavern ("The Ordinary")

The Silver Thatch Inn

Toliver House

AUTUMN HILL VINEYARDS Located on the plateau of a hill northwest of Charlottesville, with a clear view of the Blue Ridge Mountains, are the first vineyards of Autumn Hill Vineyards and Winery. This is the view and the land which two couples from the city fell in love with in the late 1970's

Ed Schwab and his wife, Avra, and Gunther and Anita Gaede were looking for a different lifestyle and wanted to move away from the fast pace of life on Long Island. Not only were the two couples friends, but the men were in business together. Ed Schwab, a graduate of Lehigh University, joined his father's interior decorating firm and eventually took over the business. However, he was getting tired of the pressures of running a very intense business and concluded that farming provided a more relaxing lifestyle. Growing grapes and wine seemed to be the logical answer.

Gunther Gaede, who is still involved in the interior decorating business, immigrated to the United States from Germany in the mid 1950's. His wife Anita, who was born and raised in Switzerland, became interested in wine grape growing at an early age. She spent many summers working on a family vineyard. The Gaedes also eventually want to live in the country. The two couples spent considerable time looking for property to purchase, and were encouraged by the Virginia Farm Winery Laws. After looking in the various winegrowing regions of Virginia, they selected 90 acres near Earlysville.

The plan was for Ed to retire from the business and leave Long Island. Ed would be in charge of the vineyards and the winery until such time when the Gaedes would also move to Virginia. In preparation for becoming a vintner and winemaker Ed took 40 college credits at night in plant science and agriculture. In 1979 the two couples planted the first stage of their vineyards. Five acres were planted in Chardonnay, Riesling and Cabernet Sauvignon. Gabriele Rausse, a pioneer in vinifera grape growing in Virginia, encouraged them to plant only vinifera grapes.

A viability study of the vineyard soil and climate proved the location of the vineyard site to be an excellent choice. The vineyard, situated on the hill is frost protected. "The cold air seems to run off, " says Ed.

Since the original planting of the vineyards the two couples have each constructed their own homes on the property – side by side. The Gaedes come down from Long Island for a long weekend every other month. The Schwabs live there permanently. Avra is a third grade and special education teacher in the local school system.

Ed Schwab, who is also a sales representative for a decorative fabrics firm, has built a small winery as a "start-up" operation. In a couple of years they will build a larger winery facility near the road. The small winery, which is partially underground, will eventually be used for aging of red wines.

European style wines with an American accent is the goal of Ed Schwab's winemaking. The first releases of Chardonnay and Riesling in 1986 are both designed to be food wines. The Chardonnay is cold fermented and aged in stainless steel. Ed does not age his Chardonnay in oak since he feels that the wine becomes "too big" and does not pair well with food.

The ultimate goal for Autumn Hills Vineyards is 20 acres of vines and a larger winery with a large tasting room and picnic facilities for visitors.

The Schwabs and the Gunthers like experimenting with recipes to pair with their wines. Avra Schwab serves her chicken with their newly released Chardonnay.

TOURS
➡

Autumn Hill Vineyards, *Route 1, Box 199 C, Standardsville, VA 22973, 804-985-3081*
Directions: *15 miles north of Charlottesville, from Route 29 north, go west on Airport Road to Route 606; then north on Route 743 to Earlysville, left at Route 663 for 5.5 miles (follow green signs to Dyke), then right at Route 603 for 2.2 miles to vineyard on the right.*
Visitation: *By appointment*
Principals: *Anita and Gunther Gaede, Avra and Ed Schwab*
Wines Produced: *Chardonnay, Riesling, Cabernet Sauvignon Blanc*
1987 Production: *450 cases*

CHICKEN IN WINE SAUCE

Serve with Chardonnay

Avra Schwab likes to serve this chicken dish – a quick and easy company entreé--with rice and a green vegetable.

10 pieces of chicken, thighs and breast pieces, or 10 chicken cutlets	1 lb. fresh mushrooms, sliced
Salt and pepper to taste.	1 cup chicken broth
2 eggs	1 cup Chardonnay
1 cup bread crumbs	2 tablespoons flour
6 tablespoons butter	1/4 cup water

Place the eggs in a medium size bowl and beat well. Have bread crumbs on wax paper for easy breading. Sprinkle chicken with salt and pepper and dip chicken pieces in egg and then in bread crumbs.

Heat 4 tablespoons of butter in a large skillet over medium high heat. Add chicken pieces and brown well on all sides. Transfer chicken to a large flat pyrex baking dish.

In a medium size saucepan melt 2 tablespoons of butter and sauté mushrooms for 3 to 4 minutes. Add chicken broth and simmer for 5 to 10 minutes. Add wine. Mix flour with water to form a smooth paste and slowly add to sauce stirring constantly over very low heat. Simmer until smooth and slightly thickened.

Pour sauce over chicken and bake in preheated 350 degree oven for 45 minutes to 1 hour or until chicken is tender. *Serves: 4 to 6*

Author's note: For additional flavor add 2 chopped green onions to the mushrooms and sauté as directed.

BACCHANAL VINEYARDS Located on the southwest slope of Afton Mountain, Bacchanal commands a beautiful view of Rockfish Valley below and of the Blue Ridge Mountains to the west.

David and Betty Mefford purchased this property of 25 acres in 1977. They wanted not only to establish a retirement home, but also a small business that would supplement their retirement income. The Meffords had searched for over a year in many of the counties of Virginia for the proper location for a vineyard. They were looking for the right combination of soil and climatic conditions.

David has a degree in chemistry and works full time as a pharmaceutical analyist for a company in Richmond. The Meffords live in Richmond, but spend their weekends at the winery.

In 1978, the Meffords planted 7 acres of vinifera – Chenin Blanc, Riesling, Semillon, Gewurztraminer, Chardonnay, Pinot Noir, Zinfandel and Cabernet Sauvignon – on their property.

The vineyard is located on the slope of the mountain at an elevation of about 900 feet. This slope provides good air drainage for the vines. The silt loam soil has permitted the roots to go deep and find water when needed, so that in the dry weather of summer irrigation is not required. David Mefford says that neither irrigation nor fertilization has been necessary for the vineyard.

The vines are set on an 8x10 foot spacing – vines set every 8 feet with rows 10 feet apart. They are trained to a double bilateral cordon system on two wires for maximum production and ease of harvesting. There is room on the property for expansion of the vineyard.

Bacchanal Winery was bonded in 1984 and did its first crush that year. David with his chemical background is the winemaker. He did some home winemaking and has visited wineries all over Europe as well as the eastern seaboard and California.

The winery, designed by a Washington, D. C. architectural firm, utilizes solar panels for hot water. This is a first for a winery in Virginia. The building blends with the surroundings and is constructed of vertical cedar planks plus hand placed field stones.

David Mefford is one of the few vintners to produce a Chenin Blanc. It is cold fermented, aged in stainless steel for 6 months and released in the spring. Like the Riesling, it is a young wine.

Although David Mefford has had health problems and is trying to sell the winery, he will do a fall 1987 crush if the winery operation is not sold. He has enjoyed every aspect of being a vintner – viticulture, winemaking and marketing and wants to see Bacchanal Vineyards remain in operation. For the Meffords, the vineyard and winery have been a way of life. Their three children and spouses have been actively involved over the years.

Betty Mefford shares her husband's enthusiasm for Bacchanal Vineyards and enjoys pairing traditional Virginia recipes with their wines.

Bacchanal Vineyards, *Route 2, Box 860, Afton, VA 22920, 804-272-6937*
Directions: *From Charlottesville take I-64 west to Crozet exit. Turn west on Route 250 for 8 miles. Go left on Route 6 East for 7 miles. Route 6 splits with Route 151. Continue north on Route 151. Turn left on Route 631 to Bacchanal.*
Visitation: *By appointment*
Principals: *Betty and David Mefford*
Wines produced: *Chenin Blanc, Semillon, Gewurztraminer, Riesling, Chardonnay, Pinot Noir, Zinfandel, Cabernet Sauvignon*
1987 Production: *Approximately 2000 cases*

SPRING CHICKEN

Serve with Riesling

Virginia is famous for its Smithfield hams. The same ham curing process has been used for generations and the Smithfield ham is produced only in the town of Smithfield, Virginia. The hogs, however, can come from the surrounding area. This dry-cured ham, which was served by Martha Washington, has been enjoyed over the centuries topped with a brown sugar and sherry glaze. In this recipe the ham is combined with chicken and covered with a light cream sauce.

1 cup finely chopped Smithfield ham	1/4 cup butter or margarine
1/4 cup flour	1/4 cup chopped onions
1/2 teaspoon salt	1 tablespoon dried parsley flakes
1/8 teaspoon pepper	1/4 cup flour
4 whole boned chicken breasts, split	1 cup milk
1/4 cup butter or margarine	1 cup half and half
1 cup dry white wine	1 3 oz. jar sliced mushrooms, drained

Place ham in a lightly greased 13x9x2 inch baking dish. Cover with foil and bake in a preheated 325 degree oven.

In the meantime mix together 1/4 cup flour, salt and pepper. Dredge chicken in the flour mixture. In a large skillet over medium heat, melt 1/4 cup butter and cook the chicken in it until golden brown on all sides. Add wine, cover and reduce heat. Simmer for 20 minutes or until chicken is done. Remove chicken and keep warm.

Add the other 1/4 cup butter to the pan drippings and add onion and parsley flakes. Sauté until tender. Add the other 1/4 cup flour and stir until smooth. Gradually add the milk and the half-and-half, stirring until thickened. Add mushrooms.

Divide ham into 8 equal portions. Place one piece (one half) of chicken on top. Cover with the sauce and serve. Serve with rice and a green vegetable. *Serves: 6 to 8*

BARBOURSVILLE WINERY There are two sides to the story of the Barboursville Winery. One is associated with Virginia history and the other with pure guts and perseverance of the modern Italian pioneers who created the winery.

In 1976, 37 year old Gianni Zonin, the president of the largest private wine company in Italy, visited Charlottesville. He was accompanied by his attractive wife and several other international business men. They visited Monticello and heard about Jefferson's ill fated efforts to grow European grapes. They also heard about Zonin's fellow countryman, Filippo Mazzei, who more than two hundred years ago had brought vines and workers from Italy to establish vineyards near Monticello.

It became evident that Zonin was in the Charlottesville area to purchase more than a small grape arbor. It was suggested that Zonin should buy the Barboursville Plantation which was for sale. This would not only provide the land he required but would also renew the efforts to grow vinifera grapes in the Charlottesville area, where his Italian countryman had tried so long ago. He purchased the 800 acre plantation, including the old plantation house designed by Jefferson. Unfortunately the house was gutted by fire on Christmas Day in 1884. The manor house was never rebuilt and the ruin still stands. In fact, it dominates the label of the Barboursville Winery. James Barbour, the owner of the plantation, was governor of Virginia from 1812 to 1814.

Gianni Zonin had three reasons for purchasing the property. He wanted to own a winery and make wine in the United States, preferably on the East Coast. He was also enough of a romantic to want to renew the efforts of Mazzei. Third, and probably the most practical reason, the winery would give Zonin an American bottling site for his Italian wines if taxes on imports were to increase substantially. The Zonin family owns 6 large wineries in Italy. Their wines are sold throughout the United States.

Negotiations for the Barboursville property were conducted in secret. There were unconfirmed rumors that if the Italian communists won the elections at that time, Zonin's wine company would be ripe for a takeover. Zonin hurriedly purchased all except 100 acres of the plantation; a total of 700 acres.

Gianni Zonin sent over from Italy a young Italian agronomist named Gabriele Rausse. He had a degree in plant pathology from the University of Milan and was given the task of establishing vinifera vineyards on the Barboursville Plantation.

It was only with sheer guts and determination that the project finally succeeded. Gabriele faced many obstacles. It was almost as if someone had thrown down a gauntlet and dared anyone to make wine from vinifera grapes in Virginia. In 1976 Gabriele planted 3,000 vinifera vines – Cabernet Sauvignon, Pinot Noir, Chardonnay and Riesling. The project got national attention with write-ups in the *New York Times* and the *Washington Post*. "It was as if the President of Kenya had decided to plant bananas in Alaska," Gabriele recalled. "Everybody thought we were crazy."

Within several months four out of every five of the plants died. At that point the British investment firm, who was one of the original investors in the project, backed out. This did not stop Gabriele Rausse or Gianni Zonin, however.

The U. S. Department of Agriculture and the Virginia Polytechnic Institute had constantly discouraged vinifera grape growing and expressed opposition to the project. There was even an official condemnation issued that insisted that only Concord grapes and hybrids could be expected to grow in the area. However, in spite of state and federal opposition, Gabriele Rausse was not the only one interested in growing vinifera varietals. There were twenty other landowners who had applied for and who eventually received farm wine permits, and who watched Rausse's progress with great interest.

As if the official public discouragements were not enough, Gabriele was confronted with the enemies of nature in his grape growing efforts: the winter cold, the spring frost, the Black Rot and the Japanese beetle all took their toll on the early Barboursville vineyards. The old phylloxera problem had been solved with the use of American root stock. The disease and insects could be controlled with modern fungicides and pesticides. However, to add to the problems of vinifera growing, the soil for the vineyard is primarily a dense clay which retains water and restricts the downward growth of the vine roots. This also makes the vines susceptible to Odium – a killing fungus disease also called powdery mildew.

A trenching plow was brought from Italy for deep cultivation, thus encouraging deep root growth. This aroused the anger of VPI and the local people who thought those responsible for this act should be put away in a madhouse. History has proven that the Barboursville vineyards, which are trenched in depth, have had no attacks of Odium. Also, deep trenching has made the vineyards more productive. After all, this method of cultivation has been used in Italy for many centuries.

After the loss of most of the initial plantings, budding vinifera shoots were purchased from other parts of the country and a nursery was established so that the new vines could be kept free of viral infection. The varieties planted were selected on their ability to grow in the soil and climate north of Charlottesville – rather than on the basis of what was currently selling in the marketplace. Cabernet Sauvignon, Chardonnay, Riesling, Gewurztraminer, Malvasia, Merlot, Barbera, Zinfandel and Pinot Noir were planted in 1978.

However, that was not to be the last of Gabriele's obstacles. There was the matter of the posts for the vineyard. In Italy, concrete is used for posts because wood is scarce. The vineyards last for many generations and so must the posts. Zonin insisted on the same posts as in Italy for his Virginia vineyard. Rausse requested bids for the posts from local contractors, who were disconcerted by the request and gave him an outrageous price for their manufacture. Consequently, Gabriele had the posts shipped from Italy. To the local population, the concrete posts in the newly planted fields looked like cemetery markers.

While the vines were growing, Gabriele Rausse readied an existing building on the property for the winery. Stainless steel tanks and a few oak barrels were purchased in anticipation of winemaking. Since some of the earlier vines had survived, there were enough grapes to make an historic vintage in 1978. It was just a drop in the bucket, however. The next year proved to be not quite a "gusher." However, the quiet young man from Italy, Gabriele Rausse, who had enough guts to keep trying, was able to make a statement to the world by producing 500 bottles of Barboursville Virginia vinifera wines.

Even though the winery was partially destroyed by fire in September 1979 – arson was suspected--Barboursville Winery has been accepted as a pioneer in the new Virginia commercial wine community. It seems that the people who did not want the winery to succeed, failed.

Since that historic vintage of 1979, there have been three other winemakers at Barboursville – all from Italy. In 1982, Adriano Rossi became winemaker and general manager of Barboursville Winery. Two years later, after fullfilling her teaching contract, Adriano's wife Luisa and their thirteen year old son joined him in Virginia. Adriano comes from a long line of winemakers in Italy -- his father was one and so was his grandfather.

There are now 50 acres of vineyards at Barboursville Winery with basically the same vinifera grape varieties that were planted in 1977 – only more of them. All of the vineyards face north. This makes the vines bud later and avoids some of the spring cold weather damage.

"There's more freedom here in Virginia. Not like in Italy. Here I get involved in everything from planting to harvesting to winemaking to bottling to distribution," said Rossi. He even helps out with the cattle and the farm if needed. In Italy the winemaker works only inside the winery. In Virginia, Rossi has the opportunity to express his own personality in his winemaking. Adriano feels that winemaking is part science, part art and part Mother Nature.

Traditional European techniques are used in the making of Barboursville wines. The Cabernet Sauvignon, for instance, is aged for 3 years after fermentation, alternating between large and small wooden casks. It is also bottle aged before release. The winery uses Yugoslavian wood for all of its aging. "That is traditional in Italy," says Luisa Rossi who is very much involved in the winery. Luisa has a masters degree in biology and does all of the laboratory analysis work needed by the winery. She also does a great deal of the administrative work.

Since that first memorable vintage of 1979, Barboursville Winery has won many medals in wine competitions in the East, nationally and even in Italy. It is a great credit to the foresight and perseverance of Gianni Zonin and his fine and persistent "Italian" Virginia wine pioneers.

Luisa Rossi likes to prepare traditional Italian dishes to complement the Barboursville wines. She relies on some of her old family recipes.

TOURS
➡

Barboursville Winery, P. O. Box 136, Barboursville, VA 22923, 703-832-3824
Directions: *North of Charlottesville at intersection of Route 20 and 33, take 20 south for 200 yards, left on Route 678 and 1/2 mile, right on Route 777 for 500 yards, right at first driveway and winery sign.*
Visitation: *Wine-tastings, Monday through Saturday, 10 a.m. to 4 p.m., Tours, Saturday, 10 a.m to 4 p.m.*
Principals: *Zonin, S.p.A., Italy*
Wines Produced: *Chardonnay, Riesling, Gewurztraminer, Pinot Noir Blanc, Cabernet Sauvignon Blanc, Merlot, Cabernet Sauvignon*
1987 Production: *9,000 cases*

STUFATO WITH CABERNET SAUVIGNON

Serve with Cabernet Sauvignon

3 lbs. roast beef	1 large onion, minced
2 to 3 tablespoons butter	1 teaspoon salt
1 large stalk celery, minced	1/4 teaspoon pepper
2 carrots, minced	3 cups Cabernet Sauvignon

In a dutch oven melt the butter over medium high heat. Add the meat and brown it lightly. Add celery, carrots, onion, salt and pepper. Stir for 1 minute to mix the vegetables. Pour in the wine. Cover and lower the heat to simmer. Cook for 3 1/2 to 4 hours until meat is tender and the sauce is thickened. Serve with mashed potatoes.

Author's note: A rump, sirloin tip or seven bone chuck roast may be used. Roast may also be cooked in a preheated 300 degree oven.

RISOTTO WITH PINOT NOIR BLANC

Serve with Pinot Noir Blanc

Risotto is an Italian dish made by boiling rice in stock and flavoring it with onion, cheese, mushrooms, wine, etc. Sometimes chicken or shellfish is added. With the addition of hot cream at the end of cooking time, this recipe is different from typical risotto.

1 oz. butter	2 cups chicken broth
1/4 cup chopped onion	1/2 cup liquid hot whipping cream
1 lb. rice	1/4 cup Parmesan cheese
1 1/2 cups Pinot Noir Blanc	1/2 teaspoon salt

Melt the butter in a large frying pan. Add onions and brown lightly over low heat for about 2 minutes. Add the rice and stir to mix well. Increase the cooking heat and pour 1 cup of wine over the rice. Stir constantly. Continue to cook at medium heat; pour little by little and in alternating amounts the chicken broth and the remaining wine. Do not add more liquid until the previous addition has been absorbed. Keep stirring. When all of the liquid has been absorbed, the rice should be done, al dente.

After 15 to 20 minutes, when the rice is almost done, add the hot liquid whipping cream, Parmesan cheese and salt. Stir well and serve. *Serves: 4*

Author's note: For this dish Italian Arborio rice is preferred, if available.

PEACHES WITH CABERNET SAUVIGNON BLANC

Serve with Cabernet Sauvignon Blanc

Marinating fruit in wine is a European tradition and peaches are a particular good choice, since they impart a juice of their own during the marinating process.

2 lbs. mature peaches	2 cups Cabernet Sauvignon Blanc
4 tablespoons sugar	

Peel amd slice the peaches in a bowl. Add the sugar and mix it with the peaches. Pour wine over the mixture. Refrigerate for 1 to 2 hours before serving. *Serves: 4*

BLENHEIM WINE CELLARS, LTD. Blenheim, located several miles south of Monticello and Ashlawn, the homes of Thomas Jefferson and James Monroe, also has a distinguished history. However, its history has become rather obscure.

In 1730, for the grand sum of forty-six pounds and fifteen shillings, King George II of England gave a land grant of over 9000 acres to John "King" Carter. The grant contained a stipulation that one shilling of rent fee had to be paid for every fifty acres yearly. Also, every three out of fifty acres had to be under cultivation within three years of the date of the land grant. The fee was no problem to the Carters, but the clearing of 561 acres of forest for cultivation purposes was no small undertaking. The land was cleared and a dwelling was built.

Edward Carter, grandson of John "King" Carter, occupied the residence from about 1750 until his death in 1792. He represented the county in the House of Burgesses from 1767 to 1788 when he was succeeded by Thomas Jefferson. After the death of Edward Carter, the property was owned by the Ross family of Charlottesville.

Blenheim passed through several hands in the early 19th century and eventually was owned by Andrew Stevenson who had an illustrious career as ambassador to England. After he came back from England he resided at Blenheim and was a member of the Board of Governors of the University of Virginia. It was during this time that Roger B. Taney, Chief Justice of the United States, was a frequent visitor at Blenheim.

The original house had burned in the early 19th century and an extremely large one room library was built on part of the foundation of the house. The foundation of the library chimney is the original one used for the residence. Judge Taney spent many hours doing research in this library and conversing with his friend Andrew Stevenson. The Stevensons, who were very fond of their habitual guest, built him a separate cottage on the grounds. Legend has it that the judge was a terrible snorer and the Stevensons could not sleep under the same roof with him. The Taney cottage still stands on the grounds of the estate.

A residence was rebuilt after the fire and occupied by the Stevensons. The original part of the house is still standing and has had several additions over the last centuries.

The present owners of Blenheim are John Marquis and his son John, Jr. The elder Marquis, who had owned a large grain farming operation in Ohio, decided to move to Virginia to escape the extreme and difficult winters. He purchased Blenheim in the late 1970's. The property consists of 240 acres and is primarily devoted to cattle raising.

In 1982, John, Jr. who's background is in chemistry and business administration, decided to plant 10 acres in vinifera – mainly Chardonnay and some Cabernet Sauvignon. Although a portion of the grapes are sold to other wineries, the majority of the crop is used for Blenheim wines. John,

Jr., does all of the vineyard work and is the winemaker. His background in chemistry has been a great asset in that occupation.

Blenheim Chardonnay is "fermented in stainless steel and aged in French oak casks," says John. They do quite a bit of private labeling of the Chardonnay for restaurants. In the future John plans to also produce Cabernet Sauvignon.

The wine label of Blenheim Wine Cellars shows a reproduction of Stevenson's library and also of the Blenheim residence. Although the history of the property is one that spans generations, the present owners are pioneers in the growing of vinifera in the region around Monticello – a dream come true for an old friend. Thomas Jefferson would have been delighted to see vinifera flourishing near his home. John, Sr., a widower, is in charge of cooking. He likes to prepare simple dishes and shares this recipe.

TOURS
➡️

Blenheim Wine Cellars, Ltd., *R.D. 6, Box 75, Charlottesville, VA 22901,*
804-295-7666
Directions: *South of Charlottesville go past Monticello and Ashlawn, the Monroe home, on Route 795, continue straight on Route 627 past Lanark, take left fork onto Route 727, continue on dirt road 7/10 of a mile to large house at top of hill.*
Visitation: *By appointment only*
Principals: *John Marquis, Jr.*
Wines Produced: *Chardonnay*
1987 Production: *500 cases*

BLENHEIM MEATLOAF

Serve with Cabernet Sauvignon

Meatloaf, if it is prepared well, can be an epicurean delight. The spices and ingredients in addition to the meat can be varied to suit individual tastes. Leftovers may be reheated or served cold.

2 lbs. ground meat, part beef and part veal	1/4 cup chopped onion
1/2 teaspoon salt	1/4 cup chopped green pepper
1/4 teaspoon pepper	1 stalk celery, chopped
1 egg	1/4 teaspoon each of dried basil,
1/2 cup red wine	rosemary, thyme, and sage
1/2 cup crushed cracker crumbs	1 8 oz. can tomato sauce

In a large bowl mix all ingredients well. Using either a fork or your hands shape mixture into a loaf. Place in loaf pan or in a shallow casserole dish. Bake in a preheated 350 degree oven 1 and 1/4 hours.

15 minutes before end of cooking time, remove excess fat from pan. Pour tomato sauce over meatloaf and finish baking. *Serves: 6*

Author's note: For a flavor variation, ground ham may be substituted for part of the meat. A chopped tomato may also be added to the meat mixture.

Burnley Vineyards
1985
VIRGINIA
Riesling
Medium Dry Table Wine
Monticello Appellation

PRODUCED & BOTTLED
BY BURNLEY VINEYARDS • BARBOURSVILLE, VIRGINIA BW-VA57
ALCOHOL 10.5% BY VOLUME

BURNLEY VINEYARDS When C.J. Reeder purchased 40 acres north of Charlottesville as retirement property in 1976, he had no idea that retirement would provide him with a full time occupation and make him a pioneer in the Virginia wine industry.

Just prior to his retirement Reeder had been a full colonel in the U. S. Army. He was in command of the Foreign Science and Technology Center in Charlottesville which evaluates foreign weapons systems for vulnerability and for U. S. application. The Charlottesville region, therefore, was not unfamiliar to the family.

C. J. grew up on a dairy farm in Oregon and was also familiar with the timber industry of that state. Upon retirement, he wanted something to do outside – possibly involved with agriculture. He had an interest in wine since he became acquainted with European wines while stationed in Germany.

Shortly after the Reeders had purchased their property near Barboursville, Gabriele Rausse, an Italian viticulturist and winemaker was sent over by the Zonin family to establish a vinifera vineyard and a winery at Barboursville. Rausse was convinced that fine vinifera wine grapes would grow in Virginia.

The Reeders saw what was being done by Rausse at the Barboursville Vineyard, and they became convinced that they, too, could grow grapes. In 1976, C. J., with the help of his wife Patt, their son Lee and Rausse's technical support, planted 3 acres in vinifera – Cabernet Sauvignon and Chardonnay. They soon added more acreage and also planted Riesling and some Vidal Blanc. There are now 12 acres in grapes.

By 1981, when Colonel Reeder retired, the vineyards were producing and the Reeders started selling grapes to Virginia wineries. C.J. was quite satisfied with his lifestyle. He worked in the vineyards 7 to 8 months out of the year and the rest of the time he and Patt travelled.

However, in 1981 that lifestyle changed when Lee, who was a student at Virginia Tech., decided to become a winemaker. He had spent two years doing undergraduate research in wine technology, including a study on freezing grapes for winemaking and making apple wine in a Riesling style. Upon graduation in 1983 with an accounting degree, Lee became a full time accountant and a part-time winemaker.

Before Lee had graduated from college, he and his dad had started building the winery. They did over fifty percent of the work themselves, and in a year's time the building was ready for the 1984 crush. Lee is no longer an accountant, but rather the full time winemaker at Burnley Vineyards.

The Reeder vineyards have helped prove that vinifera could be grown in central Virginia. French hybrids are planted only on that area of the property where vinifera will not grow, mostly on low lying land. The majority of the vineyard is at 600 feet elevation and is not subject to extreme winter frosts. As a frost protection and to aid in air circulation, the Reeders have thinned the wooded part of their property.

Burnley Vineyards still sells part of its grapes. As the winery grows, however, the Reeders plan to utilize all of their production.

The first year Burnley Vineyards wines were released they won 2 medals and have been winning medals ever since. The 1984 and 1985 Chardonnay each won gold medals in the 4th and 5th Virginia Wine Competition. The Rieslings and Cabernet Sauvignons also have won their share of medals.

Lee's prime criterion in winemaking is good acid balance. The time for grape picking is determined by the acid and pH balance, which he feels is essential for the flavor of the wine.

"Burnley Vineyards Chardonnay is aged in oak," says Lee Reeder. Part of the wine is aged for 3 months in French oak and another part is aged for 6 weeks in American oak. Lee plans to designate the Chardonnay aged in French oak as the winery's Special Reserve. Burnley Vineyards Cabernet Sauvignon, after fermentation, is aged 8 to 12 months in American oak. Lee makes the Riesling semi dry with 1 1/2% residual sugar.

The generic series of wine produced by Burnley Vineyards is named after the nearby Rivanna River. The White is 100% Vidal Blanc, a French hybrid, in a semi-sweet style. Rivanna Sunset is a blush wine made from 100% Chambourcin, also a French hybrid. A blend of four French hybrids is used for the blending of Rivanna Red – Maréchal Foch, Chambourcin, Baco Noir, and De Chaunac. Since the Reeders grow only the Vidal Blanc, the other French hybrid grapes are purchased.

Burnley Vineyards intends to grow. The Reeders are planning to plant 10 more acres with Chardonnay and Riesling. They will expand their wine production.

Since the first planting of grapes on their property, both C.J. and Patt Reeder have been active in the Virginia grape growing and winery associations. Patt was instrumental in the organization and development of the Virginia Vineyards Association and was its first president from 1982 to 1984. She is presently serving her second term as vice president of the association. C.J. and Patt were both very active in the formation of the Jefferson Wine Grape Growers Society, and C. J. has been on the Board since its formation. Currently, C.J. is Chairman of the 1987 Virginia Wineries Association Wine Festival.

Even with the expansion and all of the extracurricular activities, Burnley Vineyards is still a family operation. C.J. is in charge of the vineyards, Lee is the winemaker, Patt is in charge of sales and Dawn, Lee's wife, handles all of the tastings. The Reeders have proved that vinifera grapes could be grown successfully in Virginia and a success could be made of producing wine from them.

Patt Reeder loves to cook and has won several awards with her recipes. She particularly likes to pair Burnley Vineyards wines with food. Since she leads a very busy life, she shares some easy to prepare recipes.

TOURS

Burnley Vineyards, Route 1, Box 122, Barboursville, VA 22923, 703-832-3874
Directions: *From Charlottesville go north 15 miles on Route 20, left on Route 641 for 3/10 miles, entrance on left*
Visitation: *Wednesday through Sunday 11 a.m. to 5 p.m. Other times by appointment.*
Principals: *C.J. Reeder and Lee D. Reeder*
Wines Produced: *Cabernet Sauvignon, Chardonnay, Riesling, Vidal Blanc, Rivanna White, Rivanna Sunset, Rivanna Red*
1987 Production: *2500 cases*

HOT CRAB OPEN FACE SANDWICHES

Serve with Riesling

This is one of Patt Reeder's award winning recipes. She likes to use Virginia crab meat for a quick luncheon entrée. Serve with a green salad.

1/2 lb. fresh crab meat	1/4 teaspoon mustard
1/4 cup mayonnaise	Salt to taste
3 oz. cream cheese	3 English muffins, split and toasted
1 egg yolk	2 tablespoons butter
1 teaspoon chopped onion	

In a small bowl mix crab and mayonnaise. In separate bowl, beat cream cheese, egg, onion, mustard, and salt. Spread muffins with butter, crab mixture and cream cheese mixture. Broil 5-6 inches from broiler for 2 to 3 minutes or until brown. *Serves:3*

GOULASH

Serve with Cabernet Sauvignon

Goulash is the national meat dish of Hungary. It always contains meat, onions and sweet or hot paprika. The meat can be beef or veal or a mixture of the two. Originally the word meant herdsman's stew and probably originated with the one dish meals cooked by wandering herdsmen tending their flocks. The dish with its many variations has been found in most central European countries.

Patt Reeder's version utilizes some prepared mixes for additional flavorings. This dish is particularly easy to prepare at crush. It can sit on "the back of the stove" and be ready to serve when the day's work is finished.

5 slices of bacon, chopped	Salt and pepper to taste
2 cups chopped onions	1/4 teaspoon marjoram
1 cup chopped green pepper	1 package oxtail soup mix
1 to 1 and 1/2 lbs. beef stew meat, cut into small cubes	1 package goulash soup mix
1/4 cup paprika	1 quart water

In a medium size dutch oven fry bacon over medium high heat. Remove bacon pieces and add onions and peppers. Sauté over medium heat until limp, but not brown. Remove onions and peppers and add to the bacon. Add stew meat to the pan and brown slowly, turning all pieces to brown evenly. Add paprika, salt and pepper. Return onion mixture to pan and add marjoram. Add soup mixes and water. Cover and simmer for three hours. Serve over rice or noodles. *Serves: 4*

Author's note: Add salt sparingly, since there is salt in the bacon as well as the soup mixes.

ALMOND CHICKEN

Serve with Chardonnay

This quick chicken stir fry can be done either in a wok or an electric skillet. Have all ingredients ready before starting the cooking process. Serve Almond Chicken with rice.

3 tablespoons oil	1 cup frozen peas
2 chicken breasts, skinned, boned, and diced	1/2 cup diced onions
	1 cup sliced fresh mushrooms
1/2 teaspoon salt	1 cup hot chicken broth
1/2 teaspoon pepper	1 tablespoon cornstarch
2 tablespoons soy sauce	2 tablespoons water
1 cup diced celery	1/2 cup blanched toasted almonds

In a wok or electric skillet, heat oil over medium high heat. Add chicken and sauté for 3 minutes. Add salt, pepper, soy sauce, celery, peas, onions and mushrooms. Lower heat to medium and cook for 2 minutes. Stir in broth, cover pan and cook gently for 5 minutes. In the meantime mix cornstarch and water and stir into chicken mixture until thickened. Add almonds. *Serves: 4*

ALBEMARLE COUNTY

CHARDONNAY

PRODUCED & BOTTLED
BY

CHERMONT WINERY, INC.
ROUTE 1 BOX 59 ESMONT, VA
BW-VA-35
ALCOHOL 12.5% BY VOLUME

CHERMONT WINERY There are twenty years of viticulture and enology research behind the founding of Chermont Winery. Josh Sherman spent at least that amount of time researching not only writings on American viticulture and winemaking, but also the European field.

Josh Sherman, a graduate of the Naval Academy, a career pilot and a retired Navy captain with 30 years of service, was fortunate to have access to the Department of Agriculture for his research while stationed for a period of time in Washington, D.C. After retiring from the Navy in late 1973, Josh became a financial planner. His dream, however, was to own a vineyard and a winery.

He searched for land in the Piedmont area from North Carolina to New York state. Josh came to the conclusion that the climate in Virginia was favorable to grape growing and had similarities to France. The summers in Virginia, however, were warmer and more humid than in France.

After purchasing a farm south of Charlottesville in 1977, Josh proceeded to ready the land for grape vine plantings over a period of 3 years. He planted 10 acres of vinifera grapes – Chardonnay, Riesling and Cabernet Sauvignon. The vineyards are on sloped hillsides with southeastern sun exposure. This year Josh plans to add 2 1/2 more acres in Cabernet Sauvignon.

The summers of 1985 and 1986 were not good ones for Josh's vineyards. The drought of those two summers caused fruit loss and poor quality. On the other hand, too much summer rain, as can also be the case in Virginia, causes fruit rot. Josh says, "This is particularly true with Riesling. The vines are very hardy, but the fruit is susceptible to rot." This year Josh is putting a drip irrigation system into his vineyards to help eliminate the problems caused by drought conditions.

In 1981, with the first crop of his grapes, Josh Sherman made wine in his basement. The wine turned out well and he decided to build a winery.

The building, a two story structure, was constructed into the hillside to take advantage of natural cooling. Most of the first floor is 11 feet underground. There is also a large tasting room and a fully equipped kitchen in the building to prepare food for special events.

The grapes are all hand picked during the day and then refrigerated overnight. Josh presses only cold fruit. The next morning the cold grapes are transported to a concrete area outside of the second story of the winery for pressing. Josh uses a big basket press for this task. A large hose and pump then transport the pressed juice to cold stainless steel tanks on the first level. The juice is allowed to settle and clarify overnight. Yeast is added the next morning and the fermentation process begins. Fermentation usually takes three weeks. The wine remains in stainless steel for about 3 months and is then filtered through 6 microfilters. The Chardonnay and Cabernet

Sauvignon are placed in oak for aging. The Riesling goes back into stainless steel for another 2 months.

Chermont's wines are aged in American oak. The Chardonnay remains in new oak for 7 weeks. The Cabernet Sauvignon gets 18 months of oak aging. The wines are membrane filtered before bottling.

Josh Sherman hopes to expand his wine production to 5000 cases per year. Josh, like all other Virginia vintners feels that there is a great potential for Virginia wines inside as well outside of the state.

Josh Sherman, a widower, likes to cook and enjoys preparing recipes which complement Chermont wines.

TOURS

Chermont Winery, *Route 1, Box 59, Esmont, VA 22937, 804-286-2211*
Directions: *On Route 20 south of Charlottesville at intersection with Route 626, take Route 626 toward Howardsville for 7 miles to vineyard and winery.*
Visitation: *April through October, Wednesdays through Saturdays 1 p.m. to 5 p.m., Other times by appointment.*
Principal: *John O. (Josh) Sherman, Jr.*
Wines Produced: *Chardonnay, Riesling, Cabernet Sauvignon*
1987 Production: *2500 cases per year*

BEEF POT ROAST

Serve with Cabernet Sauvignon

A pot roast, usually beef, may be either simmered, tightly covered on top of the stove over very low heat or cooked in a 300 to 325 degree oven. Josh particularly likes the technique of twice coating his meats with flour. He feels this makes a better gravy and eliminates the need for additional thickening at the end of the cooking time.

3 to 4 lb. beef rump roast
1 cup flour
1 teaspoon salt
1/2 teaspoon black pepper
1/4 cup garlic oil
2 cups water
4 to 6 small whole onions
3 bay leaves
1 tablespoon Kitchen Bouquet flavoring

1 teaspoon dry mustard
2 tablespoons hot catsup
1 1/2 cups red wine
6 medium carrots, peeled and sliced in 3
   inch pieces lengthwise
6 medium Irish potatoes, peeled
   and halved
1 tablespoon prepared horseradish

Mix flour, salt and pepper. Coat all surfaces of the roast. Let meat stand about 30 minutes and re-coat with the flour mixture.

In a dutch oven heat garlic oil over high heat. Add meat and brown all surfaces of roast until almost blackened. Remove roast, reduce heat to medium and add the water. Stir constantly to loosen and incorporate all browned residue of the flour mixture. Stir to blend and cook until sauce is smooth.

Return roast to pot, fat side up. Add onions, bay leaves, Kitchen Bouquet flavoring, catsup, mustard and 1 cup of red wine. Bring liquid to a boil, cover pot and reduce heat to simmer. If desired, the pot roast may be placed in a preheated 300 degree oven.

Cook for 50 minutes per pound. About 1 1/4 hours before end of cooking time, add carrots. About 45 minutes before end of cooking time add potatoes. At the same time turn the roast over. About 30 minutes before end of cooking time add 1/2 cup red wine. Also stir in the horseradish.

When the roast is done remove it to a warm platter, garnished with the vegetables. Serve gravy over individual servings of the roast and vegetables. *Serves: 6*

DOMINION WINE CELLARS – Virginia Winery Cooperative The Virginia Winery Cooperative is the realization of a dream for many vineyard owners who wanted to own a winery, but did not have enough capital to build and equip such a facility. They have pooled their capital, their experience, their quest for excellence, and their love of wine to build a winery which would produce the finished product of their collective vineyards.

The nucleus of the Virginia Winery Cooperative began in 1983 when several growers got together and started talking about a cooperative. A study was conducted to determine the feasability of the project. On April 4th, 1984, twenty-four wine grape growers from all over the state of Virginia met in Charlottesville to formulate plans for a cooperative. A second meeting took place in Culpeper on June 23rd to discuss the legal aspects of the organization of such a project. Eleven members pledged $190,000 and that was the start of the Virginia Winery Cooperative.

The three main purposes for the Cooperative are: 1)To provide a safe and secure market for the members' grape crops. 2)To ensure a fair profit for that crop. 3)To ensure a fair profit for the wine made at the Cooperative. The latter in turn would assure that loans could be paid and that there would eventually be dividends for the shareholders.

In subsequent years, a charter was drawn up and by-laws were prepared. The financial obligations of each member were defined. Charter members paid $5,000 per acre of grapes committed to the Cooperative. This meant that they owned 50 shares of stock in the Cooperative at a par value of $100. This same membership arrangement is still true for current grape growing members who commit vineyard acreage. There is also another type of membership available – one for the general public who

115

wants to invest in one of the premium wineries of Virginia. This is in the form of a preferred stock investment.

In the spring of 1985, the state legislature passed an amendment to the Farm Winery Act which gave the Virginia Winery Cooperative the classification as a farm winery. This is the first winery Cooperative in the United States devoted to producing premium varietals.

By the summer of 1985, there were enough members and commitments to select a site for the winery and to arrange for financing. Twenty acres of land with a frontage on Highway 29 at Culpeper were purchased for the winery site. It was decided that the location was good because of the proximity to a major traffic artery in Virginia. The Culpeper Industrial Development Authority, the county and the town approved a loan of $750,000 at a very favorable interest rate to construct the winery.

An architect was hired, land was cleared and the winery was completed for the 1986 crush. The winery building is in the French Chateau style with an enclosed courtyard. The first floor houses the winery equipment and the second floor is used for administrative offices and a large tasting room. Overlooking the test vineyards there is a deck , which will be used for entertaining. The winery opened to the public in early May, 1987.

In the summer of 1986, Steven Reeder was hired as winemaker for the new facility. Steve Reeder, a native Virginian, has eight years of winemaking experience at wineries in California, Pennsylvania and New York. In the course of his career, his winemaking has won over 30 medals – eight of them gold and several best-of-show.

Steve grew up along the "Weinstrasse" in Germany where his father was stationed with the Air Force. At an early age he learned to appreciate wine and started making home wine as a teenager. Steve always had an interest in biology and chemistry. When his father was transferred to California, Steve enrolled in the University of California at Davis. He graduated with a degree in Fermentation Science. Steve was delighted to return to Virginia and be a part of the pioneering wine industry. Instead of remaining in California, he came back East because he thinks there is much more opportunity for experimentation and expansion here.

There are currently 18 members of the Virginia Winery Cooperative with over 60 acres of vineyards committed. Each member has one vote regardless of how many acres of vineyard he or she has committed to the Cooperative.

Each year a new marketing contract is concluded with individual members. The Cooperative cannot dictate to the members how much to produce, but it can tell them how many tons per acre it will buy from them. Steve Reeder, as the general manager and winemaker, sets the grape harvesting standards as to sugar, acid and pH. If the standards are not met, he has the option to either reject the grapes or reduce the price per ton paid to the grower by the Cooperative. Steve also sets growing guidelines.

In connection with a grape growing and education effort, a 3 acre vineyard has been planted around the winery. This vineyard not only includes many varieties of vinifera, but also shows different trellis systems, canopies, and spacing. They are not only there for the benefit of the member growers, but are also educational to the general public visiting the winery. Steve works closely with the state enologist and state viticulturist on these projects.

All of the members' committed acreage is planted with vinifera grapes but some are not yet in full production. To compensate for the shortage of fruit at the initial start of the winery, Steve Reeder purchased some French hybrid grapes which will, for the moment, be blended into a second label. As the vinifera vines become productive, the winery will handle only these grapes to make wine for the primary label. Steve will only use French hybrids for blended wines, such as table wines.

Since the Cooperative is a farm winery, it is allowed to purchase outside grapes. The members are not required to sell their uncommitted grapes to the Cooperative.

There is still room for some new members. However, it is expected that the membership will be full by the crush of 1987. There is a strict quality assessment before a new member is voted in by the Board of Directors of the Cooperative. Each perspective member's vineyard and growing techniques are evaluated prior to Board action.

The members include retired military personnel (Navy pilot, a general), a retired Exxon executive, farmers, school teachers, a cattle rancher and a medical doctor. The committed acreage ranges from 1 to 6 acres per member, and the varietals are basically Riesling, Chardonnay and Cabernet Sauvignon, with some Merlot and Pinot Noir.

The Cooperative's wine label – DOMINION WINE CELLARS -- is a sunset over the Blue Ridge mountains. It is a reproduction of an aerial photograph by Robert Llewellyn. Different photographs are used for the blended wines.

At the present, the Cooperative's white table wine is a blend of 80% Seyval Blanc and 20% Chardonnay. "The proposed blush table wine will be a base of Pinot Noir and Cabernet Sauvignon with Seyval Blanc blended in," says Steve Reeder. "Eventually all blends will also be vinifera," he adds.

Steve Reeder fermented the 1986 Chardonnay in several lots – some with barrel fermentation, some with only barrel aging, and some with stainless fermentation and aging. They will be blended for the final product. The Riesling is made in two styles--one off-dry and the other semi-sweet. The former is marketed in a green bottle as White Riesling and the latter in an amber bottle as Johannisberg Riesling.

A giant step forward has been taken in the Virginia wine industry by the creation of the Virginia Winery Cooperative. It is an innovative venture which provides a unique approach to the expansion of the Virginia wine industry. As the motto of the Cooperative says, "Our roots are in Virginia."

Steve Reeder loves to cook, and is particularly sensitive to food and wine combinations. Included with each of the recipes are some of his own comments about the ingredients and the accompanying wines. The scallop recipe comes from one of the Cooperative's members, Mrs. Shirley Dorrier of Endfield Vineyards in Scottsville, Virginia.

TOURS
➡

Dominion Wine Cellars, *P. O. Box 1057, Culpeper, VA 22701, 703-825-8772*
Directions: *On the Route 29 bypass of Culpeper, at the overpass with Route 3 and Route 522.*
Visitation: *Tuesday through Saturday 10 a.m. to 6 p.m. Sunday 12 noon to 6 p.m. Closed Mondays, except major holidays*
Principals: *Members of the Virginia Winery Cooperative; Winemaster and general manager: Steven Reeder*
Wines Produced: *White Riesling, Johannisberg Riesling, Chardonnay, Cabernet Sauvignon*
1987 Production: *9,000 cases*

FOOLS CHICKEN

Serve with Chardonnay

Steve Reeder says that this is a Reeder family recipe, but he is not sure of its origin. It was very useful to him when he was a bachelor because it comes across as very elegant, but is actually very easy to make. It can be made up early in the day, stored in the refrigerator, and then placed in the oven at the appropriate time.

"The recipe is a perfect match for a dry, full bodied wine like the 1986 Dominion Chardonnay. The heavy cream sauce that is created in this recipe is equalized by the full body of the Chardonnay, while crisp acidity freshens the palate for another bite."

Steve usually serves this chicken with fresh asparagus, lightly steamed and a nice dinner roll. "Though many people feel that asparagus does not go with wine, I disagree and eat it whenever possible," he says.

1 small jar Armour dried beef	1 can cream of mushroom soup
4 boneless, skinless chicken breasts	1 pint sour cream
4 strips Virginia Smithfield bacon	

Line an ungreased 9x4x2 inch baking dish with the dried beef. Wrap each chicken breast with a strip of bacon, secure with a toothpick and place on top of the dried beef. Combine the can of soup with the sour cream and pour over the chicken. Bake for 1 1/2 hours in a preheated 350 degree oven. *Serves: 4*

FLANK STEAK MARINADE

Serve with Dominion Red Table Wine

This is Steve's conversion of some everyday marinade recipes. It goes well with all lesser beef cuts, but it complements flank steak the best. The recipe originated when Steve attended the University of California at Davis where he put something on the barbecue almost every night.

The key to the recipe is the length of time the meat is allowed to marinate and the time it is allowed to cook. The marinating allows the flavor to penetrate the meat and tenderizes the flank steak which can tend to be a little on the tough side. Steve advises that the meat be cooked either rare or medium, since the marinade loses something if the the meat is cooked done . To serve, cut the meat on the diagonal.

"A lot of people use a lesser quality wine for cooking. I believe that many fine recipes are spoiled by this. It is important to use a quality wine in cooking so that all of the fine flavors of the wine will show through into the meal," says Steve.

Marinade:

3/4 cup sunflower oil	1/2 teaspoon ginger
1/2 cup high quality red table wine	1/4 teaspoon ground pepper
1/3 cup soy sauce	Dash of tabasco sauce
2 cloves fresh crushed garlic	1 flank steak

Combine all marinate ingredients well and pour over the flank steak in a shallow glass baking dish. Allow to marinade for 24 hours in the refrigerator, turning the steak frequently. Cook over a hot flame on the grill for about 4 minutes per side to achieve a medium rare steak. Slice into strips about 3/4 inch wide with a diagonal cut across the grain of the meat. Serve with a baked potato and a green vegetable. *Serves: 3 to 4*

FRESH SEA SCALLOPS IN WHITE WINE SAUCE

Serve with Johannisberg Riesling

The Dorriers own a cottage on the seashore and enjoy pairing seafood with wine. The delicate sauce and the flavor of the fresh sea scallops are enhanced by the rich flavor of Johannisberg Riesling. Served with a fresh spinach salad, this is a perfect summertime meal.

1 large clove garlic, crushed	2 teaspoons minced parsley
12 tablespoons butter	1/8 teaspoon white pepper
1 lb. fresh sea scallops	1/8 teaspoon paprika
3 teaspoons flour	Salt to taste
1/2 cup Johannisberg Riesling	1/2 lb. thin vermicelli, cooked al dente

In a large skillet heat 6 tablespoons of butter and sauté garlic for a few minutes. Add scallops and stir, cook 3 to 4 minutes until tender. Remove scallops from pan and save butter and juices in a separate container. Melt the other 6 tablespoons butter in the same pan. Whisk in 3 teaspoons flour, stir and cook for 2 to 3 minutes. Add wine, parsley, seasonings, and juices from scallop cooking. Cook until thickened. Add more wine if too thick. Return scallops to sauce and heat. Serve over cooked vermicelli. *Serves: 4*

1986 Skyline White Virginia
GRAPE TABLE WINE

LA ABRA FARM & WINERY, INC. – MOUN-TAIN COVE VINEYARDS La Abra is the name of the winery and Mountain Cove Vineyard is the label under which Al Weed produces his wines. La Abra means the cove in Spanish. Actually La Abra is a 65 acre farm in a small valley nestled against the Blue Ridge Mountains, 35 miles south of Charlottesville.

Al Weed purchased the farm in 1973 because he wanted a change of lifestyle. He wanted his kids to grow up in the country and see where the food on their table came from. He wanted them to know what their Dad did for a living, instead of seeing him go off in the morning to an office to shuffle papers.

Al Weed was born in Brooklyn, New York, and grew up there and in northern Virginia. He had always dreamed of being a farmer and producing a farm product. After graduating from Yale and getting a Masters in Public Affairs from Princeton, Al found himself in the world of finance. A former Green Beret and a veteran of the Vietnam War, Al spent two years as an economist with the World Bank before becoming an investment banker with the Arthur Lipper Corporation in Washington, D.C.

Although Al was making a comfortable living, the then 30 year old executive decided to take the plunge and start a completely different career. Encouraged by a small winery operation outside of Baltimore, he decided that further south in Virginia would be the ideal place to farm and grow grapes. The Weed family, Al, his wife Emily and their two children left a comfortable house in Alexandria, purchased the 65 acre farm and moved to the country in 1973.

In 1974 and 1975 Al Weed planted 12 acres of grapes – all French hybrids. He had done thorough research on grape growing and came to the conclusion that the hybrids were more hardy and proliferous. They are also more resistant to rot from the summer rains in Virginia.

La Abra's first wine production was in 1976 when Al produced several thousand gallons of dry apple wine. Although his grapes were not fully developed in 1977, Al Weed made his first grape wine that year from purchased grapes. A nearby farmer had an over abundant crop of peaches, so he also produced peach wine that year. Over the years, the peach and apple wine have become a part of Al's regular wine making. He has purchased special equipment for the crushing of peaches.

The raising of grapes has not been an easy undertaking. It is a full time, 7 day a week job, but Al Weed loves it. He has had some ups and downs. In 1980 a virus struck his vineyards and he lost four acres of grape vines. In 1985 heavy rains caused much of the crop to rot. In the summer of 1986 the deer, who had been driven from the woods by the drought, ate much of the red wine crop. Even with the difficulties Al Weed loves his life as a vintner. He is proud of the medals he has won for the Mountain Cove wines.

Since Al Weed raises only French hybrids he has had to learn over time how to handle the proliferation of those varieties. He cluster-thins his grapes in June and uses various canopy techniques to control the crop.

Al Weed built most of the little log cabin tasting room and the winery himself. The winery was opened in 1977, and has been producing 4 to 5 French hybrid wines, plus two fruit wines each year. Al learned winemaking by doing. He purchased a Sears do-it-yourself kit and starting making wine. "I had 12 acres planted and I thought I had better learn to do something with the grapes," he said. Over the years his learning and experimentation has paid off. Seventy percent of the wine is sold at the winery.

The Mountain Cove Baco Noir, a red wine, is made in the Burgundy style. The juice has 10 days of skin contact and is aged for 8 months in oak after fermentation. The Villard Blanc which is cold fermented and aged includes 5% sweet reserve Riesling for body. The generic wines are blends of the hybrids in the La Abra vineyard – for instance the Skyline Rose is Baco Noir and Chancellor.

Al Weed hopes to expand his winery to 4000 cases per year. The farm is breaking even now, but the family's income is supplemented by Emily's position as an operating nurse in the University Hospital at Charlottesville. The winery is very much a family operation with Emily and the children also helping out in the vineyard. "It's hard work," says Al, "but we have achieved our dream to live on a farm and produce a farm product". Even with her busy schedule Emily Weed finds time to create recipes which pair with their Mountain Cove wines.

TOURS
➡

La Abra Farm & Winery, Inc., *Route 1, Box 139, Lovingston, VA 22949, 804-263-5392*
Directions: *From Route 29 just north of Lovingston (south of Charlottesville), go west on Route 718, follow signs for 3.5 miles to the winery*
Visitation: *Daily 11 a.m. to 5 p.m., except closed Mondays and Tuesday, January through March*
Principals: *Albert C. Weed II, Emily C. Weed and ten minor stockholders*
Wines produced: *Villard Blanc, Baco Noir, Harvest Red, Skyline Rose, Skyline White*
1987 Production: *2000 cases*

CREAM OF LEEK SOUP

Serve with Villard Blanc

The sharp flavor of Stilton cheese is a good contrast to the leeks and potatoes used in the soup.

1 teaspoon butter	1 cup cream
1 shallot, chopped	Salt and pepper to taste
1 cup leeks, well rinsed and chopped	Dash of lemon juice
1 medium potato, peeled and diced	1/8 lb. Stilton cheese, crumbled
2 cups chicken broth	

In a medium size saucepan over medium heat, melt the butter and add shallot and leeks. Cook until soft, but not brown. Add potato, and broth. Bring to a boil, reduce heat to low, cover and cook until potato is tender, about 15 to 20 minutes. Cool. Put mixture in a blender or food processor and blend until smooth. Return mixture to saucepan. Blend in cream, salt and pepper and lemon juice. Heat to boiling, but do not boil. Pour into soup bowls and top with crumbled Stilton cheese. *Serves: 4 as an appetizer*

PEACH WINE SORBET

Serve with Peach wine

This peach sorbet may be served as a light refreshing dessert, accompanied by a piece of cake or a cookie. Fresh sliced peaches and mint leaves may be used as a garnish.

2/3 cup sugar	1 1/2 cups Peach wine
1 cup boiling water	1 teaspoon lemon juice

Melt sugar in boiling water. Add Peach wine and lemon juice. Pour into a 9x6 inch pan. Place in freezer. Every 20 minutes stir mixture to aerate by breaking ice formations with a fork. Do this for two hours, then allow mixture to freeze. *Serves: 6*

RABBIT WITH ALMONDS AND RAISINS

Serve with Skyline Rose

Although popular in Europe for years, the rabbit is only recently gaining acceptance in the United States. The meat has a low fat content and is similar in flavor to chicken.

2 tablespoons butter
1/2 cup blanched whole almonds
3 tablespoons olive oil
3 tablespoons butter
2 large onions, sliced
1 teaspoons salt

1/2 teaspoon coarsely ground pepper
1/4 teaspoon saffron
1/8 teaspoon cayenne
2 rabbits, cut up in parts
1/2 cup raisins, soaked in water
1 tablespoon lemon juice

In 2 tablespoons butter, saute almonds until browned. Set aside. Heat oil and 3 tablespoons butter in a heavy pot or dutch oven over medium high heat. Stir in the onions and the seasonings. Add the rabbit pieces, and turn to coat each piece well. Cover and simmer until tender about 1 to 1 1/2 hours, turning rabbit occasionally. Remove rabbit to heated serving dish. Keep warm. Cook sauce on medium high heat, until well blended. Add almonds, drained raisins and lemon juice. Pour over rabbit. Serve with rice. *Serves: 4*

Author's note: For additional flavor, the raisins may be soaked in wine.

MISTY MOUNTAIN
1986

ESTATE BOTTLED
VIRGINIA CLARET
MONTICELLO
PRODUCED AND BOTTLED BY
MISTY MOUNTAIN VINEYARD, INC.
AYLOR, VIRGINIA BW/VA 65
ALCOHOL 12.5% BY VOLUME
NET CONTENTS 750 ML

MISTY MOUNTAIN VINEYARD WINERY, INC.

The Misty Mountain Winery is one of the newest in the state of Virginia. It is owned by Mr. and Mrs. Michael J. Cerceo.

In 1982 the Cerceos purchased a large farm situated against a mountain east of Madison. At times, the morning fogs are prevalent in the area, and not only the mountain but the entire farm is shrouded in a misty fog. Thus the name Misty Mountain.

Michael Cerceo, president of ISCS, a computer consulting firm in Chantilly, Virginia, purchased the farm in 1982. Inspired by their love of wines, the Cerceo's decided to plant a vineyard with the eventual hope of establishing a winery. Mrs. Cerceo, a native of Australia, grew up with wine and was familiar with the wines of her native country.

In 1983, two acres of vinifera and French hybrids were planted. Although some of the Riesling grapes were lost due to severe winters, most of the plantings flourished and Michael Cerceo decided to remodel the old barn on the property for a small winery. He invested $200,000 in the building and winery equipment and hired Eric Brevart as winemaker. Eric is a graduate of Lille University in France and makes wine in the classical French style.

Since both sugar and acid can be added to the winemaking process in Virginia, Eric picks the Misty Mountain grapes on acid. "Virginia grapes are high in acidity," he commented. Eric believes that this is the key to the flavor and aroma of the wine. "Sugar can be added if necessary half way through the fermentation process," he says.

Eric likes to blend various varieties of grapes and feels that the art of winemaking is in the blending. He is making a Virginia Chablis in the French style. It is a blend of 30% Seyval Blanc, 60% Vidal and 10% Riesling. The Riesling was added to give the wine a fruity character.

Michael Cerceo is expanding his vineyard by planting 8 more acres of grapes, including 3 in Seyval Blanc. Until all of the Misty Mountain vineyards come into full production Eric Brevart will purchase Virginia grapes. In the next couple of years Cerceo plans to build a winery and craft center on Route 29 near Shelby. In the next five years Misty Mountain winery will be producing 12,000 cases of wine per year and Michael Cerceo plans to retire from his business activities to become a full-time vintner. Although Misty Mountain is one of the newest Virginia wineries, it intends to quickly become a factor in the marketplace.

Eric Brevart likes to cook his native French recipes and pair them with Misty Mountain wines.

TOURS
➡

124

Misty Mountain Vineyard Winery, Inc., *Star Route 2, Box 458, Madison, VA 22727, 703-923-4738*
Directions: *From Madison take Route 231 east for 2 miles, then left on Route 651 for 2 miles, take Route 652 at sharp curve, take gravel Route 698 on left for .5 mile through farm, past maintenance sign to winery on left*
Visitation: *By appointment*
Principals: *Mr. and Mrs. Michael J. Cerceo*
Wines Produced: *Chardonnay, Riesling, Seyval Blanc, Merlot, Cabernet Sauvignon, Virginia Chablis*
1987 Production: *1200 cases*

VEAL BLANQUETTE

Serve with Chablis

The French word blanquette is derived from the word blanc meaning white. Blanquette is a white stew of chicken, lamb or veal. It is a traditional dish and typical of "home cooking" in France. A blanquette is enriched with egg yolk or cream and flavored with a bouquet garni, onion and lemon juice. Noodles, rice, or boiled potatoes usually accompany this entreē.

2 1/2 lbs. of veal, cut into 1 and 1/2 inch cubes	Salt and pepper to taste
1 onion, quartered	1/4 cup butter
1 carrot, cut into 1 inch pieces	3 tablespoons flour
1 stalk celery, cut into 1 inch pieces	1 lb. small button mushrooms
2 cups chicken broth	2 teaspoons lemon juice
2 cups white wine	12 small white onions, parboiled until just tender
Bouquet garni, consisting of 1 bay leaf, 1/2 teaspoon thyme, 4 sprigs parsley	2 egg yolks
	1/2 cup heavy cream

Soak veal in cold water for 1/2 hour before cooking. Drain and pat dry.

Place veal in dutch oven or flameproof casserole. Add onion, carrot, celery chicken broth, white wine, bouquet garni and salt and pepper. Bring to a boil and remove any scum which forms. Reduce heat to simmer, and simmer for 1 to 1 1/2 hours or until meat is tender, but not overcooked. Remove meat and vegetables from the liquid. Strain the liquid.

In a saucepan melt the butter and add the flour stirring with a metal whisk. Slowly ladle 4 cups of the stock, into the butter mixture, stirring constantly until thickened. If not enough stock add some white wine. Add mushrooms and lemon juice and cook over medium heat for about 5 minutes. Add veal and onions to the sauce. Carrot pieces may be added, if desired.

Beat egg yolks and cream until well blended. Stir some hot liquid into egg yolk mixture, then add to the sauce. Stir to blend. Heat but do not boil. Adjust salt and pepper, if necessary. Serve with noodles, rice or boiled potatoes. *Serves: 4*

MONTDOMAINE CELLARS A bottle of wine usually evokes good comradeship and good conversation. In this instance, however, a bottle of wine at Christmas was the christening of an idea – a new winery in Virginia. Steve Bowles, his brother Michael and his sister-in-law were discussing a recent article which had been written about Gabriele Rausse and his success at establishing a vineyard at Barboursville. By the end of the evening and the bottle of wine, they had decided to become vintners. Montdomaine Cellars was born.

That was in 1976, when Steve Bowles was 26. He sold his construction business in Danville, Va. and went to work for Gabriele Rausse to learn all he could about vines and vineyards. He soon learned that "grape growing is just like farming – hard work." He planted his first vineyards in 1977 with all vinifera grapes.

By 1980, there were several others like Steve Bowles who were growing grapes and wanted to own a winery. None of them, however, felt they could do it singled-handedly. Thus the concept of establishing a winery corporation to handle their grapes was born. By 1984, the building and winery facility, which today is Montdomaine, came into existence.

The winery building is partially built into a hillside for natural cooling. It has separate fermentation and barrel aging areas. An expansion to house the shipping department is scheduled for the near future.

There are four satellite vineyards with a total of 48 acres, which sell all of their grapes to Montdomaine. In return there is a group policy set for vineyard management, which includes such items as when and how to prune, how to trellis and when to pick. There are also other smaller investors in the group beside the four vineyard owners.

Waldemar G. Dahl is president of the corporation. Shep Rouse, Montdomaine's winemaker, sets the policy for not only the winemaking but also the vineyard management.

A graduate of Washington and Lee University, Shep became interested in wine when he was in Germany in 1976-77 on a Fulbright Scholarship. When he came back to Virginia, he took a job as a wine steward in Colonial Williamsburg. "I learned wine as a connoisseur and became so interested that I wanted to become involved," Shep said.

This decision led Shep Rouse to the University of California at Davis where he earned a Masters Degree in Enology. Shep stayed in California and worked at such prestigious wineries as Carneros Creek, Chateau St. Jean and Schramsberg. He came back to Virginia in 1986 and joined Montdomaine Cellars.

Shep Rouse feels that the biggest obstacle to Virginia vinifera grape growing and winemaking is the climate. Many vineyards have serious winter kill every four years and a spring frost every 2 to 3 years. Then there is also the problem of bunch rot from high humidity in the late summer when the grapes are ripening. Part of the rotting problem, he feels, can be solved with trellising which allows air flow through the vines.

Winemaking can be a problem when the grapes have bunch rot. "There is only a limited amount of treatment you can use in that case," said Shep. The winery workers really have to be on their toes and watch the grapes which go into the crusher.

Shep Rouse uses some innovative techniques in his winemaking. Oak chips are added to the Riesling for two days after fermentation to add complexity. The Montdomaine Chardonnay is partially fermented in oak. It remains on the lees for about 5 months.

Montdomaine has become known for its Merlot. It is an extremely difficult vinifera to grow in Virginia, since it is sensitive to winter kill. The Cabernet Sauvignon, too, has gained a good reputation for Montdomaine. Both are aged in French oak.

The Montdomaine Blush is a blend which contains 31% Cabernet Sauvignon. The Cabernet is crushed and given several hours of skin contact to get enough color for the blush wine. It is a light and fruity wine.

In the 1987 Virginia Wine Festival, all of Montdomaine's wines won medals – three bronze and two silver.

Shep Rouse entered the world of wine as a consumer and became a connoisseur and then a winemaker. It can truly be said that he has followed in the steps of his ancestral great, great, great, ...great uncle Thomas Jefferson, the first American wine connoisseur.

JoLind Eckstein, wife of the marketing director of Montdomaine Cellars, has created this entree to accompany Montdomaine's Riesling.

TOURS

Montdomaine Cellars, *Route 6, Box 168 A, Charlottesville, VA 22901, 804-971-8947*
Directions: *Take Route 20 south of Charlottesville for 11 miles, right on Route 720 for 1/2 mile to entrance on right.*
Visitation: *April 1 through October 31, 7 days a week 10 a.m to 4 p.m. November 1 through March 31, Monday through Friday, 10 a.m. to 4 p.m.*
Principals: *Waldemar G. Dahl, president of Montdomaine Corporation*
Wines Produced: *White Riesling, Chardonnay, Cabernet Blanc, Merlot, Cabernet Sauvignon*
1987 Production: *6600 cases*

CATFISH

Serve with Riesling

Catfish which has been popular in the South for many years is now being raised commercially. It is usually baked or fried.

4 large farm cultured catfish filets	3/4 teaspoon garlic salt
1/2 stick margarine, melted	1 teaspoon seasoned pepper
3/4 cup bread crumbs	

Dip filets in margarine. Then roll in crumbs which have been mixed with the seasonings. Place in shallow greased pan and bake in preheated 450 degree oven for 15 minutes. Reduce heat to 350 degrees and continue baking for 20 to 30 minutes or until fish is done and flakes easily to the touch of a fork.

Serve with mint flavored peas and cauliflower with cheese and butter. *Serves: 4*

MINT PEAS

1 pkg. frozen peas	Mint leaves, dried

Cook frozen peas in small amount of water until just tender. Drain. Sprinkle a pinch of dried mint on peas. Stir to blend flavor.

CAULIFLOWER

1 head cauliflower	Thin sliced wedges of Cheddar cheese
1 to 2 tablespoons margarine	

Cook cauliflower in covered saucepan with small amount of water until just tender. Place on ovenproof dish and put flakes of margarine between florets. Arrange wedges of cheese on top. Place under broiler just long enough to melt the cheese or place in microwave oven to melt cheese.

OAKENCROFT VINEYARD & WINERY The matriarch of the Virginia wine industry is Felicia Warburg Rogan. Not only is she the founder and owner of Oakencroft, one of the most prestigious wineries in the state, she has been a staunch supporter and promoter of the entire industry.

Mrs. Rogan was instrumental in the establishment of the Monticello viticultural appellation by the federal government. This appellation includes the nine wineries centered around Charlottesville.

Felicia Rogan is the founder and first and only President of the Jeffersonian Wine Grape Growers Society which promotes quality grape growing in Virginia. Each fall the society holds a Bacchanalian Feast to celebrate the grape harvest. This is followed the next day by the Monticello Wine and Food Festival. Both events are held at the Boar's Head Inn in Charlottesville.

In 1985, an act of the Virginia General Assembly established The Virginia Winegrowers Advisory Board to which Felicia Rogan was appointed by the governor. The Board supports programs in education, research and marketing of the Virginia wine industry. Felicia Rogan was elected the first Chairman of the Board and has already served in this capacity for two years.

Another wine-related project of Felicia Rogan's was the establishment of the Virginia Wine Museum, located in the General Store at Historic Michie Tavern near Monticello. The museum gives an account of Jefferson's interest in the growing and making of wine and also tells the story of the production of Virginia's famed Claret in the late 1880's.

Although there is a spirit of competition among the 34 wineries in the state, there is also a great deal of cooperation. Mrs. Rogan feels any standardization of quality and information about grape growing and winemaking will help the entire industry."What benefits one, benefits all," she says. This year she has written a book entitled "Virginia Wines – A Vineyard Year."

This interest in wine is not new to the attractive 60 year old grandmother who grew up in New York and learned to appreciate fine wines as an integral part of everyday life. When she married John Rogan and came to Virginia 10 years ago, Mrs. Rogan became interested in horticulture, especially the growing of orchids. John Rogan is a land developer and owner of the prestigious Boar's Head Inn in Charlottesville.

In 1978, Felicia and John decided to also plant some vines in the garden of their Polled Hereford farm. The 25 vines flourished and they enjoyed grape growing so much they planted an acre vineyard. The grapes proved to be of commercial winemaking quality. It was time to think about expansion and the possibility of going into a commercial operation. In the meantime, the Rogans had been making wine in their garage. The wine worked out well the first year and was even better the next year. This, too, encouraged Mrts. Rogan's decision to establish a winery.

In the spring of 1980, Felicia Rogan advertised for a gardener in the local paper. She needed help with her plantings of roses, bulbs, orchids and the grape vines. The ad was answered by Deborah Welsh who was hired for the position.

Gardening is one of the interests of Deborah Welsh, this multifaceted young woman who was a literature major at the University of Virginia. After graduation she tried a variety of jobs in order to find a career that suited her. She worked in a law library which helped her make the decision not to go to law school. Then Deborah waited tables, tended bar, drove a United Parcel truck, and worked in construction. She had also done some gardening.

Deborah is an avid reader and soon after starting work for the Rogans, she learned everything she could about orchid growing. Deborah also became involved in the grape growing which consisted of about 100 vines at the time. Her fruit growing experience had been limited to some apple trees, and she proceeded to read anything and everything on grape growing and winemaking. She attended classes at Virginia Tech and received winemaking instructions from Jacques Recht, a wine consultant and enologist at Ingleside Plantation Vineyards.

Oakencroft vineyards were expanded to 17 acres of Seyval Blanc, Chardonnay, Merlot and Cabernet Sauvignon. At this point grape growing and winemaking had stopped being an experiment and the Oakencroft Vineyard and Winery Corporation was established.

Oakencroft is a true farm winery. It sits on the Rogan's 250 acre Polled Hereford farm. The winery building is a converted smoke-house that was enlarged. It looks like a large barn and is painted a pleasing red. A large pond with duck and geese complete the tranquil scene. The winery was bonded in 1983 with a first production of about 400 cases of wine.

Felicia Rogan, who is the sole owner and only stockholder of Oakencroft Vineyards and Winery, admits it takes a great deal of courage and money to start a winery. It is very capital intensive, and returns are not realized for a number of years. Oakencroft Winery is well equipped with stainless steel tanks, French oak casks and a modern laboratory. There is also an attractive, antique filled tasting room and visitor's center.

Although Philip Ponton is vineyard manager, Deborah Welsh is very much involved in the grape growing. She believes that work done in the vineyard will reflect on the quality of wine which is being produced. She is also constantly experimenting with ways to circumvent vine damage from extreme winter cold.

Deborah likes to ferment the white wines in stainless steel for a fruitier taste. Some of the Chardonnay, however, has been partially fermented in oak. Both the Chardonnay and Cabernet Sauvignon receive oak aging. The former about two months and the latter one year. Both of these wines are bottle aged before release.

Felicia Rogan and Deborah Welsh have similar taste in wine styles and their goals are the same. Admittedly, both prefer reds, but are very proud of their Seyval Blanc and Chardonnay. At the 1987 Virginia Wine Competition at the Homestead, the Oakencroft Seyval Blanc won a silver medal as did the Chardonnay. The Cabernet Sauvignon won a bronze medal.

Mrs. Rogan plans to increase Oakencroft's production to 8000 cases per year in the next two or three years. At the present time the demand exceeds the supply, and she hopes that the two will coincide in the future.

In March of 1987, Felicia Rogan participated in the bicentennial celebration of Jefferson's trip through Burgundy. The weekend festivities in Burgundy culminated with an address by Mrs.Rogan in French to the Academy of Science and Letters in Dijon. She spoke on the "World of Wine of Thomas Jefferson." The highlight of the celebration dinner was the introduction in Burgundy of a Virginia grown wine produced in Jefferson's own Albemarle County – Oakencroft's 1986 Seyval Blanc.

If anyone deserves to be called the matriarch of the family of Virginia vintners, it is Felicia Rogan. She has tirelessly promoted Virginia wines and the raising of quality standards within the industry. A gourmet cook, she likes to serve fresh seafood complemented by Oakencroft Seyval Blanc or Chardonnay.

TOURS
➡

Oakencroft Vineyard & Winery *Route 5, Charlottesville, VA 22901 804-296-4188*
Directions: *From Route 29, north of Charlottesville, at Barracks Road light, turn west on Barracks Road and go 3 1/2 miles to winery sign on split rail fence on left*
Visitation: *April through December, seven days a week, 10 a.m. to 4 p.m.; January through March, by appointment only*
Principals: *Felicia Warburg Rogan*
Wines Produced: *Seyval Blanc, Chardonnay, Cabernet Sauvignon*
1987 Production: *2500 cases*

OAKENCROFT MUSSEL BISQUE

Serve with Seyval Blanc

Mussels are very popular in Virginia, although the early settlers, whose food heritage included mussels, did not eat them. The Rogans enjoy this Mussel Bisque as a winter Sunday night supper, particularly after having had a large lunch in the middle of the day. Mrs. Rogan also serves this as a summer luncheon dish at her summer home. Serve with a green salad with a mild dressing.

3 tablespoons butter	1 tablespoon flour
2 cloves garlic, minced	2 cups whipping cream
3 tablespoons minced shallots	1/4 cup chopped parsley
1/2 bottle Seyval Blanc	1 egg yolk
2 lbs. fresh mussels, medium size	

Scrub mussels in cold water and use only the ones which are tightly closed. Remove beards on the mussels. Keep mussels in water until ready to use. Choose a large pot deep enough to hold mussels, so that it is only half filled when the mussels are put into it.

In this pot melt 2 tablespoons butter over medium high heat and then add garlic and shallots. Cook until soft, but not brown. Add half bottle of wine and cook for two to three minutes. Remove mussels from water and put in pot. Cover with a tight fitting lid. Cook over medium to high heat, shaking pot occasionally to make sure mussels are covered with wine and seasonings. When they are all open (which takes about 4 minutes), remove mussels with a slotted spoon to a large pyrex dish.

When cool enough to handle, remove top shell of each mussel and discard. Leave mussels attached to one shell and cover with foil. Take pot with wine liquid and pour through a strainer into a clean bowl. Pour the clean liquid into a medium size sauce pan and put on medium heat. In a small bowl blend 1 tablespoon of soft butter and the tablespoon of flour. Add 2 cups of cream to the wine sauce and bring to a low boil over medium heat, stirring to blend cream into wine sauce. Add parsley and butter-flour mixture, stirring rapidly with a wire whisk. At the last minute add egg yolk and stir briskly so egg will not curdle. Remove from heat. Place mussels and shells in deep soup dishes, pour cream sauce over them, and serve hot with French bread. *Serves: 4*

DEVILED EGGS AND SHRIMP IN MORNAY SAUCE

Serve with Chardonnay

This recipe is a luncheon favorite of the Rogans. It is served with buttered rice and a side dish of chopped fresh endive salad mixed with julienned canned beets.

6 hard-boiled eggs	1/2 cup mayonnaise
1/4 teaspoon dry mustard	1 1/2 cups small cooked shrimp
1/3 cup chopped parsley	3/4 cup freshly grated Parmesan cheese

Mornay Sauce:

3 tablespoons butter	3/4 cup light or heavy cream
3 tablespoons flour	4 oz. Gruyere cheese, grated
3/4 cup chicken broth	1 tablespoon dry sherry

Preheat oven to 350 degrees.

Cut eggs in half lengthwise and put yolks in a bowl. Thoroughly mash yolks and mix in mustard, parsley, and about 1/2 cup of mayonnaise, or enough to make a smooth paste. Fill each egg white half with the egg yolk mixture.

Place the eggs in a buttered ovenproof serving dish and distribute the shrimp evenly around the eggs.

Prepare sauce: Melt butter and stir in flour until well blended. Gradually add chicken broth and cream stirring over low heat until sauce is thickened and smooth. Add the Gruyere and heat, stirring until cheese melts. Add sherry. Spoon sauce over eggs and shrimp. Sprinkle with Parmesan cheese and heat in oven for 15 minutes to warm thoroughly. Remove from oven and place under broiler for 3 to 5 minutes or until top is golden brown. *Serves: 6*

OAKENCROFT FARM PIE

Serve with Cabernet Sauvignon

Meat pies have been a traditional part of Virginia's culinary repertoire since colonial days. This particular one is a Rogan family favorite. It may be served either as a luncheon or a dinner dish. Serve with a spinach salad, sprinkled with bacon bits and tossed with a light salad dressing.

1 large onion, coarsely chopped	1 bay leaf, crumbled
1 clove garlic minced	1/2 teaspoon dried sage, crumbled
2 tablespoon butter	2/3 cup Cabernet Sauvignon
2 lbs. ground lamb	Salt to taste
3 large carrots, julienned	3 cups mashed potatoes
2 tablespoons tomato paste	1/2 cup grated Cheddar cheese,
1 teaspoon finely chopped parsley	medium sharp
1/2 teaspoon dried thyme	1/2 cup grated Parmesan cheese

Preheat oven to 375 degrees. In a large skillet sauté onion and garlic in butter until limp. Add lamb and cook, breaking up meat with a fork until it is brown. Stir in carrots, tomato paste and the herbs. Add wine and season with salt to taste. Simmer gently for about 30 minutes.

Spoon the mixture into a well-buttered, deep, oval baking dish. Spread the mashed potatoes on top. Mix the cheeses together and sprinkle them on top of the potatoes. Bake for 8 to 10 minutes or until the cheese is melted and golden. If desired, slip the dish under the broiler briefly to brown it nicely. *Serves: 4 to 6*

PRINCE MICHEL
vineyards

VIRGINIA
Chardonnay

1986 VINTAGE VIN BLANC
Grown, vinted and bottled by VaVin, Inc., Leon, Virginia
Contains sulfites   Alc: 12% by vol.

PRINCE MICHEL VINEYARDS With one hundred and ten acres in vineyards, Prince Michel is the largest winery operation in the state of Virginia. In the next several of years the production of the winery is expected to double to 50,000 cases per year.

Beautifully situated on rolling hills south of Culpeper, the vineyards are planted in Chardonnay, Cabernet, and Pinot Noir, with some Merlot and Cabernet Franc. The winery, built in 1985 is a very impressive French Provincial style brick building. The winery equipment is state of the art.There are tours of the winery and a museum to acquaint the visitor with a history of winemaking. The museum contains wine related historic items, many of which were brought over from France. There is also a tasting room and an attractive gift shop.

Prince Michel Vineyards is owned by Omni Services,Inc. a Culpeper-based holding company. The principal stockholders of Omni are Jean Le-Ducq of France and a Culpeper businessman, Norman B. Martin. Joachim Hollerith, Prince Michel's general manager is a stockholder in the winery. The name Prince Michel was chosen for the winery in honor of the son of the exiled king of Poland who is a friend of Monsieur LeDucq.

Rapidan River Vineyards was purchased by LeDucq in 1985. The two wineries, however, are separate entities, each having their own style of wines – Rapidan with a German style and Prince Michel with a French style.

Joachim Hollerith, whose German family has a three hundred year history of winemaking, is the general manager and one of the winemakers at Prince Michel. He is a graduate in vitaculture and enology from Geisenheim University in Germany – a famous school for winemakers. He came to Virginia in 1978 to work as vineyard manager and winemaker at Rapidan River Vineyards, but left there in 1983 to plant the vineyards of Prince Michel. Joachim, a seasoned winemaker with 10 years of experience at the age of 33, has pioneered some of the first commercial winemaking in the state of Virginia.

Alan Kinne is the other winemaker at Prince Michel with dual duty at Rapidan River. Alan is a graduate of the University of Michigan and has 10 years experience in winemaking both in Virginia as well as on Long Island in New York.

The Prince Michel property was a former a cattle farm with good soil. Lime was added to prepare the soil for grape planting. Although the climate of the vineyard is not as severe as in other grape growing sections of Virginia, winter precautions for the vines are taken. To withstand winter frost each vine is hilled up to cover the graft and protect the vinifera graft union. In order to insure against spring freezing and damage, two canes are usually left until May 15th, when additional pruning is done.

Prince Michel Vineyards is the first in the state to have a mechanical harvester for its grape crop. The harvester, a Braud, was made in Germany and also does routine vineyard work, such as spraying, cultivating and hedging. A mechanical planting machine will be utilized to plant the additional 40 acres of vineyards targeted for 1990. Prince Michel's vineyards are more intensely planted than unusual. The vines are on a 8 and 1/2 by 3 and 1/2 foot spacing, resulting in 1450 to 1500 vines per acre. Tonnage yield per acre is also increased over the normal planting of 1200 vines per acre. An umbrella trellis system has been found to be the most effective.

At harvest time the mechanical harvester uses its finger-like prongs to pick the grapes in whole clusters and dump them into a six ton gondola truck. "It takes 4 hours from vine to juice in the tank," says Alan Kinne. "There is no fruit damage with a mechanical harvester, because the stem is the weakest point of the grape and easily broken," he added. Most of the grapes are picked early in the morning, with also some night picking. This assures cool juice for fermentation.

The Prince Michel crusher-stemmer, which de-stems the grapes first and then lightly crushes them, can be programmed as to the percentage of the grape load to be crushed. In this way whole berries can be easily left and added to the fermentation. The press, too, can be programmed as to the amount of pressure to be used.

Prince Michel has a separate room for stainless steel fermentation and holding tanks, and a another room for barrel aging.

One of the most popular wines at Prince Michel is the White Burgundy made in true Burgundian style. "It is a blend of 75% Chardonnay and 25% Pinot Noir," says Alan Kinne. "The Pinot Noir is lightly pressed to give the wine a young fresh feeling." Blush de Michel is 85% Riesling and 15% Cabernet.

"We make our Chardonnay light in style with some oak aging. In this way it is not overpowering and complements food," Alan commented. "Depending on the vintage we blend some Merlot and Cabernet Franc with our Cabernet Sauvignon. This is a traditional Bordeaux style and the wine is aged at least 12 to 16 months in French oak," he explained. "All aging is done in French oak, because the grains are tighter and add more complexity to the wine," Alan explained.

In the future, Prince Michel will be making a Riesling and a champagne using the traditional French cuvee – Chardonnay and Pinot Noir. The champagne will be made by methode champenoise.

Prince Michel, a recent addition to the Virginia wine scene, has entered it in a big professional way and will certainly help make Virginia become recognized as a foremost producer of premium wines in the East. Joachim Hollerith and Alan Kinne have already won many awards for their wines and will certainly continue to do so.

Both Mrs. Hollerith and Alan Kinne enjoying cooking. Mrs. Hollerith uses some of her traditional German recipes, while Alan enjoys putting ingredients together in an informal way and likes that style of entertaining.

TOURS
➡

Prince Michel Vineyards, *Star Route 4, Box 77, Leon , VA 22725, 703-547-3707*
Directions: *Winery located on west side of Route 29, 10 miles south of Culpeper and 8 miles north of Madison.*
Visitation: *Daily, 10 a.m. to 5 p.m. Weekends, 10 a.m. to 6 p.m.*
Principals: *Omni Services, Inc..*
Wines Produced: *Chardonnay, Cabernet Sauvignon, Pinot Noir, Blush de Michel, White Burgundy*
1987 Production: *20,000 cases*

COLD PASTA SALAD

Serve with White Burgundy

Pasta salads are very popular for informal entertaining and give the cook a chance to be creative. Shrimp, ham or leftover meat may be added and the vegetables may be varied. Spiral pasta known as fusilli or rotelle is used in this recipe, since the dressing easily combines with the crevices of the pasta.

12 oz. spiral pasta rotelle, preferably a combination of grain, spinach and tomato	1 small sweet red pepper, seeded and thinly sliced
1 small head of broccoli	**Herbs and Spices:**
8 oz. small black olives, pitted and sliced	3 tablespoons chopped fresh parsley
2 to 3 tablespoon minced green onion or chives	3 tablespoons chopped fresh marjoram
1/3 cup freshly grated Parmesan cheese	3 tablespoon chopped fresh dill
1/3 cup freshly grated Romano cheese	1/8 teaspoon chopped fresh cilantro
	1/8 teaspoon paprika

(other fresh herbs such as basil, rosemary or thyme may be substituted)

Dressing:

Juice of 1 to 2 lemons (about 4 tablespoons)	1/2 teaspoon dried mustard
2 cloves of garlic, crushed and minced	Dash of ground pepper
1/2 teaspoon dried tarragon	4 oz. olive oil

Cook pasta in boiling water until al dente. Drain in colander and rinse with very cold water. Steam broccoli until slightly crisp. Do not over cook. Drain broccoli and rinse with cold water. Mix dressing ingredients, adding oil last, whisking to blend all ingredients. Set dressing aside.

Shake colander with pasta well to eliminate extra water. Place pasta in a large bowl. Add olives, onions, cheeses, red pepper and herbs and spices. Toss lightly to combine. Add dressing and toss again. Cut up broccoli, taking care not to break up florets. Add to salad and chill until serving.

Small cooked shrimp, radishes, or sunflower seeds may also be added to the salad. *Serves: 4 to 6*

PORK TENDERLOIN IN ROSEMARY

Serve with Chardonnay

This is a traditional Southern German method of cooking pork tenderloin. It is simple, yet elegant.

4 whole pork tenderloins	1/2 cup white wine
Salt, pepper and paprika	3/4 cup cream
2 tablespoons of fresh rosemary leaves	

Place tenderloins in a fairly flat casserole dish and season well with salt, pepper and paprika. Sprinkle with rosemary leaves. Add wine and cook in a preheated 400 degree oven (middle rack) for 25 minutes. Turn meat and cook for an additional 25 minutes. Add cream and cook for 15 minutes.

Serve and garnish with fresh rosemary sprigs. *Serves: 8*

VERY FINE RASPBERRY CREME

Serve with Blush de Michel

The Holleriths are fortunate enough to have raspberries growing on their property. Other berries in season may also be used for this recipe.

3 lbs. very ripe raspberries	1/2 cup sugar
1 cup semi-sweet white wine	12 eggs

Mash raspberries and strain through sieve. In a medium saucepan, heat wine, sugar and strained raspberries to boiling. Remove from heat, cool slightly and add eggs one at a time, mixing well after each addition. Place mixture in top of a double boiler and cook until mixture starts to thicken, beating constantly. Remove from heat and place top of double boiler containing the raspberry mixture in ice water. Beat well for 15 minutes.

Pour into serving dish and refrigerate for 3 hours before serving. Garnish with whole raspberries. *Serves: 8*

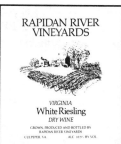

RAPIDAN RIVER
VINEYARDS

VIRGINIA
White Riesling
DRY WINE

GROWN, PRODUCED AND BOTTLED BY
RAPIDAN RIVER VINEYARDS
CULPEPER, VA   ALC. 10.5% BY VOL

RAPIDAN RIVER VINEYARDS Local legend says that in the 1700s a group of German settlers planted vines along the bank of the Rapidan River. Supposedly, these settlers continued to grow grapes and make wine until mildew and *phylloxera* killed the vines. Over 250 years later, wine is again being made along the Rapidan River.

In 1976, a German surgeon named Gerhard Guth came to Virginia and purchased a large farm on the Rapidan River, southeast of Culpeper. Most of the farm was and still is devoted to a dairy operation. Being a true German and lover of wine, he decided to plant a vineyard and start a winery.

In 1978, for this purpose, Dr. Guth hired and brought to Virginia Joachim Hollerith, a young winemaker from Germany. Not only has Hollerith's family been making wine since 1678, he is a graduate of the University of Geisenheim, a famous winemaking school in Germany.

Assured that vinifera grapes would grow in the Rapidan region, Gut had 25 acres planted. These were primarily Riesling, with some Gewurtztraminer, Chardonnay, and Pinot Noir. Another 25 acres were planted in 1984. Dr. Guth's original plan was to have 250 acres in vinifera grapes by about 1990 with a total investment of about 6 million dollars, including the winery equipment.

Rapidan's vineyards are structured in the German manner. There are 1200 vines per acre. The trellising system is higher than normal, allowing good air circulation and more light to reach the vines. This six wire trellising system guarantees a good canopy management.

The winery is a modern, well-equipped facility in an old brick building which existed on the property when Dr. Guth purchased the farm.

Joachim Hollerith stayed at Rapidan River Vineyards for five years, making wine in the German style, after which he left to start another Winery - Prince Michel Vineyards. In 1984, Steven Warner, a graduate of Fresno State University in California, joined Rapidan as winemaker. He continued to make wines in the German style.

The Riesling, the most popular wine, is made in both a dry and semi-dry style. Rapidan River has established a reputation for its Rieslings and has won many awards for this wine. The Chardonnay, too, is made in a dry style as is the award-winning limited release Gewurtztraminer. The winery's entire selection is sold out completely every year.

In July, 1985, Dr. Guth sold the vineyard and winery to Jean Leducq, one of the owners of Prince Michel Vineyards, keeping the rest of the 1500 acre farm and dairy operation. Joachim Hollerith once again became the winemaker at Rapidan, still retaining the same position at Prince Michel. Alan Kinne, associate winemaker at Prince Michel, has taken over many of the winemaking duties at both facilities.

There are plans to plant another 25 acres at Rapidan River and expand production. The German style of winemaking continues to be employed and there are plans to produce a Sekt – Champagne made from Riesling wine – by méthode champenoise.

Rapidan River Winery is fulfilling the dreams of those German settlers of long ago who tried to grow grapes and make wine along the Rapidan River.

Mrs. Hollerith, Joachim's charming, petite wife and the mother of their two small children, still prepares a great number of her native German dishes. They go particularly well with Rapidan River Vineyard's German style wines.

TOURS
➡

Rapidan River Vineyards, *Route 4, Box 199, Culpeper, VA 22725 703-399-1855*
Directions: *From Culpeper take Route 3 east, then take route 522 south over the Rapidan River bridge, left on Route 611 and go 4 miles to vineyard sign on left. Turn left on Route 620 for 1.3 miles to vineyard sign on right*
Visitation: *Daily from 10:00 a.m. to 5:00 p.m.*
Principals: *Jean Leducq*
Wines Produced: *White Riesling, Gewurtztraminer, Chardonnay*
1987 Production: *6,000 cases*

SCHWARZWURZEL (SALSIFY)

Serve with semi-dry Riesling

Salsify is another name for oyster plant, which is a white root vegetable similar to a parsnip in shape. It has a lightly sweet flavor which is supposed to resemble the flavor of oysters. It is more prevalent in Europe than in the United States where it is usually found only in gourmet shops. Steamed asparagus may be substituted for the salsify in this recipe.

3 quarts of water　　　　　　　　　　　2 1/2 lb. of black salsify (oyster plant)
2 tablespoons vinegar

Sauce:

4 tablespoons butter　　　　　　　　　1 cup sweet cream
2 tablespoons flour　　　　　　　　　　2 egg yolks
1/2 cup vegetable broth　　　　　　　　Salt, pepper and nutmeg

Add vinegar to the water and clean the salsify by scraping it. Immediately put the salsify into the water to prevent any discoloration. In a medium size saucepan bring water to a boil and add the cleaned salsify. Cook until done - not too soft. The salsify may either be boiled whole or cut into 2 to 3-inch pieces before boiling. Adjust cooking time accordingly. If not previously cut into pieces, do so and serve warm with the following sauce.

To make sauce: In a small saucepan melt the butter over medium-high heat. Add flour and brown it to a light golden brown. Slowly, while stirring constantly, add the vegetable broth. Add cream and cook gently for about 3 minutes. Beat the egg yolks and add some of the hot sauce to them. Then stir egg yolk mixture into the sauce mixture, stirring constantly to prevent egg yolks from curdling. Season with salt, pepper and nutmeg. *Serves: 8*

Author's note: Peeled, sliced broccoli stems may also be used instead of the salsify. Cook broccoli until tender and serve with sauce.

WINE ROASTED POTATOES

Serve with Chardonnay

This German style potato dish is a nice accompaniment to broiled or roasted meat.

2 1/2 lbs. potatoes　　　　　　　　　　2 cups white wine
4 tablespoons butter or margarine　　　Salt, pepper and nutmeg
2 onions, minced

Clean potatoes and boil them unpeeled. Peel the boiled potatoes and cut them into little cubes. In a large, heavy skillet over medium high heat, melt the butter. Add potatoes and onions and roast them until they get crispy. Add wine and season with salt, pepper and nutmeg. Simmer uncovered until wine is almost completely absorbed. Add more seasoning if necessary. *Serves: 8*

SIMEON VINEYARDS, LTD. Two hundred years ago Filippo Mazzei attempted to grow European vines on property given to him by Thomas Jefferson adjacent to Monticello. Neither Mazzei nor Jefferson succeeded but Jefferson continued to believe it could be done even after Mazzei returned to Europe. This dream has finally come true. Vinifera grapes are being raised, and wine is being made on the same property Mazzei owned.

The estate is named Colle, and the original site is still part of a larger farm owned by Stanley Woodward who in the 1950's served as U. S. Ambassador to Canada. The vineyard and winery are located on the property. The Woodwards raise all types of crops on their farm and in 1981 engaged Gabriele Rausse as their farm manager.

Gabriele Rausse, an agronomist graduate of the University of Milan, had come to Virginia in 1976 to help start a winery on the old Barboursville Plantation. He had been sent by Gianni Zonin, owner of the property and president of Italy's largest privately held wine company.

Up until that time, mostly native and French hybrids were grown in Virginia, with small quantities of vinifera. Gabriele, who is considered the sage of grape growing in Virginia, was sent over by Zonin on a 40 day visa to determine if vinifera could be grown in the Charlottesville area. After three years and many obstacles, he was able to give his boss a positive answer. The rest is history.

Gabriele Rausse was instrumental in establishing modern viticulture practices in Virginia. In 1976, the USDA advised him not to plant grapes. All he was going to do was to get the farmers unnecessarily excited. However, Gabriele felt that the area around Charlottesville was well suited for grape growing. The soil had good drainage, the sloping hills were ideal for vines and modern technology and pest control could alleviate the problems that his fellow countryman, Mazzei, had faced two hundred years ago. In the fall of 1978 he made the first wine at Barboursville. He also established a nursery to propagate more vines for Barboursville's own use as well as some for sale. Ninety thousand vines were grafted, and all were sold in one month.

In 1981 Gabriele, his wife and children desired a change of pace from the hectic pressures of working for a large cooperation. Mrs. Woodward, who has since passed away, was very impressed with Gabriele's accomplishments. The Woodwards had an interest in wine and wanted a small vineyard on their property. They needed someone, however, who was knowledgeable in agriculture to manage their property and other farming operations. The Woodward farm consists of 750 acres and raises apples, peaches, chickens and cattle.

In 1981 Gabriele planted a small vineyard of Zinfandel, Pinot Noir and Barbera on the Woodward property. He has since expanded the vineyard to 8 acres adding Chardonnay and Cabernet Sauvignon. There are plans to increase the vineyard acreage to 15 acres. Gabriele believes that grapes must be picked when there is a decent acid content. "You cannot always bring up the grapes to high sugar," he said. Many times the crop can be destroyed by rain or rot if the grapes stay on the vines to reach maximum sugar content.

"Different soils and climate conditions produce entirely different wines from the same grape variety," Gabriele emphasized. He believes that many of the early Virginia vineyards were planted on the wrong soil. "The worst is heavy organic soil," he added. "Young volcanic soil with minerals and chemicals is best. That type of soil has good drainage and the vine roots can go deep." Gabriele also believes in proper soil preparation before any vines are planted. "You just cannot plow three feet deep in clay, plant vines and expect your vines to flourish," Gabriele commented. "Virginia has good soil, and it will produce top quality wine."

In order to keep the full time employees of the farm busy during the winter months, Gabriele Rausse established a nursery for vinifera vines. The buds are stripped from a 12 to 16 inch piece of vinifera vine and grafted onto a native, disease resistant root stock. The V-cut graft is sealed with wax. The root is then placed in peat moss, put in a dark warm place until the graft heals and roots begin to form. The roots are then planted in a nursery area and allowed to grow for about 1 year before being sold.

As the vineyard began to flourish and the grape crop became larger Gabriele Rausse started making wine in 1983 in one of the farm buildings. The winery operation soon outgrew the small building and a larger one, completely insulated, with modern winery equipment was finished in 1986. Gabriele produces Chardonnay and Cabernet Sauvignon in the classic French style. Some Merlot is blended into the Cabernet Sauvignon. The Chardonnay has been released and is available in local markets. The Cabernet Sauvignon will be released soon. Gabriele is also making Pinot Noir and Zinfandel – both of which are aging in French oak. These will be released within the next several years. He is also growing Barbera in the vineyard and will probably make it into a blush type of wine – fruity and light.

The Woodwards want to keep a low profile for the winery, even with their famous winemaker, who also prefers to remain in the background. Obscure or not, Gabriele Rausse has done for the modern Virginia wine industry what his predecessor, Filippo Mazzei, had not been able to accomplish for the colonial Virginia wine industry. The following are some of Mr. Woodward's favorite dishes to accompany the Simeon wines.

TOURS
➡

Simeon Vineyards, Ltd., *RFD 9, Box 293, Charlottesville, VA 22901, 804-977-3502*
Directions: *South of Charlottesville, 1 1/2 miles past Monticello*
Visitation: *Not open to the public. Retail outlet at Simeon Farm Market store on Route 53 between Monticello and Ashlawn.*
Principals: *Stanley Woodward*
Wines Produced: *Chardonnay, Cabernet Sauvignon*
1987 Production: *600 cases*

WATERCRESS SOUP

Serve with Chardonnay

Watercress as its name implies grows in cold running water. It is a native of Europe but has immigrated to North America. There are many legends concerning this salad green which was thought to provide magical cures in ancient and medieval times. "Eat cress and have more wit," was taken seriously by the Romans. Today watercress is grown commercially. The leaves have a slightly hot, peppery taste which in this recipe provides an interesting flavor.

2 tablespoons butter	3 medium potatoes, peeled and cubed
1 bunch well washed water cress, leaves and tops only	Pinch of salt
	1/2 cup heavy cream
6 cups boiling water	2 egg yolks

Melt butter over medium heat in a pot; add watercress tops and stir until wilted. Add boiling water, potatoes, and a pinch of salt. Simmer mixture for 30 minutes or until potatoes are done. Put in blender and blend until smooth. Return soup to pot. Just before serving, mix egg yolks and cream together, blending well. Slowly add to simmering soup stirring constantly until well blended and hot. Do not boil. *Serves: 6*

OSSO BUCCO

Serve with Cabernet Sauvignon

The translation of Osso Bucco is "hollow bone." The dish is prepared with pieces of veal shank which after cooking do have a hollow bone. This typical Italian dish is usually served with pasta or rice.

3 carrots, finely chopped	salt and pepper
1 large onion, chopped	Flour
1 tablespoon butter	3/4 cup white wine
4 tomatoes, peeled and chopped	Thyme, rosemary, bay leaf, handful of chopped parsley
1 1/2 lbs. veal shanks	
2 tablespoons olive oil	1 teaspoon each grated orange zest and lemon zest
6 sage leaves	
6 basil leaves	

In a large pot over medium heat saute carrots and onion in butter for ten minutes. Add tomatoes and continue to cook on low heat.

While cooking tomato mixture, sauté veal in a separate frying pan in olive oil on each side. Then sprinkle flour over the meat and continue cooking until flour is lightly colored. *Serves: 2*

Add meat mixture to the larger pot containing the tomatoes. Add wine and increase heat to medium. Add all herbs, salt and pepper to taste and enough water to barely cover the meat and vegetables. Cover and simmer for 1 1/2 hours. Serve with noodles or rice, arranging vegetables around the veal. The juices may be thickened if desired.

Author's note: If fresh sage and fresh basil is unavailable, substitute 1/4 teaspoon dried sage and 1/2 teaspoon dried basil.

THE BAVARIAN CHEF German settlers have a long and varied history in Virginia.One of the earliest contingent being those who came at the invitation of Governor Spotswood in 1714 to work the iron mines near the Rappahannock River. In the 1730's German settlers from Pennsylvania, fleeing from persecution in Europe, came to settle in the Shenandoah Valley. A colony of Germans settled on the Rapidan River in the 1770's and produced both red and white wine.

In modern times, too, German immigrants, such as the Thalwitz family came to Virginia via Pennsylvania. In 1951 Eckhard Thalwitz, a German chef from Bavaria who was trained in international cuisine, and his bride Bruni came to America on their honeymoon. While in Pennsylvania he was offered the job as chef at a very exclusive golf and country club. Due to the good auspices of their sponsor, an aunt of Jacqueline Kennedy, the nation's First Lady at that time, the young couple was able to stay in America. Eckhard worked as a chef in Pennsylvania for 23 years, where the couples' son Jerome was born.

Wanderlust – an urge for a change of scenery – overtook them and they came south to Virginia in 1974, as some of their countrymen had done two centuries previously. They liked the mountains and the countryside of Greene County. It reminded them of their home in Bavaria. The Thalwitz family wanted to settle there and open a restaurant.

A realtor helped them find the property. It was an old truck stop which needed quite a bit of refurbishing. After several months of renovation the building was transformed into a Bavarian-looking house. The brown framework with gingerbread trim on the outside and the stained glass windows give a feeling of "gemütlichkeit" – coziness.

In 1983, twenty-one year old Jerome Thalwitz and his wife Diane joined the family business. Jerome had graduated from the Woodberry Forest School in Virginia and had returned from a four year apprenticeship at the well-known Vier Jahreszeiten Hotel in Berchtesgaden, Bavaria. Not too long ago the elder Thalwitzes retired, leaving Jerome and his wife in charge.

Jerome is carrying on the family tradition of serving fine German cuisine, intermingled with some international dishes. There are daily specials on the menu. Jerome is a very innovative chef. Some of his German specialties include a Champagne pate served with a sauce of currants, strawberries and brandy; Mandelschnitzel, a pork tenderloin breaded and fried with almonds in the breading, topped with a strawberry gin sauce. Red cabbage and spaetzle are always on the menu. Jerome makes all of his desserts which include cheesecake, creme and fruit tortes and apple strudel.

Jerome Thalwitz states that German-style white wines – several of which are produced in Virginia – pair well with his German cuisine.

Like many of their countrymen generations ago, the Thalwitzes have made Virginia their home and have shared their cuisine with their many friends and patrons.

DINING

The Bavarian Chef, P. O. Box 375, Madison, VA 22727, 703-948-6505
Directions: 20 miles north of Charlottesville on Route 29
Meal Times: Sunday 11:30 a.m. to 10 p.m. Wed. thru Saturday 4:30 to 10 p.m.
Principals: Jerome and Diane Thalwitz

JAEGERSCHNITZEL

Schnitzel, literally is the German word for "little cut of meat." However, it has been commonly accepted as the word for veal – veal that has been carefully chosen, pounded, breaded, fried or sautéed and served with a sauce or topping. Each version is a different dish, but all have a fine piece of veal in common.

1/2 lb. bacon, sliced into small strips	1 teaspoon cornstarch
2 small onions, finely chopped	1 pint heavy cream
1 lb. fresh mushrooms, sliced	2 veal fillets, or top round,
3 tablespoons lemon juice	8 to 10 oz. each
Salt and pepper to taste	Flour.
1/8 teaspoon garlic powder	1 egg beaten
1 cup double strength chicken stock	Salt and pepper
	2 tablespoons butter

In a large skillet over medium high heat, sauté bacon until it is transparent. Add mushrooms and lemon juice. (The lemon juice helps mushrooms retain their color.) Cook until mushrooms release their juices and the liquid is reduced. Season with salt and pepper to taste and add garlic powder. Add cornstarch to stock, and then add mixture to sauce. Add cream and stir until blended. Lower heat to simmer, and keep sauce warm while preparing the veal.

Pound veal until even in thickness – 1/4 to 1/2 inch thick. Dip in flour and then in beaten egg. Season with salt and pepper to taste. Melt butter in large sauté pan over medium heat. Add veal and sauté until just done. Serve with sauce spooned over the top. *Serves: 4*

RED CABBAGE

In Germany red cabbage is traditionally served with duck, goose and roasted meats. The tanginess of this recipe is particularly pleasing to the palate.

2 heads red cabbage, cored and	4 bay leaves
thinly sliced	2 cups sugar
1 large onion, minced	Salt and black pepper to taste
4 tart apples, peeled and sliced	1 cup duck fat or lard
2 cups red wine	1 tablespoon cornstarch
2 cups red wine vinegar	1/3 cup water
4 whole cloves	

Combine all ingredients in a large pot. Bring to a slow boil, then reduce heat to low and cook until cabbage is soft. (30 to 45 minutes.) Blend cornstarch and water and thicken juices. *Serves: 8*

The Old Mill Dining Room at THE BOAR'S HEAD INN

The Boar's Head Inn is not only a complete resort complex, but is an elegant "country inn" suited to modern times. The style of the Inn, which was built in 1965, is country English.

Although the Boar's Head Inn was built in modern times it has a link to the past history of the Charlottesville area. The link is an old flour mill that has been a part of Charlottesville since 1834, located on a stretch of the Hardware River, near Monticello. For years farmers brought their grain to the mill to be ground into flour.

During the Civil War, the mill was almost destroyed when General Grant and General Custer marched through Charlottesville. They gave their men the order to destroy any and all manufacturing and transportation facilities. The mill was spared, however, because of its strong construction. Rains on the previous days made the wood so wet that it would not burn when Yankee soldiers tried to torch the building.

A retired Confederate Captain, R. J. Hancock, purchased the mill after the Civil War and operated it for 60 years. The mill ceased operation in the 1930's.

In the early 1960's, John B. Rogan, a local land developer and President of The Boar's Head Inn, recognized the special significance of the mill and its historical value to the Charlottesville area. He purchased the old mill and had it carefully dismantled, numbering each piece. The mill was reconstructed on the Boar's Head property and became in integral part of the Inn.

Today the old grist mill is one of the focal points of The Boar's Head Inn. The carefully restored edifice serves as the main dining room – The Old Mill Room–and a comfortable social room--The Ordinary. The heartwood pine beams, the original plank flooring and the carefully preserved paneling from the old mill have added to the charm and grace of the Boar's Head Inn.

The public rooms of the Boar's Head Inn are furnished in English antiques which have been carefully selected by John Rogan. The Old Mill Dining room is decorated in traditional English furnishings with accents of blue.

Also on the premises of the Boar's Head Inn is an extensive Sports Club, featuring tennis courts, swimming pool, exercise facilities and a restaurant. The Sports Club operates on a membership basis, but it is also available to guests of the Inn. The mushroom soup recipe included below is from Chef Ledford of the Sports Club.

The name Boar's Head stems from the boar's head which is a part of the Rogan family crest. Also, it serves as a reminder that wild boar were hunted around the Charlottesville area in the past.

Melvin Frye is the chef at The Boar's Head Inn. He began his career at the Inn seventeen years ago and emphasizes a Continental cuisine with traditional Virginia accents. Many of the ingredients used in the preparation of the meals are raised locally. Mushrooms are grown in nearby Buckingham County and all produce is fresh. Frye has perfected the cooking of local Virginia ham and serves it many different ways, including fried with red eye gravy for breakfast. Chef Frye has included his Virginia wine selections with his recipes.

The wine list at The Old Mill Dining Room is extensive. There are more than 30 Virginia wines on the list. The Boar's Head Inn is also very active in the promotion of Virginia wines. Each fall the Monticello Wine festival is held on its premises. John Rogan has another tie to the Virginia wine industry since his wife, Felicia Warburg Rogan, is the owner of Oakencroft Vineyard and Winery.

The Boar's Head Inn not only has a link to the past with the old mill, but it also provides encouragement to the new and growing industry of Virginia winemaking.

DINING
➡

The Boar's Head Inn, *Ednam Forest on Route 250, P. O. Box 5185, Charlottesville, Virginia 22905, 804-296-2181*
Directions: *On Route 250, 1 1/2 miles west of Charlottesville*
Principals: *John B. Rogan*
Meal Times: *Breakfast: 7 a.m. to 10:30 a.m. Monday through Saturday Sunday Breakfast: 7:30 a.m. to 10:30 a.m. Lunch: 12 noon to 2 p.m. 7 days a week Dinner: 6 p.m. to 9:30 p.m. Monday through Saturday Sunday dinner: 6 p.m. to 8:30 p.m.*

MUSHROOM SOUP

This mushroom soup is a flavorful first course or may be served for a luncheon with a green salad.

2 tablespoons shallots, finely chopped	1/4 cup white wine
1 clove garlic, finely minced	1/2 teaspoon chopped fresh thyme
1 medium onion, finely chopped	1/2 teaspoon fresh chopped marjoram
3 tablespoons butter	Salt and pepper to taste
2 tablespoons flour	1/2 cup heavy cream
3 cups chicken or light beef broth	Thinly sliced mushrooms and chopped
1 lb. mushrooms	parsley for garnish

In a large saucepan, sauté shallots, garlic and onions in 3 tablespoons melted butter. Add flour to make a pale roux. Add broth and cook until thickened.

Clean and coarsely grind mushrooms in a food processor. In another saucepan, combine mushrooms and wine. Cook over medium heat to sweat the mushrooms. Add to thickened stock and season with the herbs and salt and pepper. Simmer for 20 to 25 minutes to blend flavors. Add cream and simmer to blend. Serve garnished with sliced mushrooms and chopped parsley. *Serves: 4*

BRIOCHE OF OYSTERS, SWEETBREADS AND MUSHROOMS

Serve with Naked Mountain Chardonnay

Chef Frye says that "this recipe reflects the great variety of local Virginia products and was created as an example of the originality of the culinary efforts of Thomas Jefferson. The recipe utilizes Chesapeake Bay oysters, local salt cured ham and shitake mushrooms. Adding this mixture to the brioche shell is a reflection of the French influence enjoyed by Mr. Jefferson. The final product is indicative of the innovation that was characteristic of Monticello."

Brioche Dough: Any brioche dough recipe or crusty white bread recipe will do. Prepare the brioche larger than usually called for. (A recipe for 16 will yield 10 oversize rolls.) Bake as per normal.

Filling:

4 oz. Virginia country ham	4 oz. Chardonnay
2 oz. butter	6 oz. heavy cream
1 oz. shallots, chopped	2 lobes veal sweetbreads, blanched*
9 fresh oysters, smoked	Salt and pepper to taste
3 to 4 large shiitake mushrooms, sliced	Parsley and lemon wedges for garnish

To prepare the filling dice the ham into small squares or thin strips. Melt the butter in a skillet over medium heat and saute the ham and shallots until tender. Remove ham and shallots. Add oysters and cook until puffy, 1 to 2 minutes, and remove to a plate. Add the mushrooms and sauté only until they begin to moisten. Remove the mushrooms and deglaze the skillet with the Chardonnay. Add the heavy cream and reduce by half. Return the oysters, mushrooms, ham mixture and blanched sweetbreads to the sauce. Season to taste with salt and pepper. Simmer 1 to 2 minutes.

After the brioches have cooled cut the tops off around the topknot and hollow out. Right before serving return the brioches to hot oven until slightly crisp. Spoon in filling mixture, replace the top, garnish with parsley and lemon wedge. Serve as an appetizer or accompanied by vegetables as a main course.

* Blanching sweetbreads: Soak the sweetbreads in cold water for 2 hours. Drain and remove all possible membrane. Recover with cold water and soak 1 1/2 hours more. Drain and repeat pulling off membrane. Place in a pan or skillet. Cover with cold water, a dash of salt, and juice of 1/2 lemon and bring to boil. Reduce heat and simmer for 5 minutes. Cool and cut into bite size pieces. *Serves: 4 to 6*

THE BOOK GALLERY RESTAURANT "Food for thought," – that is what many books provide. Food, thinking, reading, recipes, cookbooks, dining they all seem to go together. That is what Marshall McKenzie thought when he opened his Book Gallery Restaurant. It is an integral part of his Book Gallery bookstore. Yes, you can actually take your book to the table and read if you want to, without someone disapproving.

Marshall McKenzie, a native of Kentucky, spent most of his career as the Corporate Director of Human Resources and Administration of the Stepan Chemical Company near Chicago, Illinois. The company manufactures emulsifiers and is also credited with the secret ingredient in Coke. Marshall, who had been with the company for a number of years, had become tired of the job routine and decided to seek another career.

For several vacations Marshall and his wife Jackie had driven to Florida. On their way back to Illinois, they usually managed to route their trips through Virginia, particularly the Charlottesville area. The mountains, the rolling hills, the climate and the community appealed to them. In 1982 they started looking at residential property and almost purchased a house a few miles west of Charlottesville. A few months later the real estate agent contacted the McKenzies and told them of a business that was for sale. It was a bookstore. Marshall, on his next trip East, stopped to look at it and negotiated for the purchase. That was in September of 1982, when the existing Book Gallery took on new ownership.

The store was located a block away from its present location. In 1986, the restaurant on the corner of Emmet and Barracks Road was put up for sale and Marshall decided to combine a restaurant and his bookstore. The bookstore is in one section of the building and the attractive restaurant and bar are adjacent, but not separate. There is an open fresh feeling to the restaurant with its cream and blue decor. Although each is a separate entity, there is a comfortable flow of traffic from one to the other. Diners are not bothered by book browsers and vice versa. This is an unique and exciting dining combination.

Martin Wolf, who is a third generation chef, presides over the kitchen. He was raised in a restaurant owned by his parents and grandparents. Martin, a graduate of the University of Michigan, fits right into the bookstore atmosphere since he is a published poet. His dishes, too, are poetic and he draws inspirations for his creations from the American, French, Italian and Oriental cuisines.

Sandy High is the restaurant manager. Sandy was trained in France and at the Philadelphia restaurant institute. According to Marshall McKenzie, "Sandy is the key ingredient in my recipe for success."

Virginia wines are an integral part of the Book Gallery Restaurant wine list. The McKenzies and Martin Wolf are continually looking for wines which will complement their dishes and be familiar to their diners. Some of the Book Gallery's wine suggestions are included with their most popular dishes.

Chef Wolf has not included any salt in these recipes; he assumes that either the diner or cook can add it to taste.

DINING

The Book Gallery & Restaurant, *1207 Emmet Street, Charlottesville, Virginia 22901, 804-971-4696*
Directions: *North of Charlottesville center, on business Route 29 at corner of Emmet Street and Barracks Road.*
Principals: *Marshall and Jackie McKenzie*
Meal Times: *Monday through Saturday Continental Breakfast: 9 a.m. to 11 a.m., Lunch: 11 a.m. to 2:30 p.m. Tuesday through Thursday Dinner: 5 p.m. to 9 p.m. Friday and Saturday Dinner: 5 p.m. to 10 p.m. Sunday Brunch: 11 a.m. to 3 p.m.*

FETTUCINE ST. ANDRE

Serve with Oakencroft Seyval Blanc

St. Andre is a triple cream cheese, similar to Brie. If you cannot obtain St. Andre, any of the white rind cheese of the Brie family will work in this recipe. Also, any other shape of pasta may be substituted. This is the "ultimate macaroni and cheese."

1/2 lb. fettucine, fresh or homemade	1 cup mushrooms, sliced
1/2 lb. St. Andre sliced	Parsley for garnish

Cook the pasta and rinse with hot water. Drain well. Place fettucine in a baking dish or casserole, and cover top with sliced mushrooms. Remove the white rind from the St. Andre and cover top of the pasta with the sliced cheese. Bake in a preheated 350 degree oven until the cheese is nearly completely melted. Garnish with parsley and serve. *Serves: 3*

BOOK GALLERY MINESTRONE

Although there are countless versions of minestrone in Italy, the soup has come to mean a thick vegetable soup, usually with pasta and tomatoes. Diners phoning for reservations often ask if the minestrone is on the Book Gallery menu for the day.

1 large onion	1 large can (28 oz) diced tomatoes in juice
1 green pepper	2 cups tomato juice
1 teaspoon fennel	1 cup red wine
1 tablespoon oregano	4 cups water
1 tablespoon fresh basil	1 cup cooked garbanzo beans
1 tablespoon chopped fresh garlic	2 cups cooked pasta
1/2 teaspoon black pepper	1 cup julienned zucchini
1/2 cup olive oil	Grated Parmesan cheese

Chop the onion and green pepper. In a soup pot sauté onion and green pepper with herbs, garlic, and pepper in the olive oil. Add the tomatoes, tomato juice, wine, water, and garbanzo beans. Bring to a boil and simmer for one hour. Add the pasta and the zucchini just before serving and garnish with Parmesan cheese. *Serves: 6 to 8*

BEEF TENDERLOIN AND SNOW PEAS

Serve with Ingleside Cabernet Sauvignon

Oriental cuisine inspired Chef Wolf to create this traditional stir fry recipe.

1 lb. beef tenderloin, cut in small pieces	1 tablespoon soy sauce
1/2 lb. snow peas	1 tablespoon sherry
1/2 lb. mushrooms	Peanut oil
1 teaspoon chopped fresh ginger	2 tablespoon chopped scallions
1 teaspoon chopped garlic	

Slice the mushrooms and remove the ends and strings from the snow peas.

Pour enough peanut oil into the bottom of a wok or large skillet to just cover the bottom. Add ginger and garlic. When the ginger and garlic are sizzling, add the meat. Quickly brown the meat, add sherry and soy sauce. Cook for a minute or two. Add snow peas and mushrooms and cook just long enough to heat them and wilt the snow peas. Serve on a platter garnished with scallions. Serve with rice or Chinese noodles. *Serves: 4*

"THE ORDINARY" at Historic Michie Tavern

Servants were ordered to sing each time they brought meals to The Ordinary from the log kitchen not too far away. Since they were singing they could not nibble at the food along the way. Times have changed. The food is no longer prepared in the log cabin outside Michie Tavern and the singing is now in the form of praise of the old Southern fare served at The Ordinary. Visiting Michie Tavern and its restaurant, The Ordinary, is like taking a journey back in time.

It was the winter of 1777 when young Corporal William Michie (pronounced "Micky") received an urgent message to return home. He made the long journey home only to find that his father had passed away. William inherited his father's land holdings, which were once a part of Patrick Henry's lands in Albemarle County. The land was located on Buck Mountain with a road and a stream nearby. William settled in a log cabin and started raising wheat and tobacco.

The Buck Mountain Road became a popular stagecoach route from the coast. The Michie cabin became a convenient place to rest and spend the night. Since resting places along the road were few and far between, there were many nights when William gave up his own bed to "strangers," as they were called in the 18th century. These visits by strangers became more and more frequent and William Michie decided to build a proper Tavern that could offer respectable accommodations and food. Although country inns at that time were considered poor seconds to their city kin, Michie Tavern rivaled any accommodations in town.

Not only did Michie Tavern become a place to stay, but it it also became the center of political and social life of the community. It had a ballroom where, the guests as well as the town folk could dance on Saturday night. On Sunday morning, however, that same ballroom was used for church services. There was a gaming room in the Tavern where the gentlemen could enjoy a game of cards. The bar served the guests on the inside from one window and the local tradesmen or carriage drivers from the window facing the outside.

One of the most important rooms in the Tavern was the keeping room, or dining room as it would be known in modern times. It is a very large room at Michie Tavern with the original fireplace where some of the food was kept warm and a little preparation was also done. The majority of the food, however, was prepared in the log kitchen just up the hill from the outside door of the keeping room. All of the cooking, roasting and baking was done there and the finished dishes were brought to the keeping room to be served to the guests.

The Mitchie Tavern became so popular that William built a "hyphen" or connecting corridor between the Tavern and his own cabin. This, in effect, added two more sleeping rooms. In those days people slept four and five to a bed – crossways. One of the tavern rules was that no one could go to bed with their boots on. People hesitated in taking them off for fear that the boots would be stolen during the night.

As the Tavern became more prosperous a grist mill was added as well as a general store. In 1927, Mrs. Mark Henderson, a local business woman expressed an interest in purchasing Michie Tavern. At that time the building was in a remote location and it was in bad disrepair. Mrs. Henderson, however, felt that it was the ideal place for her vast collection of antiques. The rise of the popularity in automobiles and the consequent tourist industry prompted Mrs. Henderson's decision to purchase the old inn. Also at that time there was a movement toward preservation. Monticello had been open for some time and was drawing thousands of visitors.

Mrs. Henderson decided to move Michie Tavern to a more accessible location – to the foot of Carter Mountain, one half mile from Monticello. In three months time the Tavern was dismantled, moved by horse and wagon seventeen miles to its present location. The Tavern opened as a museum in 1928 and once again welcomed "strangers" to its doors, as well as to The Ordinary.

On the same premises, over the grist mill, is the Virginia Wine Museum, which traces the early Jeffersonian history of winemaking in Virginia. During the Thanksgiving and Christmas holiday season a traditional colonial meal is prepared and served to invited guests.

Otherwise, there is only one meal – lunch – a day served at The Ordinary and the menu is always the same. It is served buffet style with one of the best selections of Southern food in Virginia – fried chicken and all the trimmings. Virginia wine is also served – Blenheim's Chardonnay, Oakencroft's Seyval Blanc, and Montdomaine's Riesling.

DINING

The Ordinary, *Route 53, Monticello Mountain, Charlottesville, Virginia 22901, 804-977-1234*
Directions: *On Route 53 southeast of Charlottesville, just before Monticello*
Principals: *Michie Tavern Corporation*
Meal Times: *Daily, except December 25th and January 1st. Lunch only 11:15 a.m. to 3:30 p.m., in summer 11:30 a.m. to 3 p.m. in winter*

COLONIAL FRIED CHICKEN

Chicken was as popular in the 18th century as it is today. Cooks, in that day used as much imagination in the preparation of poultry as they do now.

1 2 to 3 lb. fryer, cut up	1 1/2 tablespoons oregano
3 cups shortening	1/2 teaspoon garlic salt
3/4 cup flour	1/4 teaspoon pepper

Wash and pat dry chicken pieces. Combine all dry ingredients. Roll the chicken pieces in the flour mixture. Using a Dutch oven or other heavy deep fry pan, fry chicken in shortening at 350 degrees for 12 minutes on each side or until tender. *Serves: 4*

STEWED TOMATOES

Our forefathers once considered the tomato poisonous. They also believed that one bite of this vegetable would stimulate lust. It is therefore called the "Devil's Apple." Thomas Jefferson was one of the first to accept the tomato as a normal ingredient in daily fare..

4 cups whole tomatoes, peeled and quartered	1/2 stick butter, melted
1/2 cup sugar	1/2 teaspoon salt
	6 baked biscuits

In a bowl mix together the tomatoes, sugar, butter and salt. Crumble the biscuits and add to the mixture. Pour into a saucepan and cover and cook over medium heat for 15 minutes. *Serves: 6*

POTATO SALAD

Fried chicken and potato salad just naturally go together, whether at a picnic or in The Ordinary.

6 large potatoes	1 small onion, diced
1/2 stalk of celery, finely minced	1 whole sweet pimento, diced
1 teaspoon sugar	1 teaspoon pepper
3/4 cup mayonnaise	2 tablespoons prepared mustard
1 teaspoon salt	1 cup sweet relish or 1 sweet pickle, diced

Dice potatoes and cook until tender. Drain, rinse with cold water and drain again. Add celery. Let cool for 1 hour. Mix together the rest of the ingredients and stir gently into the diced potatoes. Refrigerate until serving time. *Serves: 6 to 8*

CORN BREAD

Cornmeal was used in various breads in colonial days – corn bread, spoon bread, corn sticks and eventually hush puppies. Many Southern meals were not complete without corn bread.

1 cup sifted flour	4 teaspoons baking powder
1 cup self rising white cornmeal	1 egg
1/4 cup sugar	1 cup milk
1 teaspoon salt	1/4 cup shortening, melted

Sift together flour, cornmeal, sugar, salt and baking powder into a large bowl. Add egg, milk and shortening. Beat with a rotary beater until smooth, about 1 minute. Bake in greased 8 inch square pan in preheated 425 degree oven for 20 to 25 minutes. Remove from oven and dot with butter while hot. Cut into squares and serve. *Serves: 9*

THE SILVER THATCH INN The story of the Silver Thatch Inn spans more than two centuries. The first part of the lovely white clapboard building was constructed by Hessian soldiers in 1780 during the Revolutionary War. These soldiers were part of a contingent captured by General Horatio Gates at the battle of Saratoga in New York state. They were marched south to Charlottesville and upon finding that there were no facilities to house them, they were forced to build their own barracks (or detention facilities). The Hessian soldiers built a two story log cabin on the site of a former Indian settlement.

This log cabin was eventually incorporated into a larger structure which is the present Inn. The timber in the log cabin built by the Hessians is original from 1780. Today that room is used for dining and has been named the Hessian Room in honor of its builders.

In 1812 there was an addition to the original house or cabin and for many years this building served as a boys' school. In the nineteenth century the building was used for various purposes. At one time it was the plantation house for a tobacco plantation. The property was also a melon farm in the latter part of the century.

A final wing was added to the house in 1937 by Dean B. F. D. Runk, a former dean of the University of Virginia. This historic building was the home of the Runk family until his retirement in 1969, when it became the Hollymead Inn, specializing in "country-style" food.

In 1984 the property was purchased by Tim and Shelley Dwight, a young couple from New Jersey with hotel and restaurant experience. Tim Dwight, a native of Florida and a graduate of Boston University, did graduate work at the University of Nevada Hotel and Restaurant School in 1977-78. For six years Tim worked in administration of hotels and casinos in Atlantic City.

Shelley Dwight, a New Jersey native, is a graduate of the Atlantic Culinary Academy and has been in the restaurant business since graduating from high school. While she was working as a chef at a large casino hotel, she met Tim who was in the administration part of the hotel. After they were married, they decided to make a change in their lifestyles – but not in their careers. They wanted to own a small inn and restaurant and proceeded on a search to find just the right place. After looking up and down the East Coast from Maine to Florida they found "their country inn" in Charlottesville and renamed the property, The Silver Thatch Inn.

Many months were spent doing extensive renovations and redecorating of not only the three dining rooms, but also the seven bedrooms available for overnight guests. The colonial theme of the inn has been maintained throughout. In addition to the "Hessian Room" there is also a "Williamsburg Room" and an "English Room." All are furnished in colonial style and used as dining rooms.

There is a division of labor in the Dwight family. Tim is the innkeeper and is in charge of the extensive wine cellar which features Virginia, California, French and German wines. In 1986 the Wine Spectator presented a Grand Award of Excellence to The Silver Thatch Inn for their extensive and outstanding wine list.

Shelley Dwight is the chef de cuisine and is fast gaining a reputation for the Inn as one of the best dining places in central Virginia. Shelley's culinary emphasis is country French and she features many seasonal specialties. The herbs, as well as salad greens and some vegetables, come from the Inn's garden.

Since there are many repeat dinners at The Silver Thatch, Shelley changes the entrees on the menu every week. Most restaurants change every three months. Each night there are five or six entrees which enables Shelley to give each of them her own personal touch. She treats every dish as "one of her specialties." A favorite, either as an entree or first course is the angel hair pasta prepared with a variety of sauces, mostly featuring seafood. From first course to dessert, Shelley Dwight is involved with the entire meal.

DINING
➡

The Silver Thatch Inn, *3001 Hollymead Road, Charlottesville, Va. 22901, 804-978-4686*
Directions: *Eight miles north of Charlottesville on Route 29*
Meal Times: *Dinner hours: 5:30 to 9:30, Tuesday through Saturday, Reservations requested*
Principals: *Tim and Shelley Dwight*

The following recipes highlight the menu at The Silver Thatch Inn:

APPETIZER PASTA ANGELINA

The use of Virginia ham in this recipe is a pleasant complement to the shrimp and cream sauce. If using medium size shrimp, double the amount.

1 teaspoon butter	3 oz. white wine
1 teaspoon shallots, finely chopped	1 1/2 cups heavy cream
1/4 cup Virginia ham, diced	1 tablespoon Parmesan cheese
1 teaspoon garlic, finely chopped	Flour
2 large shrimp. shelled and deveined	Butter
1 tablespoon green peppercorns	Salt and pepper, to taste
1 teaspoon tomato paste	3 1/2 oz. Angel hair pasta, cooked
	al dente

Melt butter in a sauté pan over medium high heat. Add shallots, ham, garlic, shrimp, peppercorns and tomato paste. Saute until shrimp begin to cook and turn pink. Add wine and cook a few minutes longer until shrimp are just done. Do not over cook. Remove shrimp and keep them warm. Reduce liquid by one half. Add heavy cream and Parmesan cheese. Thicken with a roux made with equal amounts of flour and butter. Season with salt and pepper. Add cooked pasta and heat. Top with the shrimp, a dash of Parmesan cheese and garnish with some fresh chopped parsley.

Author's note: To make the roux -- which is known as beurre manie, a classic thickener in French cuisine--combine equal amounts of flour and softened butter. Form into very small balls and drop several into the sauce, stirring constantly until desired thickness. *Serves: 2 as an appetizer*

CIOPPINO

Cioppino, this basically Italian fish stew, originated with Italian immigrant fishermen in California. In the old days wives of the fishermen waited their return on the shore, brewing pots of the bubbling sauce. The seasonings varied according to the area and the individual tastes of the families. The fish also varied according to the catch of the day. Today, in California, the Dungeness crab is usually a main ingredient in Cioppino. The Italians traditionally used red wine in this dish. Shelley Dwight's version uses a lighter white wine and saffron in addition to the traditional seasonings. French bread is a necessity to accompany this meal.

3 tablespoons olive oil	1/2 cup chopped parsley
1 1.2 cups chopped onion	1/2 teaspoon oregano
1 green pepper, seeded and chopped	1/2 teaspoon basil
1/2 cup chopped celery	1 bay leaf, crumbled
2 cloves garlic, minced	Salt and pepper, to taste
1 1 lb. 12 oz. can of tomatoes	
1 8 oz. can tomato sauce	Seafood as desired:
3 oz. Pernod	1 lb. shelled and deveined shrimp
2 cups white wine	2 lb. firm fish (snapper, flounder or
1 tablespoon saffron	grouper), cut into serving size pieces

Heat oil over medium heat in a large heavy dutch oven. Add onion, green pepper, celery and garlic and cook for 5 minutes until onion is transparent. Add tomatoes, tomato paste, Pernod, wine, saffron, 1/4 cup of chopped parsley, herbs, salt and pepper. Lower heat, cover and simmer for 30 minutes.

Add raw shellfish and cook over low heat for five minutes. Add fish and cook for 5 more minutes or until fish and shell fish are done. Add rest of parsley and serve hot as a stew or over pasta. *Serves: 8*

Author's note: Pernod is an aperitif and is named for a French firm which used to distill absinthe. Today it is based on aniseed since absinthe is prohibited in France. Pernod is usually served with three parts water to one of Pernod.

BOURBON PECAN BUTTERSCOTCH PIE

Shelley Dwight presents a different version of the Southern favorite pecan pie.

1 9-inch unbaked pie shell	1 cup sugar
Butterscotch chips for bottom of pie shell	1/8 teaspoon salt
3 eggs	1 teaspoon vanilla
1/2 cup sour cream	2 oz. Bourbon
1/2 cup dark corn syrup	1 3/4 cup pecans, chopped

Preheat oven to 400 degrees.

Cover bottom of pie shell with butterscotch chips. In a medium size mixing bowl combine eggs, sour cream, corn syrup, sugar, salt, vanilla and Bourbon. Mix well to blend ingredients and until mixture is smooth. Add pecans. Pour into the pie shell with chips. Place in oven and immediately turn down temperature to 350 degrees. Bake for 50 minutes or until firm and a knife comes out clean when inserted in the center.

Author's note: If using extra large or jumbo eggs, use a 10 inch pie plate. If a less sweet pie is desired sugar may be reduced to 3/4 cup.

TOLIVER HOUSE "Come Meet a Virginia Winemaker" is a monthly feature and event at the Toliver House Restaurant in Gordonsville, Virginia. This event pairs the wines of a specific Virginia winery with a specially designed six course dinner. Each month the wines are different and so is the menu. Many months there is a theme to the menu such as Cajun food or typical Southern specialties.

The dinner starts at approximately 7:30 p.m. The winemaker of the selected winery is present and ready to answer any questions the diners might have. With each course, a different wine is served and the winemaker discusses each particular wine and its winemaking process. In the middle of the dinner, between courses, there is usually a short slide presentation of the vineyards and the winery. Michael DeCanio, the owner of the Toliver House feels that this is an excellent way for the public to experience food and wine and in that way become better informed about the wines and operation of one of Virginia's wineries.

Mike DeCanio is a newcomer to the restaurant business and to Virginia. He has owned the Toliver House for two years. Mike has always wanted to own his own business. When his wife, Pat, who is a native Virginian, suggested they move to the quiet region of the Piedmont area of her native state, they struck a deal. They would move from the Chicago area if Mike could go into business for himself. The agreement was reached, but Mike did not know what type of business he wanted to pursue. He had twenty five years experience at various professions – teaching, business management, and human relations.

Mike and Pat began looking in the Charlottesville area. The real estate agent remembered Pat's love for old houses and Mike's role as the cook in the family. The agent suggested the Toliver House in Gordonsville, which was for sale. It seemed perfect – there was a restaurant downstairs and an apartment upstairs for the DeCanio family.

The Toliver House was built in 1870 and received its named from the first owner – E.F. Taliaferro, pronounced Toliver in Virginia at that time. Over the past hundred years, the house changed hands eleven times. In 1983 it was purchased by a Mrs. Margaret Siracuse who opened a restaurant in the downstairs. She named the restaurant Toliver House in honor of the first owner. The DeCanios acquired ownership in April of 1985.

At first, Mike was the cook and he still helps out occasionally. Dorothy Wright, however, is the full time chef. She gained her culinary knowledge by practical experience, working in several restaurants in Texas and Virginia.

Toliver House specializes in Virginia cuisine – crab cakes, fritters, Brunswick stew, and spoonbread, to name a few. The menu changes every week to take advantage of seasonal foods which are available fresh. All of the desserts are homemade by Dorothy. She enjoys working with desserts and has perfected several types of cheesecakes.

All of the recipes are for dishes that have been served at the monthly Winemaker's Dinners. Mike DeCanio has included the wine selections that were served with each dish.

DINING ➡

Toliver House, *209 North Main Street, P. O. Box 299, Gordonsville, Virginia 22942, 703-832-3485*
Directions: *In the center of Gordonsville, to the west of the railroad overpass*
Principals: *Michael J. DeCanio and Patricia O'Rourke*
Meal Times: *Tuesday through Saturday Lunch: 11:30 a.m. to 2:30 p.m. Dinner: 5:30 p.m. to 9 p.m. Sunday Brunch: 11:30 a.m. to 2:30 p.m.*

SHRIMP IN HERB BUTTER WITH ANGEL HAIR PASTA

Serve with Burnley Chardonnay

This shrimp and pasta dish is a simple and elegant preparation. It may also be used as a luncheon entree for 4. A green salad with a vinaigrette dressing would be a nice accompaniment.

1 cup walnuts, chopped	1/2 cup fresh basil leaves, finely shredded
1/2 stick butter	1/4 cup minced fresh parsley
1 stick butter	8 oz. angel hair pasta
1 lb. medium shrimp, shelled and deveined	

In a medium size skillet sauté walnuts in 1/2 stick butter until the nuts are lightly browned and very crisp. Set aside.

In a large skillet melt 1 stick of butter, then add shrimp and herbs. Sauté until the shrimp are just done and opaque.

In the meantime cook the pasta until al dente. Drain and place in a warm bowl. Top with shrimp and herb butter and toss to coat pasta. Sprinkle walnuts on top and serve. *Serves: 6 as a first course*

ROAST LOIN OF PORK WITH FRUIT STUFFING

Serve with Barboursville Cabernet Sauvignon

This recipe, although European in origin, has been in the Virginia culinary repertoire for many years. The stuffing not only adds flavor to the pork, but it and the cooking technique also add moisture.

1 package dried fruit (8 oz.)	2 cups apple cider
1 cup hot water	1/2 stick butter
1 whole boneless pork loin (about 6 lbs.)	3 tablespoons cornstarch dissolved in 2
Salt, pepper and ground ginger	tablespoon cold water

In a bowl soak fruit in the hot water for 30 minutes. Pit the prunes.

Cut pork loin open lengthwise, but do not cut through. Cut slits down where pork is still thick so you have an even rectangle. Sprinkle meat with salt, pepper and ginger. Drain fruit and reserve soaking water. Arrange fruit down the center of the meat. Fold roast back together and truss tightly. Melt the butter in a heavy skillet and brown roast on all sides. Place roast on a rack in a roasting pan. Add cider and water in which fruit was soaked. Cover tightly with pan lid or aluminum foil. Bake in a preheated 375 degree oven for 1 to 1 1/2 hours or until meat thermometer registers well done. Remove meat to a platter and keep warm.

Put all pan liquids in a blender. Add cornstarch mixture and blend until smooth. Heat gravy in saucepan, stirring constantly until mixture thickens slightly. Season to taste. Slice pork thinly and serve sauce on the side. *Serves: 8*

RASPBERRY MOUSSE

Serve with Ingleside Champagne

The Raspberry Mousse may also be made with other berries. One pint of fresh raspberries may be substituted for the frozen ones.

1 package frozen raspberries in syrup, thawed	1 cup whipping cream
1/2 package plain gelatin	1/3 cup sugar
1/2 cup egg whites (from 5 eggs)	2 tablespoons Chambord

Rub raspberries through sieve or food mill to remove seeds. Soften gelatin in 1 tablespoon water and add raspberry puree. Cook over low heat until gelatin is dissolved. Let cook until syrupy. Add Chambord.

Beat egg whites, adding sugar gradually, until stiff peaks form. Beat in raspberry mixture. Whip cream until almost stiff, fold in egg white mixture. Let chill until almost set. Then pile into cookie cups and serve immediately. *Serves: 12*

LACE COOKIE CUPS

The cookie cups can be made well in advance and stored in tins. Handle them carefully since they are very fragile. Fill just before serving.

2/3 cup ground blanched almonds	1 tablespoon flour
1/2 cup sugar	2 tablespoons milk
1/2 cup butter	

Combine all ingredients in saucepan. Cook, stirring until hot and blended. Drop by level tablespoons onto buttered and floured cookie sheet, at least 5 inches apart. Bake in preheated 350 degree oven until golden brown, about 5 minutes.

Let cool about 1 minute, then carefully remove from baking sheet and drape over a small cup. Let cool and remove carefully. If cookies harden on the sheet, put them back in the oven for a few seconds.

Eastern Region

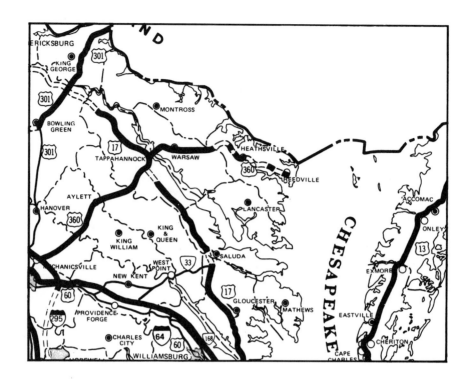

WINERIES:

Accomack Vineyards

Ingleside Plantation Vineyards

The Williamsburg Winery

RESTAURANTS:

Chimneys

The Eastville Inn

The Inn at Montross

The Smythe's Cottage

The Trellis

Williamsburg Inn (The Regency Dining Room)

Williamsburg Taverns

Accomack Vineyards

ACCOMACK VINEYARDS Is Virginia's Eastern Shore the best region of the state to grow vinifera grapes? Jim Keyes certainly believes so. It was a long awaited dream for Jim Keyes that became reality when on Valentine's Day, 1987, the first bottles of his Accomack Vineyards wine were released for public sale. For more than a decade Jim Keyes had dreamed of growing European vinifera grapes on Virginia's Eastern Shore and producing his own wine.

The Keyes' interest in wine began as consumers. A career U. S. foreign service officer, specializing in agricultural practices, Jim began learning about wine while on various overseas assignments. As his interest in wine and growing grapes increased, he began studying textbooks to determine ideal climate and soil conditions for the growing of wine grapes.

In the mid 1970's, Jim and his wife Gerry, an attorney working for the Federal government, decided to look for eventual retirement property on which they could grow grapes. Jim procured temperature charts from the state experimental station at Painter on the Eastern Shore and proceeded to study them. He also analyzed the soil conditions of the region from the USGS quadrangle maps and a Department of Agriculture soil survey map. Jim Keyes believes that soil and climate are both contributing factors in the production of excellent wine grapes.

The Keyes, who were living in Washington, D.C. were impressed with Virginia's Eastern Shore on their first trip to the area in February 1975. The lower part of the peninsula had sandy soil and a more moderate climate than the rest of the state. Both of these conditions were similar to the Medoc region of Bordeaux, France.

In 1977, the Keyes purchased a 57 acre farm south of Painter and restored the 150 year old farmhouse on the property. The house, a very comfortable one, also has a spacious office for Gerry who is a practicing attorney in Accomack County. After the purchase of the property Jim had to go overseas on another assignment and Gerry, with some help, proceeded to plant the test plot of grapes in 1979.

An eye problem prompted Jim to take early retirement from the Foreign Service in 1981. He decided to become a full time vintner, concentrating his first major grape growing effort on Merlot. Currently, he has two acres planted with 1800 vines. When Jim became satisfied that vinifera could be grown on the Eastern Shore he proceeded with plans for a winery.

Jim believes that the Eastern Shore will become an important growing area for vinifera grapes. As Jim says, "The water – the Atlantic on the east and the Chesapeake Bay on the west – acts as a heat sink and moderates the climate. It delays the spring so that bud growth does not come too early and stretches out the fall so that we don't have to worry about an early frost. This milder climate permits healthy development of the grapes." There is usually a 10 degree variation – cooler in summer and warmer in winter –

on the Eastern Shore as compared to the rest of Virginia. In recent years several nurseries and two other vineyards have established operations on the Eastern Shore to take advantage of these conditions..

In addition to the area's favorable growing climate, the sandy soil is similar to the gravel soil of the Medoc region of France. The soil structure basically is one foot of sandy loam, with one foot of sandy clay underneath and coarse sand under that. The top foot of soil tends to hold moisture and the underlying coarse sand allows the vine roots to go deep which is ideal for grape growing.

Once Jim became convinced that the area could produce premium wine grapes, he started his winery, although on a small scale. Jim soon realized, however, that the job of winemaker would be too time consuming and would limit his other activities. Consequently, he hired Thomas J. Payette as winemaker and enlarged the winery to handle 4000 gallons. Tom has a B. S. degree in Food Science Technology from Virginia Polytechnic Institute and has had a long interest in winemaking. That interest started when as a teenager he was a grape picker for a vineyard near Rapidan – his hometown. In 1985-86, prior to joining Accomack Vineyards, Tom worked as an assistant winemaker at Ingleside Winery.

The Keyes grow part of the grapes used in their wine production and have a lease agreement with two other vineyards on the Eastern Shore. One vineyard, owned by Geoffrey and Carole Grubb, was planted in 1978 and has supplied award winning grapes to many of Virginia's wineries. Suzanne Wescoat's vineyard in Northampton County will be producing its first harvest in 1987.

The first releases of Accomack Vineyards are Riesling and "Old Dominion White." Tom Payette explained that the "Old Dominion White" is a blend of two thirds of the French hybrid Seyval Blanc and one third Chardonnay. In the fall of '87 there will be releases of Chardonnay and Cabernet Sauvignon. The Cabernet Sauvignon will be a blend of 90% Cabernet and 10% Merlot.

Tom Payette believes that gentleness in handling of the grapes is essential to producing good wine. All grapes are given a light press, after automatic destemming and crushing. The juice then goes into stainless steel tanks for fermentation and aging. The reds, however, are aged in French oak.

The Accomack label says it all. The seagull on the label indicates where the area is located; the blue is the sky and the water; and the green denotes the land. There is also a small map of the area on the label.

Jim Keyes is convinced that grape growing is going to be the big industry on the Eastern Shore. "I think we'll get a crop 99 years out of a hundred, and we won't have winter frost kills," he added.

Suzanne Wescoat, one of Accomack's contract grape growers has provided the following recipes which feature Eastern Shore seafood and were especially designed to be accompanied by Accomack wines.

Accomack Vineyards, *P. O. Box 38, Painter, VA 23420, 804-442-2110*
Directions: *From Route 13 (south of Painter), take Route 607 east for 1/2 mile*
Visitation: *Tuesday through Sunday, 10 a.m. to 4 p.m.*
Principals: *James D. and Geraldine Keyes*
Wines Produced: *Riesling, Chardonnay, Cabernet Sauvignon, Old Dominion White Table Wine*
1987 Production: *2500 cases*

HOT CRAB DIP

Serve with Riesling

1 8 oz. package cream cheese	1 teaspoon Worcestershire sauce
1 cup mayonnaise	2 pounds cooked fresh crab meat
1 and 1/2 cups grated Cheddar cheese	Freshly ground pepper, to taste

Depending on the sharpness desired, use either mild, medium or sharp Cheddar cheese. The cream cheese will tone down the sharpness of the Cheddar to some extent. Melt the cream cheese in a small saucepan over low heat. In a medium size bowl combine the rest of the ingredients. Fold in melted cream cheese and mix well. Place dip in a chafing dish to keep warm. Serve with crackers. *Makes 4 to 5 cups*

CURRIED OYSTERS

Serve with Old Dominion White Wine

The Chesapeake Bay has been famous for its oysters and its oyster dishes since early colonial times. Scalloped oysters were often served for breakfast and are still a popular item on Sunday brunch menus. This dish combines curry and its traditional rice accompaniment with oysters in an easy to prepare casserole. A green vegetable, such as broccoli, completes the main course.

1 6 oz. package of long grain and wild rice mix	1 cup light cream
1/2 cup butter	1 1/2 tablespoons onion powder
4 dozen oysters, shucked and drained	3/4 teaspoon thyme
1 10 1/2 oz. can cream of chicken soup	1 tablespoon curry powder

Cook rice mix according to package directions. While hot add butter and stir lightly until butter is melted and blended into the rice. In a 2 quart casserole, place 1/3 of the rice mixture, add 1/2 of the oysters, then another 1/3 of the rice, and top with remaining oysters. Spread the remaining rice on top.

In a medium saucepan mix together the soup, cream, onion powder, thyme and curry powder. Warm over medium heat to blend. Pour over the rice mixture in the casserole. Bake in a preheated 300 degree oven for 45 minutes. *Serves 4 to 6*

INGLESIDE PLANTATION WINERY Jacques Recht is the dean of Virginia winemakers. He is the winemaker at Ingleside Plantation Winery. Not only did he help establish Ingleside as an important entity in the state wine industry, he has served as a consultant to many Virginia wineries.

His Ingleside wines have received over 70 medals in the last six and a half years. At the 1987 Virginia Wine Competition at the Homestead, Ingleside's Cabernet Sauvignon won the only two gold medals in the competition – one for the wine and the other for Best of Show. In addition, Ingleside received two bronzes for its champagnes, a bronze for the Chesapeake Blanc and a silver for its Chardonnay.

It was probably a stroke of fate that brought Jacques Recht and his wife Liliane to the Northern Neck of Virginia. Jacques Recht had retired from an enology career in Europe and found himself with a brand new one in Virginia – at Ingleside Plantation Winery.

Ingleside Plantation is just what the name implies – a plantation of 2000 acres which in modern times has become one of the largest landscape nurseries on the East Coast. The original house was not only a plantation home, but it was also a boys' school in the nineteenth century. During the Civil War it served as a command post, at one time or another for both sides.

The Flemer family purchased the property before the turn of the century. The present generation of Carl Flemer and his two sons, Fletcher and Douglas, operate the nursery operation and the recently added vineyard/winery. Doug Flemer is in charge of the winery. Over 100 acres of the plantation are devoted to nursery production with over 100 greenhouses. Vineyards occupy 53 acres with 10 more to be added this year.

In 1976, Carl Flemer, who had an interest in wine, decided to plant a five acre experimental vineyard. With the Flemer's expertise in agriculture, the vines prospered. Carl Flemer experimented with home winemaking. By 1980, there was a substantial crop of grapes available to make into wine. As harvest was approaching, Carl Flemer sent Doug to France to either find a winemaker or learn all he could about winemaking.

A few years previously on the other side of the Atlantic, Jacques and Liliane Recht, native Belgians living in Brussels, decided to sail around the world. Jacques, who was a competitive sailor in the North Sea for the Belgian government, and his wife had built their own 36 foot catamaran with the intention of taking two to three years on their round the world journey. They eventually planned to retire in southern England.

Jacques Recht had just retired as a professor of wine chemistry and technology after 25 years of work in the field of enology. He had been a winemaker and consultant in Bordeaux, where many of the wine chateaux are owned by Belgians. Jacques taught wine technology at the Institute of Fermentation Science in Brussels. He had also worked with Booz Allen, an American consulting firm, to re-establish the vineyards in Algiers that had been damaged during the second World War. At age 48, Jacques retired to his second love – sailing.

The Rechts set sail from Belgium in early 1979 to cross the Atlantic via the Spanish Coast, Gibraltar, the Canary Islands and into the Caribbean. It was while they were in the Caribbean Islands that Jacques acquired a copy of James Michener's book "Chesapeake." The book's description of the area fascinated him and he wanted to sail up the Chesapeake Bay and into the Potomac River. After all it was only going to be a little diversion from their set course. The Rechts were planning to sail along the East Coast of the United States and then up the St. Lawrence River to visit friends in the Great Lakes area.

The day in late August was hot and humid when the Rechts landed at the little riverfront town of Kinsdale on the lower Potomac, in Westmoreland County. It took them a year and a half to come from Belgium to the Chesapeake Bay. They quickly became acquainted with the local folks and were told about Carl Flemer who was trying to make wine. The next day the people who had befriended the Rechts took them to meet Carl Flemer.

Over a glass of homemade Seyval Blanc, Carl and Jacques discussed grapes, soil, climate and winemaking. Jacques was impressed with the Seyval's similarity to the white "Muscadet" of the Loire River Valley in France. After much discussion, Jacques and Liliane agreed to stay for three weeks to help with the first crush at Ingleside Plantation. When Doug Flemer returned from his trip to France without a winemaker, he found that his father had already engaged a "temporary" one. The "temporary" winemaker has been at Ingleside ever since. With the first vintage of 1980 he started winning medals with the Ingleside wine.

The 53 acres of vineyards at Ingleside Plantation consist of both French hybrids and vinifera. Jacques initially planted experimental plots of 33 varieties to determine which ones would do best on the Northern Neck. He felt that the climate and soil of Ingleside were similar to an area of Bordeaux. This land, too, is situated between two rivers – the Potomac and the Rappahannock. Jacques has also experimented with different trellis systems. For some of the Chardonnay he uses a Burgundian style where the wires are 18 inches above the ground and the plants are spaced much closer – only 3 feet apart. This method gives the grapes a higher sugar content and heartier body.

Thirteen farmers in the area surrounding Ingleside have been encouraged by Jacques to put in vineyards. "The gravelly soil of both the Northern Neck and the Eastern Shore are good areas for wine grape growing," Jacques said. The temperature of both areas is also more moderate than the rest of the state.

Jacques has been particularly impressed with the area's ability to grow fine Cabernet Sauvignon. On the Northern Neck there is a long growing season upon which the Cabernet grape thrives. "You should let grapes grow slowly for good wine," says Jacques.

During fermentation Jacques Recht does a complete analysis of the fermenting wines twice a day. He strictly monitors the fermentation temperature, using both portable heat exchangers and jacketed stainless steel tanks for precise control.

Jacques feels that the art of winemaking is in the blending and also in the use of various oaks for aging. He uses both American and French oak. He feels that various oaks implant certain subtleties and flavor components into the wine.

One of the wines Jacques Recht likes to make is Cabernet Sauvignon. During fermentation he pumps the juice over the cap instead of punching it down. The amount of time the juice remains on the skins varies, since Jacques carefully analyzes the amount of tannins in the wines. The tannin in wine is the result of the skin contact. Cabernet Sauvignon is aged for 12 to 18 months in French oak. Jacques prefers to fine his wines with egg white rather than filter to remove any impurities. Some Cabernet Franc and Merlot, when the latter is available, is blended into the Cabernet Sauvignon in a true Bordeaux style. The Merlot is difficult to grow in Virginia since it is susceptible to winter damage.

One of the most popular Ingleside wines is the Chesapeake White. It is basically Seyval Blanc with 10% Chardonnay which lightens up the finish. Another popular table wine is the Williamsburg Red which is made in a nouveau beaujolais style using the carbonic maceration technique. It is a light fruity wine, consisting mostly of Chambourcin, and has no oak aging. The Ingleside Claret, a blend of Chancellor and 10% Cabernet Sauvignon, is aged in American oak for 8 months.

The Ingleside Chardonnay is half barrel aged and half is aged in stainless steel. The wine goes through malolactic fermentation. This is a secondary fermentation that converts malic acid to lactic acid and helps reduce the harshness of wines as well as stabilize them.

Jacques Recht was the first to make Champagne by the traditional methode champenoise in Virginia. He believes that the state's future in Champagne production is unlimited. "To produce Champagne you need tart grapes – grapes that are lower in sugar than those for still wine," he explained. Virginia's climate is very close to the Champagne Region of France where the winters are cold.

There are two styles of Champagne made at Ingleside – a Brut and a Rose. Both of the Champagnes are hand produced following the traditional French methods. They remain on the yeast for 14 to 18 months and are hand riddled. The cuvee of the Brut is 100% Chardonnay and the final product has less than 1% residual sugar. The Rose is a blend of Chardonnay, Chenin Blanc, and Cabernet Sauvignon. It is discreetly pink, or to quote Jacques "nearly the color of the inside of the thigh of a nymph."

Liliane and Jacques Recht have become acclimated to the land once again. Liliane, who is very much involved in the Virginia wine industry, is not only helping Jacques when needed but has her own business of importing French wine barrels. She has also planted a three acre vineyard which she tends by herself. After seven years, the Rechts are almost permanent residents – they are building a house not too far from the winery.

This temporary stop on the Chesapeake has resulted in a permanent position for Jacques Recht at Ingleside. He is a vice president of the corporation. It has been through his and Liliane's efforts that Ingleside has gained the reputation of being one of the premier wineries in the state of Virginia. Jacques Recht has earned the friendship and respect of his fellow Virginia vintners.

Liliane Recht is an excellent cook. Not only is she versed in her native European culinary style, but she has added many Virginia recipes to her repertoire. Nancy Flemer, Carl's wife, is also an excellent cook and likes to match her dishes with the Ingleside wines. She often designs recipes for special tastings.

TOURS
➡

Ingelside Plantation Winery, *P. O. Box 1038, Oak Grove, Va. 22443, 804-224-8687*
Directions: *South of Fredericksburg, take I-95 or Route 301 to Route 3, take Route 3 to Oak Grove, then south on Route 638 for 2 and 1/2 miles to the entrance of the winery on the left*
Visitation: *Monday through Saturday, 10 a.m. to 5 p.m., Sundays, 12 noon to 5 p.m., except major holidays*
Principals: *Carl Flemer, Jr.*
Wines Produced: *Riesling, Chardonnay, Cabernet Sauvignon, Champagne, Chesapeake Blanc, Williamsburg White, Virginia Blush, Wirtland Rose, Williamsburg Red, Chesapeake Claret*
1987 Production: *20,000 cases*

CHAMPAGNE OYSTER LOAF

Serve with Brut Champagne

The original oyster loaf, known as La Mediatrice or the "peacemaker" is said to have originated in New Orleans. The story goes something like this: Every husband who lingered too long in the French Quarter and felt a bit guilty would stop at a French market on the way home and get an oyster loaf to pacify his wife. There are versions of the original recipe, which was a hollowed out loaf of bread filled with sauteed oysters.

1 1 lb. loaf of French bread	3 dashes tabasco sauce
1 16 oz. jar sweet pimentos, diced	2 tablespoons olive oil
4 green onions, finely diced	2 cups oysters, drained and reserve
1/4 cup black olives, sliced and diced	the juice
4 cloves garlic, minced	4 tablespoons butter
2 tablespoons chopped parsley	1/2 cup Brut Champagne
Pinch of thyme	1/2 cup grated Parmesan cheese
Salt and pepper to taste	Olive oil
Juice of 1 lemon	

Cut the French bread in half and scoop out the insides of both halves, hollowing it out much like bread canoes. Grind the removed bread pieces into fine bread crumbs. Combine the crumbs with the pimentos, green onions, black olives, garlic, parsley, thyme and salt and pepper to taste. Add the lemon juice, tabasco sauce, and olive oil and mix well.

In a medium size saucepan bring 4 tablespoons butter and 4 tablespoons reserved oyster juice to simmering. Add the oysters and poach for 1 minute. Add the Champagne and cook the oysters until they begin to curl, 3 to 4 minutes. Remove oysters and drain them. Chop the oysters coarsely and add to bread mixture. Mix well. Add the Parmesan cheese and toss.

Brush olive oil lightly on hollowed out bread, particularly the edges. Pack oyster mixture into bread hollows. Mound mixture in the center. Place halves with oyster mixture together as if bread were whole. To do this place the two halves side by side and roll up to each other. Do not place one on top of the other. Wrap loaf tightly in foil. Refrigerate overnight or for 24 hours.

To serve cut into 1/4 to 1/2 inch slices with a serrated knife. *Serves: 10 to 12 as an appetizer*

CHESAPEAKE BAY MEDELY

Serve with Chesapeake Blanc

Seafood and asparagus have been a natural combination for many years. The combination is also found in numerous Chinese recipes.

24 asparagus	Salt, pepper and a pinch of cayenne
8 tablespoons butter	pepper
3 shallots, thinly sliced	1 1/4 lb. scallops
2 cups Chesapeake Blanc, white wine	1 pint oysters, drained
1 3/4 cup heavy cream	Chopped parsley

While the sauce is being prepared, cook asparagus until al dente. Drain them and keep warm.

In a medium size saucepan over medium heat, melt 2 tablespoons butter. Add shallots and cook until transparent. Add wine and boil down to half its volume. Add cream and heat gently, stirring from time to time. Season with salt, pepper and a pinch of cayenne pepper. Remove sauce from heat and add butter, a little at a time, whisking the sauce to mix well. Place the sauce back on the heat and add scallops and oysters. Poach over medium heat for 3 to 4 minutes or until oysters begin to curl and scallops are done. Do not overcook the seafood.

To serve: Place 3 spears of asparagus on each plate and add seafood. Cover both with the sauce and sprinkle chopped parsley on top. *Serves: 8*

WESTMORELAND VENISON

Serve with Chesapeake Claret

Liliane says that the marinade in this recipe may also be used for a leg of deer which is roasted after it has been marinated. She usually serves this venison stew with boiled or mashed potatoes. A frequent side dish is a baked apple filled with cranberry sauce.

4 pounds deer meat, cut into 1 1/2 by 2 inch cubes	1/2 teaspoon thyme
2 to 3 carrots, chopped	1/2 teaspoon rosemary
2 to 3 onions, chopped	Salt and coarsely ground pepper
2 stalks celery, sliced	Flour
1 bottle Chesapeake Claret, red wine	3 tablespoons butter
2 tablespoons olive oil	2 slices Smithfield ham, cut in small pieces
2 bay leaves	1 lb. pearl onions, blanched
	1 lb. mushrooms, quartered

In a large bowl combine the deer meat cubes, carrots, onions, and celery. Cover mixture with the wine. Add olive oil, herbs, salt and ground pepper. Stir to mix. Cover and let marinate in cool place (or refrigerator) for 24 hours. The next day, dry the deer cubes with a paper towel. Dredge them in flour. Strain the marinade, removing all of the vegetables. Melt butter in a dutch oven over medium high heat and sauté meat quickly until brown. Add ham on top of meat. Cover with the strained marinade. Bring to a boil, cover and simmer for 2 hours. After 1 1/2 hours add the onions and mushrooms and cook for the additional 1/2 hour.

Adjust seasonings, if necessary, and thicken gravy, if desired. *Serves: 8 to 10*

THE WILLIAMSBURG WINERY In the not too distant future there will be a winery in Williamsburg. A test plot of 3 acres of vinifera grapes (Chardonnay) was planted in 1985 by Patrick and Peggy Duffeler on their 290 acre farm. This is the first commercial planting of grapes in the area since the early settlers tried to grow wine grapes in Jamestown in the early 17th century.

Patrick Duffeler, an international entrepreneur, and his wife Peggy purchased the farm in 1983 and immediately began to plan their vineyard and winery. There was some historical evidence that grapes had been grown on one of the slopes of the farm.

The Duffelers plan to start construction of their winery in order to be ready for the 1987 crush of their Chardonnay which will have reached maturity and be producing its first crop. The resulting wine should be ready for release in mid 1988. Pat also plans to purchase grapes for his 1987 winemaking venture.

Jeanette Smith, a V.P.I. graduate in horticulture, recently joined the Duffeler enterprise as the vineyard manager. She is experimenting with various trellising systems in order to provide the most air flow for the grapes during the hot, humid summers. To further facilitate air flow, the rows of vines are spaced ten feet apart and are allowed to grow to a height of 4 to 5 feet.

Another 11 1/2 acres of vines were planted in the spring of 1987. These included Chardonnay, Seyval Blanc, Cabernet Sauvignon and Cabernet Franc. In the following years more vineyard acreage will be added to bring the total up to 40 acres.

Pat Duffeler is in the process of engaging a winemaker. The Williamsburg Winery will feature mainly dry wines made in the French style. Pat indicated, however, that the Seyval Blanc would be a semi-dry style, making it a picnic wine. Hopefully, what the early settlers did not accomplish over 350 years ago, will finally come to be a reality – a winery in Williamsburg, the colonial capital of Virginia.

Since the Duffelers have lived all over the world while Pat was pursuing his international marketing career, Peggy Duffeler's recipe collection has an international flavor.

TOURS
➡

The Williamsburg Winery, P. O. Box 1573, 2638 Lake Powell Road, Williamsburg, VA 23185, 804-229-0999
Directions: *Take road to Jamestown, at intersection of Route 199 turn left, turn right on Brookwood Lane, then left on Lake Powell Road, .6 mile to dirt road on left*
Visitation: *Tuesday through Sunday, 10 a.m. to 4 p.m. starting in January, 1988*
Principals: *Patrick and Peggy Duffeler*
Wines Produced: *Chardonnay*
1987 Production: *Unknown*

CAMARAO PERNAMBUCANA

Serve with Chardonnay

This Brazilian shrimp dish is a typical seafood dish of Bahia, the old capital of Brazil on the north coast. Onion, green and red peppers, celery, or okra is often added for variety to the basic ingredients.

1 cup shredded coconut	2 tablespoons butter
2 cups milk	1 tablespoon curry powder
1 cup rice	1 to 2 tablespoons sugar
2 cups water	1 1/2 tablespoons cornstarch
2 lbs. medium shrimp, peeled and deveined	

In a medium saucepan bring coconut and milk to a boil. Remove from heat and set aside while preparing other ingredients.

Cook rice in water until done. Keep warm.

In a large skillet melt butter and sauté shrimp until they turn pink and are barely cooked. Add coconut milk, curry and sugar. Cook over low heat to blend ingredients. Do not overcook the shrimp. Dissolve cornstarch in a little water and stir into sauce, cooking until thickened. Serve over hot rice. *Serves: 6*

Author's note: Watch shrimp carefully when sautéing so as not to overcook them. Remember that the shrimp will continue to cook while the coconut milk is added and also when the sauce is being thickened.

ZWETSCHENKUCHEN

Serve with Cabernet Sauvignon

This fresh prune cake is an Austrian recipe similar to the tortes frequently served in the Konditoreis of Vienna when the fresh Italian prunes are in season.

2 to 3 lbs. fresh Italian prunes, pitted and quartered	1 1/2 tablespoon butter
	1/2 cup sliced almonds

Kuchen Crust:

2 cups plus 2 tablespoons flour, leave 2 tablespoons aside	Pinch of salt
1/2 cup sugar	1 egg
7 tablespoons butter or margarine	Milk
1 1/2 teaspoons baking powder	1/2 cup sliced almonds

In a bowl combine 1 cup flour and the rest of the ingredients. Add enough milk to make a smooth dough. Then work in the remaining cup of flour, kneading the dough to make it smooth. Grease an 8 inch tart pan and sprinkle bottom with bread crumbs. Flour a pastry board with the 2 tablespoons of flour and roll out the crust to fit the tart pan, pushing dough up the sides of the pan.

Arrange plums on top of crust. Cover with filling.

Kuchen Filling:

2 eggs, separated
1/2 cup sugar
1/2 teaspoon vanilla extract

1/4 cup flour
1 teaspoon baking powder
1/2 teaspoon vanilla extract

In a bowl beat egg yolks with sugar; add vanilla. Combine flour and baking powder and stir into egg mixture. Beat egg whites until they form soft peaks. Fold gently into egg yolk mixture. Pour filling on top of plums. Top with crumbs.

Kuchen Crumbs:

1/2 cup sugar
2/3 cup bread crumbs

Dash of cinnamon
Milk or fruit juice to moisten

Combine the crumb ingredients with a fork and just enough liquid to form crumbs the size of large peas. Sprinkle on top of filling. Dot with butter and sprinkle with sliced almonds.

Bake in preheated 350 degree oven for 40 to 45 minutes. *Serves: 6*

Author's note: If Italian plums are not available, any firm plum may be substituted. Do not use an extremely juicy plum, since the juices will overwhelm the filling.

CHIMNEYS The house known as The Chimneys is generally regarded as one of the finest examples of Georgian architecture in Fredericksburg. The residence was built in 1769 by Charles Yates, a local businessman.

Two years later, however, he sold the property to John Glassell, a Scottish merchant and a Loyalist. The selling price was 200 pounds sterling in British money and 100 pounds in then current Virginia money. When the Revolution broke out and as fighting became widespread, Glassell returned to Great Britain.

The Chimneys is a well balanced structure with a chimney on each side. Its appearance has changed with the social customs of the community. Like many of the grand homes in Fredericksburg, The Chimneys originally fronted on the river. A porch dominated the facade. By 1805, the porch was removed. As Fredericksburg's importance as a port declined, business and social activities relocated to Caroline Street. In 1818 the change was made final by the addition of a kitchen to the main house. The original porch foundation, on the riverside, was used for the kitchen. A small porch was added on the street side and the entrance placed on Caroline Street.

The home remained a private residence until 1967 when it was purchased by the Historic Fredericksburg Foundation. For a number of years it served as the association's headquarters. In 1983, the house was bought by a local businessman for the purpose of restoration and conversion into a restaurant, which opened in early 1985. However, The Chimneys changed hands again in October of 1985, when the partnership of Williamson, Hayes and Muir purchased the restaurant. John Williamson, as general manager, and David Haynes, as executive chef, have established a restaurant that has rapidly developed a reputation for fine food.

Much of the elegant interior of the house has been maintained, although revisions in the interior were made over the years before it became a restaurant. The back porch and patio have recently been opened for casual dining. Outdoor service is provided when weather permits.

John Williamson, who has been in the food business for 14 years, had gone back to the academic world for a Ph.D. in English when The Chimneys came on the market. He could not pass up the opportunity, particularly since David Haynes, a chef of some renown, agreed to join in the enterprise.

Chef David Haynes, a graduate of the Culinary Institute of America, has 20 years restaurant experience on the East Coast. His forte is American regional cooking with classical techniques. The menu at The Chimneys features traditional entrees matched with seasonal fresh vegetables. Southern regional dishes are also featured.

The Chimneys' wine list is extensive, with a number of Virginia wines. The house wine is from nearby Ingleside Plantation Vineyards. John Williamson, who is frequently a judge at wine competitions, has made Virginia wine suggestions to accompany the following recipes.

DINING
➡

Chimneys, 623 Caroline Street, Fredericksburg, Virginia 22401, 703-371-9229
Directions: *In center of town near the Information Center.*
Principals: *John Williamson, David Haynes and Angus Muir*
Meal Times: *Tuesday through Saturday, Lunch: 11:30 a.m. to 3 p.m. Sunday Brunch: 11:30 a.m. to 3 p.m., Tuesday through Friday, Dinner: 5:30 p.m. to 9:30 p.m. Saturday and Sunday, Dinner 5:30 p.m. to 10 p.m. The Backporch Cafe and Patio serves light fare year around on Tuesdays through Sunday from 11:30 a.m. to last call.*

OYSTERS RAPPAHANNOCK

Serve with Piedmont Virginia Semillon

Oysters have been a food for man almost as long as civilization has existed. The ancient Chinese dried the bivalve on bamboo sticks and kept them for future use. Chinese cuisine includes scores of dishes using oysters and they also use oyster sauce in cooking. The Lynnhaven variety of oyster was popular in Colonial days, but is not as plentiful today. However, other varieties have become favorites. This recipe is similar to the ever popular Oyster Rockefeller that originated in New Orleans.

1 dozen oysters on the half shell	Salt and pepper, to taste
2 shallots, minced	1/4 cup Pernod
2 tablespoons sweet butter	1/2 cup grated Parmesan cheese
1 lb. chopped and drained wilted spinach	6 lemon rounds and parsley for garnish
1/2 lb. cream cheese	

Prepare a baking pan with a bed of rock salt on which the oyster shells will be placed. (The rock salt keeps the oysters upright while they are cooking.) Preheat oven to 450 degrees.

In a medium size saucepan melt butter, add shallots and saute over low heat until soft. Add spinach and cream cheese. Stir until blended. Season with salt and pepper. Splash each oyster with Pernod. Top with spinach mixture and sprinkle with Parmesan cheese. Bake in preheated 450 degree oven until top is lightly browned, about 4 to 5 minutes. *Serves: 6*

PASTA KALANTY

Serve with Virginia Gewurztraminer or a "big style" Chardonnay

Although this recipe takes some time to prepare all of the individual parts, it is well worth the effort. Andouille sausage first became popular in New Orleans, and is now available in most delicatessen and large supermarkets. It is becoming more popular in modern Virginia cuisine.

2 lbs. red pepper pasta (see following recipe)	2 roasted red peppers, julienned (see following recipe)
1 lb. Andouille sausage, cut into bite-size pieces	4 cups heavy cream, heated and reduced by 1/3rd
2 tablespoons chopped shallots	24 fresh basil leaves, chiffonade (cut in thin strips)
1/2 cup white wine	Salt and pepper, to taste
32 asparagus spears, blanched and cut into 1 inch pieces	8 oz. fine grated Parmesan cheese

Boil pasta in salted water to just under al dente. In a large skillet saute Andouille until brown. Add shallots and deglaze with the wine. Add asparagus and peppers. Reduce liquid to 1 tablespoon. Add cream and reduce. Drain pasta and add to sauce, mixing gently. Add basil, season with salt and pepper to taste. Then add cheese and gently stir to mix. Serve.

Red Pepper Pasta:

4 cups flour	2 eggs
3 fl. oz. red pepper purée (about 1/4 cup)	2 tablespoons olive oil

In kitchen aid or food processor mix flour until light and fluffy. Add puree, eggs and olive oil. Mix until it forms a ball. Then turn dough onto floured pastry board. Knead and add flour as necessary until dough is no longer wet and is smooth and elastic. Wrap dough in plastic wrap and rest in refrigerator for 1 hour. Roll out and cut into fettucine. Dry pasta on a board which has been lightly dusted with cornmeal.

Roasted Red Pepper Purée – Makes 1 to 1 1/2 cups

6 sweet red peppers	1/8 to 1/4 cup red wine
1 shallot	

Over open flame, blacken red peppers all over in order to remove skins. Cool, skin and seed. Purée with shallots and red wine. Heat mixture and reduce in volume by one third. *Serves: 8*

Author's note: An easy way to remove the skins from red peppers is to place them in a brown paper bag. Seal bag tightly and place on a cookie sheet in a 250 degree oven overnight. The next morning peel the peppers.

BLACK CAV CAKE

Serve with Virginia Champagne

This cake is an extra special dessert which is a grand finale to the meal. Black Cav Cake is made in three parts and can be prepared early in the day, then stored in the refrigerator.

Chocolate Mousse:

10 oz. bittersweet chocolate
1 oz. sweet butter
1 oz. rum

4 eggs, separated
1 cup heavy cream

Melt chocolate and butter in top of double boiler over hot water. When melted remove from heat and stir in yolks and rum. Whip egg whites to stiff peaks. Beat one third of egg whites into chocolate mixture to thin the mixture. Fold in the rest of the egg whites. Beat cream until stiff and fold into chocolate mixture. Cover with plastic and place in refrigerator until ready to use.

Génoise:

6 eggs, at room temperature
1 cup sugar

1 cup all purpose flour

Butter and flour 2 - 9 inch cake pans. Preheat oven to 375 degrees.

Hand beat eggs and sugar over boiling water to 112 degrees. Transfer to mixer and beat at high speed until triple in volume, about 6 to 8 minutes. Carefully sift and fold in flour in thirds. Pour batter into cake pans and bake in preheated 375 degree oven until cake is springy and begins to pull away from sides of pan. Cool cake in pans on racks, then turn out and cool completely.

Icing and Garnish:

2 lbs. 10X confectionery sugar
2 oz. dark rum
2 egg yolks

1 lb. sweet butter
1 oz. bittersweet chocolate melted

Put the sugar in a mixing bowl and beat at low speed. Add the room temperature butter, a chunk at a time, until all of it is incorporated. Add yolk one at a time. Add rum. Beat until smooth. Melt bittersweet chocolate and reserve.

To assemble the cake: Split layers of cake in half and stack with one third of mousse between each layer. Ice sides and top with the butter cream.

Carefully drizzle melted chocolate in 4 circles on top and on edge of cake. Let it run down the sides. Draw a knife toward the center to blend circles of chocolate. Pipe 12 rosettes of icing around sides of cake for garnish and portion control. Store cake in refrigerator up until an hour before serving. *Serves: 12*

THE EASTVILLE INN There are "born heres" and there are "come heres" as Pete Musgrove will tell the diners in his Eastville Inn restaurant. He's a "come here" to the Eastern Shore, who has come to Eastville to reopen the restaurant in one of the oldest buildings in the community. Pete and Anne Musgrove are serving some of the best seafood on the Eastern Shore in the lobby of the old Inn. They have leased the old Eastville Inn that had not been operational for the last 20 some years and are once again serving food to the community.

Eastville, a small town of a little over 300 inhabitants, has the oldest continuous court records in the United States. The records of Northampton County, in which Eastville is located, date back to 1632. A courthouse as such, however, was not established in the town until 1677. Now there are two courthouses in Eastville, the modern one which was built in the 20th century and the old Flemish bond brick building which was constructed in 1731 for the cost of 50,000 pounds of tobacco. Today, the small, 23 foot by 35 foot, building and its adjacent tiny jail are used as a museum.

In colonial days since Eastville was the county seat, it was only natural for taverns and inns to be among its earliest buildings. There was always a need for meals and refreshments during the long court sessions. Rooms were needed for overnight stays, since travel to and from the county seat was difficult. Originally there was a tavern built on the present site of the Eastville Inn. It started operation in 1724.

The present building, according to the courthouse records, dates from 1780 when the lot was sold by a Williamsburg resident to a James Taylor for the purposes of an Inn. For over 100 years, the Inn was known as the Taylor House. It was a simple two story building with a basement. Over the years several additions were added to the original building and by 1900 the name was changed to Eastville Inn. In the mid 1950's, the Eastville Inn became a popular stopping place for people travelling from New York to Florida.

In the mid 1960's, a fire erupted in the kitchen and destroyed parts of the building. It was never rebuilt and became an eye sore for the town. When the Inn was about to be torn down, a plan was devised which, it was hoped, would save the building. The Board of Supervisors of Northampton County agreed to lease out the building at a very reasonable rate, provided it would be made operative, at least as a restaurant.

It is not every restaurateur who would open an operation in a partially burned building where there were no kitchen facilities. However, an energetic young couple from Texas did just that. Anne and Pete Musgrove, found the Eastville Inn while they were vacationing on the Eastern Shore. They liked the area, and were looking for a small town in which to open a restaurant. However, they did not want to go head over heels in debt and the lease arrangements for the Eastville Inn suited them. Eventually they hope to do some restorations – first the old dining room and then some of the upstairs rooms.

It has not been easy. There was no kitchen or dining room for this much needed restaurant, so the Musgroves improvised. The old registration desk became the counter of the restaurant and the area behind the desk was turned into the kitchen. The old lobby area is now the dining area. What the restaurant may lack in ambience at the present time, it makes up in the quality of its food.

Pete Musgrove had been cooking for his younger brothers and sisters since he was a teenager. Although he holds a liberal arts degree, he started working in restaurants after graduation from college. A career counselor told him to pursue the avocation he most enjoyed. Six years later he is the owner of his own restaurant. Anne, a chemist by profession, worked as a waitress while in college. She gave up test tubes for a mix master and baking pans. Anne prepares all of the desserts and also acts as hostess for the Eastville Inn restaurant.

There is a move underway to place the Eastville Inn on the National Register of Historic Buildings. This will help with the remodeling phase, but Anne and Pete intend to expand their operation only as capital permits. They want to refurbish and use the large kitchen and hope eventually to open several of the guest rooms.

Breakfast and lunch caters to the local people who daily business with the county. Dinner, however, attracts guests from all over the Eastern Shore who previously were forced to go "across the Bay" to find the blend of contemporary and classic dishes prepared at the Eastville Inn.

Pete and Anne Musgrove feature a special dinner once a month on weekends. The dinners follow a theme – either a holiday theme or a food theme. Local Virginia wines are served at the Inn and paired with the many seafood dishes Pete prepares. Fresh vegetables from local farmers are served with the entrees. Since fresh seafood is plentiful on the Eastern Shore, it is featured in all types of dishes at the Eastville Inn.

DINING
➡

The Eastville Inn, *Business Route 13, Eastville, Virginia 23347, 804-678-5551*
Directions: *In the center of Eastville on Business Route 13*
Principals: *Anne M. Gorman and William A. (Pete) Musgrove*
Meal Times: *Monday through Saturday*
Breakfast: *6 a.m. to 11:30 a.m. Lunch: 11:30 a.m. to 2:30 p.m., Wednesday, Thursday, Friday and Saturday -- Dinner: summer months only 6 p.m. to 9 p.m., Monthly Dinner weekends throughout the year*

CREAM OF CRAB SOUP

Serve with Old Dominion White from the local Accomack Vineyards

Pete Musgrove likes to prepare dishes using local crab. This soup may be served as a first course or as a luncheon entree with a colorful spring salad.

1/4 cup butter	Pinch of thyme
3/4 cup chopped onion	1 bay leaf
3/4 cup chopped celery	1 lb. crabmeat
3/4 cup chopped green pepper	Salt and pepper, to taste
1/4 cup flour	1/8 teaspoon nutmeg
2 cups half and half	Chopped fresh parsley
2 cups milk	

In a medium size saucepan, melt the butter and add the vegetables. Cook over low heat for about 5 minutes or until the vegetables loose their crispness. Add flour and stir to blend. Combine half and half with the milk. Increase heat to medium high and slowly add milk to the vegetable mixture stirring constantly. Then return heat to low and simmer the soup for 5 to 8 minutes.

Add crabmeat and heat through. Do not boil. Season with salt and pepper, and nutmeg. Garnish with chopped parsley. Serve. *Serves: 4 or 6 as a first course*

EASTVILLE INN CRAB CAKES

Serve with Eastern Shore Riesling from Accomack Vineyards

There are many recipes for crab cakes -- all of which are slightly different. Most use a special seafood seasoning. available in local fish markets or gourmet shops. This crabmeat mixture with more crumbs and less mayonnaise tends to be stiffer and also makes an excellent stuffing for fish.

1 lb. crabmeat	1 teaspoon Worcestershire sauce
1 egg, beaten	1 teaspoon baking powder
3/4 cup ground cracker crumbs	1 tablespoon lemon juice
1 tablespoon Wye River Seafood Seasoning	3 tablespoons parsley flakes
3 dashes tabasco sauce	Mayonnaise to moisten and bind
1/4 teaspoon dry mustard	Butter for frying

Pick over the crab meat, removing any loose shells. Place in bowl and add all ingredients except mayonnaise. Fold gently to mix, being careful not to break up the crabmeat. Fold in enough mayonnaise to hold mixture together.

Heat a large skillet and add sufficient butter to cover bottom. Pat the crab mixture into 8 3-inch patties. Sauté in butter until brown on one side, then turn and sauté the other side. Serve. *Serves: 8*

THE INN AT MONTROSS   The Inn at Montross was built in 1683 and some parts of the structure have been in continuous use for over 300 years. That same year the justices of Westmoreland County gave permission to John Minor to construct an Ordinary with the provision that no spirits be sold while the court was in session. John Minor and another citizen had given acreage to the county for the construction of the courthouse. Politics has not changed all that much. Even 300 years ago one hand washed the other.

In 1730 the property was sold to the Spence family and it became known as Spence's Tavern. Since that time the building has been a hotel, a home for the elderly and an inn. Though the original building was destroyed by fire around 1800, it was quickly rebuilt on the original foundation. The foundation is visible from the present wine cellar.

The Inn had been vacant for 2 1/2 years when Eileen and Michael Longman happened upon it in the summer of 1985. Both Eileen and Michael, who had been married for only 18 months, wanted a change of pace. Michael, born in England, had been in the insurance field for twenty years while Eileen had worked in public health for about the same length of time. They both wanted to own and operate a country inn, but could not decided on a location – whether Michael's native England or on the East Coast of the United States. The knowledge of American business led them to the decision to stay on this side of the Atlantic.

Upon purchasing the Inn two years ago, Eileen and Michael started a complete renovation program – from the kitchen to the attic. They put a blackboard in their front yard which informed their neighbors of their activities. It was almost like reading the weekly newspaper. After six months of hard work – scrubbing, painting and wallpapering – the Inn was ready for its grand re-opening.

Today there are six guest rooms at the Inn, all with private baths. They are furnished in the Colonial style. The Longman's antiques, along with primitive and modern art, and porcelains, add decorative touches to the house. There is a full service bar and a comfortable lounge.

The style of the restaurant could be classed as "Sophisticated Home Cooking," says Eileen Longman. "We are a country restaurant with a discerning clientele who know good food." Michael Longman, who is the chef, adds "We provide fine quality meals without pretentiousness." He has had no formal training other then gourmet home cooking. That palate for fine food has been carried over to his restaurant cuisine. Fresh seafood from the nearby shore is always a highlight of the menu.

The Virginia wines featured on the wine list are all from nearby Ingleside Plantation Vineyards. "We want to give our patrons the opportunity to enjoy the products of our local winery," said the Longmans. Jacques Recht, the winemaker at Ingleside, has assisted them in putting together the Inn's wine list.

The Inn at Montross has developed an excellent reputation for its crab specialties – colonial crab, crab imperial and of course, crab cakes. Most "land locked guests" just cannot get enough crab dishes and there are always one or two featured as specials on the menu.

The Inn's crab cakes are made according to an old Maryland family recipe which belonged to Eileen's family. It is very similar to the Rose Bower recipe, elsewhere in the book. Meat dishes, too, are featured on the Inn's varied menu.

TOURS
➡

The Inn At Montross, *Courthouse Square, Montross, Virginia 22520, 804-493-9097*
Directions: *In the center of town across from the Westmoreland County courthouse*
Principals: *Eileen and Michael Longman*
Meal Times: *Daily, Lunch 11:30 a.m. to 2 p.m., Sunday through Thursday Dinner: 5:30 p.m. to 8 p.m., Friday and Saturday Dinner: 5:30 p.m. to 9:30 p.m.*

COLONIAL CRAB

Serve with Ingleside Chesapeake Blanc

This recipe is a very typical dish of early colonial Virginia. It combines the subtle taste of Chesapeake Bay crabmeat with the sharp salty flavor of country ham. Since the dish is prepared very quickly, it is made to order at the Inn. Thus there are ingredients for only one serving. If serving more people, adjust the ingredients.

2 to 3 tablespoons butter	1 drop hot pepper sauce
5 1/2 oz. backfin (lump) blue crabmeat	Dash of thyme
1/4 teaspoon lemon juice	2 thin slices of Country Ham (approx. 2
Dash of salt	oz.)
Dash of white pepper	1 slice white bread, toasted

Melt the butter in skillet over medium heat. Add crabmeat, lemon juice, salt, pepper, tabasco sauce, and thyme. Sauté briefly until crabmeat is heated through. Cover crabmeat with the ham slices. Cover skillet and simmer for 2 - 3 minutes until edges of ham curl and flavors are blended. Serve over toast points and garnish with lemon slice and parsley. *Serves: 1*

NORTHERN NECK CRAB IMPERIAL

Serve with Ingleside Virginia Chardonnay

This slightly unusual variation of crab imperial is also an old family recipe from Eileen's family in Maryland. The dish is all crabmeat with no filler and does not have a creamy sauce covering it. Therefore, the delicate flavor of the crab comes to the forefront. This entree is the signature menu item of the Inn at Montross.

3 lbs. crabmeat, lump blue crab	1 1/2 teaspoon dry dill
3/4 cup mayonnaise	9 drops hot pepper sauce
3 teaspoons chopped pimiento	2 to 3 tablespoons butter
3 teaspoons whole capers	16 large mushroom caps
1 1/2 teaspoon Worcestershire sauce	Paprika

Place crabmeat in a large bowl. In another bowl mix mayonnaise, pimiento, capers, Worcestershire sauce, dill and hot pepper sauce. Blend well. Pour over crabmeat and toss lightly. In a large skillet melt the butter and lightly saute the mushroom caps. Place two mushroom caps per serving in individual ramekins. Divide crabmeat mixture into 8 servings and place each on top of the mushroom caps. Sprinkle with paprika. Bake in a preheated 350 degree oven for 15 to 20 minutes until lightly browned and hot throughout. *Serves: 8*

FILET MONTROSS

Serve with Ingleside Cabernet Sauvignon

This peppered filet of beef in red wine sauce is simple to prepare. The secret is not to over cook the meat, since it will continue to "cook" as it is sitting on a warm plate.

Cracked black pepper	1/2 red pepper, julienned
2 6 oz. filet beef steaks	1/2 green pepper, julienned
2 strips of bacon	1/2 cup dry red wine
2 tablespoons oil	1/2 cup heavy cream
2 tablespoons butter	

Sprinkle both sides of the meat heavily with cracked pepper. Press the pepper into the meat. Wrap each steak with one strip of bacon and secure with a toothpick.

In a skillet combine oil and butter and heat over medium high heat. The pan should be hot in order to sear the steaks. Sauté steaks on each side for 4 to 5 minutes for pink centers. Check doneness occasionally. When desired doneness has been reached, remove meat to a warm platter. Remove toothpicks. Sauté pepper strips in steak drippings until softened but not brown. Add wine to the pan and reduce to about half. Add cream to the pan and reduce until the sauce is thickened. Arrange the peppers on top of the steak. Pour sauce over the steaks and serve immediately. *Serves: 2*

THE SMYTHE'S COTTAGE Smythe's Cottage, a small blue cottage on Fauquier Street in Fredericksburg, is a pleasant place to stop for a meal while touring in the Fredericksburg area. The turn of the century cottage in the midst of colonial landmarks offers traditional American food with some Southern specialties. The restaurant, founded by Joyce Ackerman, has been in operation for 12 years. It was recently sold to the present owners, Lonny Williams and James Gibbons. The cottage has several pleasant dining areas including a glassed-in porch.

There is one curious item in the delightful cottage – and a story that goes with it. It seems that the grandfather of one of the early owners was captured by the Yankees. Young Maurice Evans was only 16 years old when he fought at the Battle of Fredericksburg as a scout for Jeb Stuart.

From his prison cell in the North he wrote to his mother and family, telling of the hard tasks he was being forced to perform. When Evans refused to dig ditches, his captors hung him by his thumbs. He did survive the ordeal and returned home after the war.

Many years later, the founder of Smythe's Cottage and granddaughter of Maurice Evans, Joyce Ackerman, decided to honor her grandfather. She knew from the letters how her grandfather had suffered and wanted to avenge that suffering. She decided to hang a portrait of Ulysses Grant – but to hang it upside down. Now at last, all was right with the world and her grandfather could rest in peace.

Dining at Smythe's Cottage is like eating in someone's home. Lonny Williams is the chef. He has worked in several restaurants and enjoys preparing some of the old traditional recipes of the area. Many of the items on the menu are prepared to order. Lonny and Jim Gibbons serve local Ingleside wine as the house wine.

Lonny Williams has researched a number of the entrees served at Smythe's Cottage and has tried to adhere to the original colonial recipes as nearly as possible. The chicken pot pie is similar to one of colonial Virginia. "In those days wild game or fowl was used in the pie," says Lonny. "Today we use chicken, but any fowl may be included in the pie." The boiled trout recipe, too, was adopted from an old colonial one. Fish and meat entrees were served in the same course in colonial days. Consequently a mild fish dish, for instance, would balance a spicy meat pie. In those days a Claret would have been served with the meal. Lonny Williams recommends the Ingleside Claret which is light and fruity and can be served with the fish.

DINING
➡

187

The Smythe's Cottage, *303 Fauquier Street, Fredericksburg, Virginia 22401,*
703-373-1645
Directions*: In center of town on a side street*
Principals*: Lonny Williams and James Gibbons*
Meal Times*: Wednesday through Monday*
Lunch*: 11 a.m. to 5 p.m.*
Dinner*: 5 p.m. to 9 p.m.*

CHICKEN POT PIE

Serve with Ingleside Chesapeake Blanc

There are almost as many versions of chicken pie as there are feathers on the bird. It may be prepared with chicken especially cooked for the pie or leftover chicken. Crusts, too, vary from the early colonial ones made with suet to the rich pastryones, as well as biscuit dough and puff pastry. Meat pies of all types have been a popular part of Virginia cuisine since early colonial days.

1-3 to 4 lb. chicken, cut up	3 carrots, diced
2 qts. water	2 stalks celery, chopped
1 teaspoon salt	1 8 oz. can sweet peas
4 oz. butter	2 cups heavy cream
1 cup mushrooms, sliced	Salt and pepper to taste
1 medium onion, chopped	1 teaspoon poultry seasoning
1/2 cup flour	1/2 teaspoon garlic powder
1 qt. chicken stock, from poaching chicken	1-9 to 10 inch pie crust
6 red bliss potatoes, diced	

Place chicken, water and salt in a small dutch oven. Bring to a boil and simmer for 50 to 60 minutes. Remove chicken from water to cool. Boil the broth down to 1 quart and reserve.

In another large saucepan, melt butter and add mushrooms and onion. Sauté until onion is transparent. Stir flour into sautéed vegetables. Add the reserved 1 quart of chicken stock. Then add potatoes, carrots and celery to the stock. Simmer until tender. Add the peas. Stir in cream and spices.

Meanwhile remove chicken meat from bones and cut into large bite size pieces. Add to stew.

Pour stew into a large 3 quart casserole dish. Place an oven proof cup in center of casserole to hold up crust. Roll out crust to fit casserole with about 1 1/2 inches overlap. Roll up the edges and crimp with a fork to make crust adhere to the dish. Put slits in top of crust to allow steam to escape.

Bake in a preheated 450 degree oven for 10 minutes, reduce heat to 350 degrees and continue baking for 30 to 40 minutes until crust is nicely browned. *Serves: 6*

THE TRELLIS The setting is Colonial Williamsburg, but the food is contemporary American and the restaurant is The Trellis. In the six years since its founding in 1980, The Trellis has become a top rated restaurant, not only in Virginia but in the United States. Its executive chef and co-owner, Marcel Desaulniers, is a recognized authority on contemporary American cuisine and is a sought-after speaker at gatherings of restaurateurs.

There are three partners in The Trellis, each from different professional backgrounds. John Curtis is the owner of The Bookpress in Williamsburg, Tom Power owns a cheese and wine shop, and Marcel Desaulniers was in the food brokerage business at the time The Trellis was founded.

The Trellis is located in Merchants Square which was developed by the Colonial Williamsburg Foundation. For some thirty years the Rexall Drug store had occupied the building that was to become The Trellis. The restaurant is a joint venture, in a sense, of the three partners and the Williamsburg Foundation. The Foundation agreed to completely remodel the building for $500,000 to provide the necessary space and facilities for the restaurant. The three partners provided the expertise of their combined restaurant experience with Marcel Desaulniers as executive chef.

Marcel Desaulniers is from a French-Canadian background and grew up in Woonsocket, Rhode Island. As a teenager he worked in various neighborhood restaurants and was inspired to become a chef by two professional chefs who were friends of the family. With the financial help of one of the local restaurateurs, Marcel was able to attend the Culinary Academy of America from which he graduated in 1965. Marcel then worked in restaurants in New York, with a two year interruption as a rifleman in the Marine Corps in Vietnam.

In 1970, Marcel came to Colonial Williamsburg and ultimately became assistant chef at The Cascades, one of the Foundation's restaurants. He later worked for the Colonial Williamsburg Food Service, serving all of the food entities within the Foundation. In 1974 he became executive vice president and co-owner of Williamsburg Food Brokers, Inc. The Trellis restaurant was founded and opened in 1980.

It was while redesigning the menu and cuisine at The Cascades that Marcel Desaulniers first became aware of traditional American dishes such as peanut soup and Brunswick stew. Although these items were removed from the menu, Marcel's interest in American food was kindled. During his travels all over the country, he sought out traditional as well as contemporary American foods. Ideas from all over the United States have influenced his creations at The Trellis.

The menu changes with the seasons and there are always chef's specials of the day. Marcel's regular seasonal menu as well as the daily specials depend on the availability of fresh ingredients. For instance, in the spring there is grilled flounder with fresh asparagus, red peppers and toasted cashews, in the winter a roulade of rabbit and country ham with toasted walnut bread, and in summer grilled chicken breast with peaches, country ham and black pepper butter – to mention only a few. Ingredients are always fresh, some come from local farmers who are under contract to provide certain items to the restaurant.

Desserts are a main feature of the restaurant. Marcel refers to The Trellis as a "theme park of desserts." A survey showed that in spite of this era of weight watching, 88% of the diners order dessert. Many of the desserts are prodigious and customers frequently take home portions in a foil wrapped package shaped like a graceful foil swan.

The Cafe section of The Trellis restaurant has its own separate menu. Basically it consists of the appetizers whose portions are somewhat enlarged and served with bread and a salad. This suits people who are looking for lighter fare. Weather permitting, there is an outdoor cafe with service of lighter entrees.

Lunch is also unique. Typical hamburgers, sandwiches, and salads are offered. The clientele at that time of day is different from those at dinner – mostly tourists who are touring historic Williamsburg. For dinner most of the clientele is local Williamsburg residents.

The Trellis serves 200 to 250 dinners per evening. To do this efficiently takes quite a devoted and well trained staff. In addition to a first chef, there are also senior and assistant chefs, as well as a pastry chef. The kitchen staff runs anywhere from 32 to 38 people.

Marcel knows the value of a well trained and loyal staff. In order to recruit new permanent staff, he has set up an apprenticeship program. Marcel developed a similar program for Colonial Williamsburg.

Each spring in order to promote Virginia wines, The Trellis holds a barrel tasting of new releases of some of the leading Virginia wineries. This is always a very successful event. The Trellis is very wine oriented – it even has grape vines growing on a trellis outside the restaurant.

Marcel Desaulniers is a master at combining ingredients for unusual and pleasing flavor combinations. He is one of the most innovative chefs to come on the American food scene in years. Marcel's cookbook, entitled *The Trellis*, is scheduled to be released in 1988.

DINING

➡

The Trellis, *403 Duke of Gloucester Street, Williamsburg, Virginia 23185, 804-229-8610*
Directions: *Near historic Williamsburg in Merchants Square*
Principals: *John Curtis, Marcel Desaulniers, and Tom Power*
Meal Times: *Seven Days a Week Lunch: 11:30 a.m. to 2:30 p.m. Dinner: 5:30 p.m. to 9:30 p.m.*

SAUTEED SEA SCALLOPS ON LEAF SPINACH

The unusual combination of scallops, sweet potatoes, hazelnuts and spinach makes this dish a memorable one. Some of the preparation of this dish may be done in advance.

3/4 lb. sea scallops	1 pound spinach
1/4 pound slab bacon	8 tablespoons butter
1 pound sweet potatoes	1 tablespoon lemon juice
1/4 pound hazelnuts	Salt and pepper to season

Remove muscle from sea scallops, slice scallops in two or three slices. Refrigerate.

Remove rind from slab bacon, slice bacon into strips and then cut strips into 1/4 inch dice. Place diced bacon on a baking sheet, then place sheet in a preheated 300 degree oven for 10 to 15 minutes. Remove bacon from sheet in a slotted spoon. Drain bacon on paper towels.

Peel sweet potatoes and cut into julienne strips. Hold in cold water.

Roast hazelnuts in a preheated 425 degree oven for 5 to 7 minutes. Allow to cool for a few minutes. Remove skins and then split each hazelnut in half.

Remove stems from spinach. Wash spinach, then drain.

To assemble the dish: Drain sweet potatoes, then sauté for 2 minutes in 1 tablespoon of butter and one tablespoon of water. Add diced bacon, and keep warm.

In a separate sauté pan, heat spinach in 1 tablespoon butter and 1 tablespoon water. Season with salt and pepper. When spinach leaves begin to wilt, remove them from the pan. Drain spinach well and portion onto 4 warm plates. Hold warm.

In yet another pan, sauté sea scallops in 2 tablespoons butter. Season with salt and pepper. Do not over cook the scallops.

Portion warm sweet potatoes and bacon over spinach leaves. Arrange scallops in the center of each plate. In a very hot pan heat the remaining 4 tablespoon of butter until butter begins to brown, add lemon juice to butter. Portion butter equally over scallops and garnish with hazelnuts over the scallops. *Serves: 4 as an appetizer*

Author's Note: The sauteed shoestring sweet potatoes make a good vegetable accompaniment to grilled meats or ham.

GRILLED CHICKEN BREAST ON BEET FETTUCCINE

Make the beet fettuccine early in the day. The cream sauce and chicken are a complement to the colorful as well as flavorful fettuccine.

1 1/2 lbs. boneless chicken breasts (4 pieces)	1 cup heavy cream
3 tablespoon dry white wine	1/4 cup sour cream
1 tablespoon lemon juice	1 bunch scallions (green tops), sliced
Salt and pepper to season	3 tablespoon unsalted butter
	Beet fettuccine

Remove skin from chicken breasts. Sprinkle wine, lemon juice, salt and pepper over chicken breasts. Cover and refrigerate until ready to cook.

Place cream in a heavy duty sauce pot and place pot over medium heat. Bring cream to a simmer, then lower heat and allow cream to cook and reduce by half of its original volume. Stir sour cream into reduced cream, blend and hold warm until ready to use.

Sauté sliced scallions for 3 to 4 minutes, in 1 tablespoon butter. When hot remove from heat and hold warm. To assemble the dish: Grill chicken over a low charcoal or wood fire. Cook chicken on both sides. When sufficiently cooked but still juicy remove for fire and keep warm.

Toss fettuccine to remove excess corn meal. Cook fettuccine in lots of boiling salted water for 3 to 4 minutes. Drain very well and toss with remaining butter. Then portion onto warm plates. Place cooked chicken breasts on top of each dish of pasta. Spoon 3 tablespoon of sour cream sauce over each breast and finish by portioning scallions over sauce. *Serves: 4*

BEET FETTUCCINE

1 large beet (about 5 oz. raw weight)	1/2 teaspoon olive oil
2 1/2 cups all purpose flour	1/4 teaspoon salt
1 large egg, plus 1 egg yolk	Cornmeal

Cover beet with cold water and cook until tender (about 25 minutes). Remove beet from water. Allow cooking liquid to simmer and reduce to one tablespoon. Peel beet, then purée in food processor with eggs, olive oil, salt and reduced beet liquor.

Place flour in large mixing bowl and add beet purée mixture. Knead mixture by hand until dough forms a ball. Remove dough ball from mixing bowl, place on floured surface and knead by hand until soft. Cover dough with plastic wrap and allow to relax in refrigerator for 1 hour.

Roll and cut dough into fettuccine. Toss fettuccine with cornmeal to prevent sticking. Refrigerate pasta until ready to use. *Serves: 4*

PEAR SORBET IN A TULIP WITH LEMON CUSTARD SAUCE

Usually designed for two, this interesting dessert is a recent addition to The Trellis menu.

2 cups water	2 tablespoons lemon juice
1 1/4 cups sugar	Lemon custard sauce
1 lb. red Bartlett pears	Tulip

Bring water and sugar to a boil. Allow to simmer for 5 minutes. While syrup is boiling, core and then purée the pear with lemon juice. Cool the syrup to room temperature and then combine with pear purée. Transfer mixture to sorbet freezer and freeze according to manufacturer's directions.

To serve the dish: Portion 4 tablespoon of lemon custard sauce onto each plate. Place tulip in center. Fill tulip with 4 small scoops of frozen pear sorbet.

Lemon Custard Sauce:

1/2 cup heavy cream	4 egg yolks
1/2 cup water	1/4 cup granulated sugar
Zest and juice of 1 lemon	1 teaspoon cornstarch

In a heavy duty saucepan heat cream, water and lemon zest to a simmer. While cream mixture is heating to a simmer, beat egg yolks, sugar and cornstarch in a stainless bowl, until thick. Pour the hot cream mixture into the egg yolk mixture. Stir gently. Place bowl over pan of boiling water and cook until mixture is thick, stirring constantly.

Remove thickened sauce from heat. Stir in lemon juice and allow to cool to room temperature. If sauce is not used immediately, refrigerate it. If refrigerated allow sauce to return to room temperature before serving.

Tulips: Makes 4 six-inch tulips

3 1/2 oz. unsalted butter
3/4 cup granulated sugar
4 drops vanilla extract

4 egg whites
1 cup all purpose flour

Cream butter, sugar and vanilla until smooth.

In a stainless steel bowl heat egg whites over boiling water, stirring constantly. When egg whites are warm (not hot!) slowly add to creamed mixture. Combine until smooth. Then add all of the flour at once and again mix until smooth.

Line a baking sheet with parchment paper. Smear four thin layers of batter into six inch circles.

Bake tulips in preheated 375 degree oven until golden brown. Remove from oven. Place individual tulips over the base of a large coffee mug. Form into shape while still warm. Hold down over coffee mug until cold. *Serves: 4*

WILLIAMSBURG INN – The Regency Dining Room The five-star Williamsburg Inn is one of America's most quietly elegant hotels. It still reflects the sense of perfection and refinement of the late Mr. and Mrs. John D. Rockefeller, Jr., who were instrumental in the restoration and creation of Colonial Williamsburg. Built in 1937 with 61 rooms, fifty years later and 166 rooms larger, the Inn has been patronized by millions of people, including many famous ones from around the world.

When Williamsburg opened to visitors in 1931, it soon became obvious that there were not enough overnight accommodations available. Originally the Raleigh Tavern was reconstructed for guest accommodations, but its 13 guestrooms and baths on the second floor were not sufficient. The Raleigh Tavern was opened as an exhibition Hall the following year. There were also some rooms in a Tavern existing in Market Square at the time. A consultant's report in 1934 urged Colonial Williamsburg to build a first-class hotel with recreational facilities for guests who opted for a longer stay than those who came primarily to view the restorations.

Mr. and Mrs. Rockefeller were determined that such a facility would not be like the ordinary hotel, but more like a home-away-from-home. This philosophy dictated not only the style of architecture and furnishings, but also the type of service provided. An architectural image was created that postdated the 18th century colonial style and looked different while blending with the rest of the town. The building also had to be large and spacious enough to provided elegance for the guests.

The inspirations for the Inn were the great 19th century hotels located in the springs and spas in the mountains of Virginia and West Virginia. The greatest inspiration was the resort hotel at Red Sweet Springs in Monroe County, West Virginia. The charm of the resort's brick arches and entranceways that were reminiscent of classical architecture were incorporated into the plans for the Williamsburg Inn.

The landscaping with large trees and the whitewashed brick of the building provides both a pleasing visual effect and a contrast to the unpainted brick buildings of the colonial area. The interior furnishings reflect a light and airy mood, yet subdued with classical motifs of Regency furniture.

Over the years, the Williamsburg Inn has been host to many celebrities and heads of state – the Queen of England, the Emperor and Empress of Japan, the Prime Minister of Japan – to mention a few. In 1983 the Williamsburg Inn was the site of the Summit Conference of Industrialized Nations hosted by President Reagan.

The quiet elegant atmosphere of the Inn is also predominant in its Regency Dining Room. Nineteenth century English decor predominates the room, which is basically decorated in shades of green. The Regency Dining Room seats 200, has a stage and a dance floor. When the dance floor is not in use, it is covered with a hand-hooked carpet made in Tryon, North

Carolina. The lyre design in the carpet was adapted from the decoration of a snuff box owned by George IV.

Hans J. Schadler, C.E.C. is the executive chef of The Regency Dining Room. Born and trained in Germany and Switzerland, Chef Schadler was associated with the Rock Resorts for many years before coming to the Williamsburg Inn. He is life-long president of the Resort Chefs Association.

Although the cuisine of The Regency Dining Room is continental, it features a lighter style prevalent in today's dining trends. Some traditional American dishes have been adapted to classical techniques. All fresh ingredients are used in the food preparation with many items either grown or produced especially for the Inn by growers all over the East Coast. For instance the turkeys used at the Inn are raised in Vermont, as are the morels. Cheddar cheese and gooseberries also come from Vermont. All of the breads and pastries are baked at the central commissary which serves all of the food entities in Colonial Williamsburg. These items, however, are made to Chef Schadler's specifications. Virginia wines currently are being added to the extensive wine list of The Regency Dining Room.

DINING
➡

Williamsburg Inn, Francis Street, Williamsburg, Virginia 23187, 804-229-1000
Directions: *Located in the historic area of Colonial Williamsburg*
Principals: *Colonial Williamsburg Foundation*
Meal Times: *7 days a week Breakfast: 7 a.m. to 10 a.m. Lunch: 12 noon to 2 p.m. Dinner: 6:30 p.m. to 9:30 p.m.*

VIRGINIA CRABMEAT, SAUTE RANDOLPH

This Virginia crabmeat dish is particularly popular for lunch at The Regency Room. The tartness of a hollandaise sauce is a good complement to Virginia ham.

4 frozen patty shells	2 teaspoons minced shallots
1/2 pound backfin crabmeat	3/4 cup hollandaise sauce
2 teaspoons lemon juice	2 teaspoons Dijon mustard
2 tablespoons butter	8 thin slices of Virginia ham

Preheat oven to 450 degrees. Place the patty shells upside down on an ungreased baking sheet. Reduce heat to 400 degrees and bake for 20 minutes. Cut away the sides of the shells, so that a flat bottom remains. If the bottoms are not nicely browned return them to the oven for a few minutes. Set the pastry rounds aside.

Pick over the crabmeat. Discard any bits of shell or cartilage. Toss crabmeat gently with the lemon juice. Melt the butter in a small skillet. Add the shallots and saute over medium heat until soft, but not brown. Add the crabmeat and saute over low heat for 2 minutes, tossing gently so that the crabmeat is well coated with butter. Combine the Hollandaise sauce and the mustard.

Place 2 pastry rounds on each of 4 warmed plates. Place a slice of Virginia ham on each round and top with crabmeat. Cover the crab with Hollandaise sauce. *Serves: 4*

VEAL REGENCY

Chef Schadler says that Veal Regency is the most popular entrée in The Regency Dining Room. It combines the mild taste of veal and crabmeat with a tangy Bearnaise Sauce.

20 oz. veal loin, cut into 8 medallions	1/2 teaspoon chervil
3 tablespoons butter	1/2 teaspoon chopped chives
4 oz. lump crabmeat	8 asparagus spears
1 tablespoon butter	Bearnaise Sauce

In a large skillet over medium high heat melt 3 tablespoons butter and quickly sauté the veal medallions. If done in two batches more butter may have to be added. In a small skillet melt 1 tablespoon butter, add crabmeat, chervil and chives. Sauté quickly to coat crabmeat. Set the veal and crabmeat aside.

Steam asparagus until crisp tender.

Top each veal medallion with a portion of the crabmeat. Place one asparagus spear on top and cover with the Bearnaise Sauce. Glaze under the broiler, but do not brown. Do not leave under broiler too long as the sauce will separate.

Bearnaise Sauce:

1 tablespoon butter	1 sprig parsley
1/4 cup green onions, minced very fine	4 egg yolks, beaten
1/3 cup white vinegar	6 tablespoons butter
4 teaspoons whole pepper	1/2 teaspoon salt
1/3 teaspoon tarragon leaves	

In a small sauce pan melt 1 tablespoon butter and sauté the green onions for five minutes. Add vinegar, pepper, tarragon, and parsley and simmer until almost dry. Cool slightly. Place over hot water and add egg yolks slowly, whisking constantly. Do not boil. Remove from heat when thick. Slowly add remaining butter and salt, stirring constantly. Strain sauce. Keep lukewarm – if too hot or cold the sauce will separate. *Serves: 4*

WILLIAMSBURG TAVERNS – Christiana Campbell's Tavern, Chowning's Tavern, King's Arms Tavern

Dining at one of the Williamsburg Taverns is like going back to the 18th century, not only in decor, but also in the cuisine served at each of the taverns. All three are operated in the 18th century style by the Colonial Williamsburg Foundation. The food of each is different from the other, as is their history. All however, relate to the late 18th century when Colonial Williamsburg was one of the centers of life in the newly created United States of America.

The taverns served as gathering places where customers could discuss business, politics, news and gossip over drinks and meals. There were also several rooms in the taverns that provided lodgings for overnight guests. In early English usage there was a difference between an Ordinary, a Tavern and an Inn, although in colonial Virginia the terms were used interchangeably. An Ordinary was an eating establishment that served a fixed meal at a fixed price. Taverns also served meals, but were primarily licensed to sell liquor. An Inn was a house for lodging, dining and entertainment – games of cards, balls, etc. In Colonial Williamsburg a Tavern served all three purposes.

"I have just opened Tavern opposite to the Raleigh at the sign of the King's Arms . . . . and shall be much obliged to the Gentleman who favour me with their company." That was part of the advertisement Mrs. Jane Vobe of Williamsburg ran in the Virginia Gazette in February of 1772 announcing the relocation of her Tavern to a prime location near the capitol. King's Arms, at that time, was still as popular a tavern name in the colonies as it was in England. During the Revolution, however, the King's Arms became known simply as Mrs. Vobe's. After the Revolutionary War the tavern was renamed the Eagle Tavern. Today the King's Arms Tavern stands on the original site. The furnishings are original to the period as are the draperies, cutlery and mugs used for ale and beer.

Being a tavern keeper was not new to Mrs. Vobe, since prior to the opening of King's Arms she operated a tavern on Waller Street. This location, near the capitol, was taken over by a Christiana Campbell, who also was not new to the business. Christiana's father had been a tavern keeper. When her husband, Ebenezer Campbell, an apothecary, died, she had to support her two children and tavern keeping was the only profession she knew. It was quite common for women in those days to be tavern keepers, following either in the footsteps of their husbands or fathers. They were respected members of the community.

Christiana Campbell became quite successful and within a few years purchased the building. Upstairs rooms in the tavern accommodated leading politicians and businessmen who came to town. George Washington was a frequent diner and overnight guest.

Chowning's Tavern, on the other hand, was not nearly as successful as the other two in colonial days. In size, clientele, and services, Chowning's Tavern was more like the small rural Virginia taverns located near ferries, crossroads or courthouses. The selection of food and drink was limited. Lodgings probably consisted of several people sharing a room upstairs. Little is known of Josiah Chowning and his family. Two years after Chowning opened the tavern in 1764, another innkeeper advertised that he had opened a tavern in the house formerly occupied by Mr. Chowning.

Food and drink available to guests were as varied as the taverns themselves. Mrs. Vobe, the most sophisticated, served her guests special meals and drinks and rented out rooms for balls, concerts and business meetings. Customers at Chowning's Tavern, on the other hand, ate whatever was served them.

Food in colonial Virginia was plentiful and the taverns usually served such items as meat and vegetable potpies, game stews, pumpkin squash, seafoods and soups. Methods of cooking varied between, boiling, baking and some rotisserie broiling in front of an open fireplace.

Tavern keepers were required to have a license, both before and after the Revolution. Rates for food and drink had to be set by the tavern keeper and posted in each tavern's public room.

Well run taverns flourished in Williamsburg while it was the capital of Virginia. However, after the seat of government moved to Richmond in the late 1700's the need for overnight accommodations and places to dine in Williamsburg declined.

Today visitors to Colonial Williamsburg can still dine at the taverns and enjoy the same food that was served in colonial days. The dishes are now prepared in modern kitchens, but the food is basically the same. Recipes (called receipts in colonial times) have been carefully and painstakingly researched in old cookbooks and letters of the period. Artifacts that have been uncovered through the archaeological research program at Williamsburg have helped to substantiate some of the food served in Colonial Williamsburg.

Now each of the taverns is known for a different type of food. King's Arms is the largest of the taverns. It serves 1000 at dinner each night in the summer and has a kitchen staff of 32. The tavern specializes in meat dishes of colonial days – particularly chicken and game. Peanut soup and Virginia ham are also featured. A broiled-fish-of-the-day entree has recently been added to conform with lighter eating styles. In season, soft shell crabs are served. For dessert there is homemade rice pudding on the menu, as well as seasonal pies. All dinners are served with relishes, salad, vegetables, Sally Lunn bread and Indian corn muffins. The latter are served at the three taverns. The bread selection, however, varies at each.

Christiana Campbell's specializes in seafood. At lunch there are crab cakes and chicken and leek pie. Jambalaya, prepared in the colonial manner, is one of the features at dinner, as is Southern fried chicken which is pan fried. Sautéed veal with mushrooms has recently become a popular entrée. Sweet potato muffins, drop biscuits and spoon bread are served with the entrées.

Chowning's, on the other hand, serves plainer food, just as the tavern did two hundred years ago. It is the type of food that would be found at smaller taverns in Williamsburg or out in the countryside. There is a game salad plate made with various types of poultry, which is a lunch specialty. Barbecued chicken with an authentic barbecue sauce is also a lunch specialty. Brunswick stew and Welch Rabbit with Smithfield ham are both popular dishes prepared from authentic colonial recipes.

Each tavern has its own executive chef who is responsible for the ordering, scheduling and food preparation. The ordering is done through a central commissary, which does all of the meat cutting and baking for all of the restaurants in Colonial Williamsburg. Christiana Campbell's, however, makes its own spoon bread and buys the biscuit dough in bulk from the commissary. Each one of the chefs uses a computer to calculate the needed supplies based on previous period's dinner occupancy rate and selection of entrees.

Herbert Foster, a veteran of 32 years in food service with the Williamsburg Foundation, is the executive chef of King's Arms. He has worked both at the Williamsburg Inn and the Williamsburg Lodge and was executive chef of the Cascades before taking over at King's Arms.

Christiana Campbell's food service is under the direction of executive chef Edward Swan. Ed's brother was a chef at the Williamsburg Inn, when he came to live with him as a teenager. Cooking seemed to come naturally to Ed and he entered the Williamsburg apprenticeship program for 2 years. After finishing the program Ed spent the next 14 years at various positions throughout the food operations at Colonial Williamsburg. He was an apprentice chef at the Lodge and sous chef at the Cascades, as well as a chef at Christiana Campbell's.

Chowning's has another veteran of the Colonial Williamsburg system. Manfred Roehr learned cooking while in the Army where he was one of the youngest chefs. He started at the Lodge as a cook and then worked in the banquet department for 5 years. Manfred was also a chef at Chowning's and an assistant manager of the tavern. In addition to Manfred who is both manager and executive chef of Chowning's, there is a staff of 7 cooks, plus a utility crew.

Wine, beer and ale were an integral part of the dining scene in Colonial Williamsburg. Today Virginia wine is served in all of the taverns.

Whether it is crab cakes, Southern fried chicken , colonial game pie, or Brunswick stew – all can be found at one of the colonial taverns in Historic Williamsburg. The preparation techniques may be modern, but the recipes are authentic to the days when Williamsburg was the capital of Virginia.

DINING
➡

Christiana Campbell's Tavern, Chowning's Tavern, King's Arms Tavern, *Colonial Williamsburg, Williamsburg, Virginia*
For reservations call 804-229-2141 Check for winter hours – January through March
Directions: *All three taverns are located in the historic area of Colonial Williamsburg. Both King's Arms and Chowning's are on Duke of Gloucester Street. Christiana Campbell's is on Waller Street across from the colonial capital building.*
Principals: *Colonial Williamsburg Foundation*
Meal Times: *All three establishments operate 7 days a week.*
Christiana Campbell's Tavern: *Brunch: 10 a.m. to 2:30 p.m. Dinner: 5:30 p.m. to 9:30 p.m.*
King's Arms Tavern: *Lunch: 11:30 a.m. to 2:30 p.m. Dinner: 5:15 p.m. to 9:30 p.m.*
Chowning's Tavern: *Lunch: 11:30 a.m. to 3:30 p.m. Dinner: 5 p.m. to 8:30 p.m.*

CORNISH GAME HENS IN CASSEROLE – King's Arms Tavern

In colonial days many meat and poultry dishes were steamed or baked in a casserole type of dish. Small chickens, or game birds were used for this entrée and vegetables varied according to the season. In the 18th century the fowl was probably roasted on a spit in the open hearth.

1/4 cup butter, divided	1 carrot, coarsely diced
4 cornish game hens	3/4 cup peas
Salt and pepper	3/4 cup string beans
1/2 lb. button mushrooms	1/4 cup white Burgundy wine
16 pearl onions	White Burgundy wine sauce

Preheat oven to 450 degrees. Butter 4 individual casseroles. Melt 3 tablespoon butter. Place the cornish game hens, breast side up, on a rack in a roasting pan. Brush with melted butter and sprinkle with salt and pepper. Reduce heat to 350 and roast the game hens until they test done, about 1 hour. Baste occasionally with the pan drippings.

In the meantime, melt 1 tablespoon butter in a skillet. Add the mushrooms and saute over medium heat for 2 to 3 minutes. Reserve. Cook the pearl onions, carrot, peas and string beans separately in boiling salted water until tender. Drain and reserve.

When the game hens are roasted, transfer them to the prepared casseroles. Remove all of the fat from the roasting pan, leaving the drippings. Add wine and bring to a boil, stirring to deglaze the bottom of the pan. Strain into the White Burgundy wine sauce and stir to blend the sauce. Preheat oven to 400 degrees. Pour the wine sauce over the game hens. Sprinkle with the reserved vegetables. Bake in 400 degree oven for 10 minutes or until heated through.

White Burgundy Sauce:

1/4 cup butter	Salt and white pepper
1/4 cup flour	1/2 cup white Burgundy
2 cups chicken stock	

Melt the butter in a saucepan. Stir in flour and cook over medium heat for 3 minutes, stirring constantly. Do not let the mixture brown. Heat the chicken stock and add it to the mixture, whisking until the sauce is smooth and thick. Add salt and white pepper to taste. Add the wine and simmer uncovered for 10 minutes. *Serves: 4*

KIDNEY BEAN RELISH – King's Arms Tavern

Relishes were an integral part of the colonial dining table. They could be either sweet or spicy and usually one of each was on the table. They were also a way of preserving some of the summer fruits and vegetables for later use.

2 cans (15 1/2 oz. each) kidney beans	1/2 teaspoon chives, snipped
2 medium red onion, thinly sliced	1/2 teaspoon oregano
1/4 cup white vinegar	Salt and freshly ground pepper, to taste
1/4 cup vegetable oil	

Drain the beans and place in a bowl. Add the onion. Combine the vinegar, oil, chives, and oregano and mix well. Pour the dressing over the beans and mix. Add salt and pepper to taste.

Refrigerate 2 hours or longer before serving. *Serves: 8*

CHICKEN AND LEEK PIE – Christiana Campbell's Tavern

Meat pies in colonial days were made with either fowl or meat. They were very popular and were eaten either hot at the main meal in the middle of the day or cold for supper.

1 lb. leeks	2 quarts chicken velouté
1 lb. mushrooms	Salt and pepper, to taste
2 lbs. cooked chicken meat, cut in bite size pieces	8 7-inch pie crusts, unbaked
	Egg wash

Clean leeks and mushrooms. Cut leeks into 1 inch pieces and slice mushrooms thickly. Blanch each separately over low heat. Drain.

In a separate saucepan heat the velouté and add the chicken meat, leeks and mushrooms. Season with salt and pepper. Heat until mixture is warm. Pour into 8 ounce crocks. Cover with pie crust. Brush lightly with egg wash.

Bake in a preheated 400 degree oven for about 15 minutes or until pie top is golden brown. Contents of pie will be bubbling. *Serves: 8*

Chicken veloute:

1 lb. butter	1/2 gallon chicken stock
1 cup flour	1 cup milk

In a saucepan melt butter over medium heat. Reduce heat to low and add flour whisking constantly. Do not brown flour mixture. Stir in chicken stock. Cook for 30 minutes and add milk. Makes about 64 ounces.

Egg Wash:

1 egg	1/4 cup of milk

Combine egg and milk, whipping to blend. Brush on top of pastry.

POACHED PEAR IN WINE – Christiana Campbell's Tavern

8 whole pears   1/2 cup sugar
1/2 bottle port wine

Peel and core pears. In a saucepan combine wine and sugar. In another saucepan poach pears in water for about 10 minutes over low heat. Drain. Then heat sugar and wine mixture over low heat. Add pears and bring to a medium boil. Cook for 30 minutes. Cool and place in refrigerator. Serve with the sauce in wide mouth Champagne glasses..

WELSH RABBIT WITH BEER – Chowning's Tavern

Welsh rabbit has no relation to rabbit, but was considered a "rare bit" in colonial days. The name Welsh was connected to the dish since it was made with English Cheddar cheese which was produced in Wales.

1 tablespoon butter   1 teaspoon dry mustard
1 lb. sharp Cheddar cheese, grated   1/2 teaspoon salt
3/4 cup beer, divided   1/2 teaspoon Worcestershire sauce
Dash of cayenne pepper or tabasco sauce   1 egg, slightly beaten

Melt butter in top of double boiler. Add cheese and all except a tablespoon of beer. Cook over hot not boiling water until the cheese melts. Combine seasonings with the remaining tablespoon of beer and stir into the cheese. Stir in slightly beaten egg. Serve immediately over toast or over broiled tomato halves. *Serves: 4*

BRUNSWICK STEW – Chowning's Tavern

Every place from the Canadian border to Georgia have claimed Brunswick stew. It probably originated in Brunswick County, Virginia. The stew was served at all public functions and became a popular tavern entrée. Originally squirrel was used to make this stew, but modern times have substituted chicken. Today a fryer is more readily available than the traditional stewing hen.

1 3 lb. fryer   2 cups corn, cut from the cob, or
1 large onion, sliced   1-1 lb. can
1 cup okra, cut into pieces   1 1/2 teaspoons salt
2 cups fresh tomatoes   1/2 teaspoon pepper
1 cup lima beans   1/2 tablespoon sugar
2 medium potatoes, peeled and diced

Cut the chicken in pieces and simmer in 1 or 1 1/2 quarts water. (One quart of water will provide a thicker stew.) Simmer for 45 to 55 minutes or until meat can easily be removed from the bones. Add the raw vegetables to the broth and simmer uncovered until the beans and potatoes are tender. Stir occasionally to prevent sticking.

Remove chicken meat from bones and cut into bite size pieces. Add to stew, along with the seasonings. Heat through and serve. If canned vegetables are used add their liquid and reduce the amount of water used to cook chicken.

Many prefer to make the stew one day and reheat and serve it the next. Long, slow cooking improves the flavors of the stew. *Serves: 4*

Southern Region

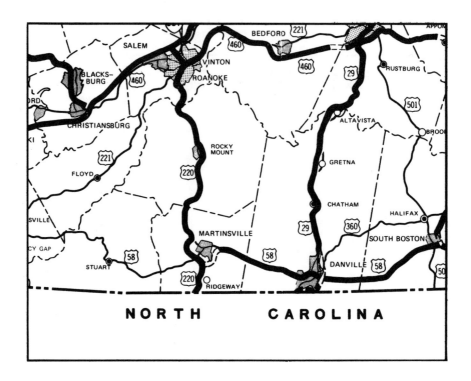

NORTH   CAROLINA

WINERIES:

Chateau Morrisette Winery

Chateau Naturel Winery

Fruit of the Bloom Farm Winery

Rose Bower Vineyard & Winery

Stonewall Vineyards

RESTAURANTS:

Emil's

The Homestead

Hotel Roanoke (Regency Room)

La Maison

Martha Washington Inn (First Lady's Table)

CHATEAU MORRISETTE WINERY Grapes have been planted almost everywhere in Virginia, even high up in the mountains on the Blue Ridge Parkway. At 3500 feet elevation there are 35 acres, mainly vinifera with some French hybrid, planted on the Morrisette family property bordering the Blue Ridge Parkway.

David Morrisette's father purchased 1000 acres in the Blue Ridge Mountains in 1978 and proceeded to plant various crops, including some French hybrid grapes. He also planted cauliflower and Christmas trees. The latter two flourished, but the grape vines were killed by winter frost the first winter. This did not stop the senior Morrisette and he proceeded to plant more grapes – two vinifera, Riesling and Chardonnay and two French hybrids, Seyval Blanc and Vidal. They fared better.

Young David Morrisette decided that if the family was going to grow grapes and establish a winery, he had better learn something about grape growing and winemaking. David enrolled at the University of Mississippi and graduated with degrees in viticulture and enology.

With a graduate winemaker in the family and with the grapes doing well the Morrisettes decided to construct a winery and make wine. Their first release was in 1983.

The vineyards which are at elevations from 1000 feet to 3500 feet actually have an excellent micro climate. "The warm days and cool nights are very similar to the growing temperatures in the wine growing regions of Germany," said David Morrisette. They do take extra precautions against winter frost damage by heavily "hilling-up" around the graft of each vine. This is a very labor intensive procedure. Even with precautions, David had extreme frost damage three years in a row.

Due to the frost loss and the unavailability of Virginia grapes, David Morrisette received a dispensation from the state to purchase more than 49 percent of his grapes outside of Virginia. He would have preferred to buy local grapes, but due to winter bud kill all over the state there were no grapes for sale. This happened both in 1985 and 1986. Some of the vines the vineyards lost were 5 year old Chardonnay which were bearing well.

However, these adverse weather conditions have not hindered David in his determination to grow grapes and produce wine. In 1985 and 1986 with the special dispensation from the state, he was able to purchase grapes from California and have them delivered in lug boxes in refrigerated trucks. Since then, he has also leased 35 acres of vineyards near Charlottesville to give him some insurance in case there is another big freeze on the mountain.

"I have never had a rot problem due to humidity," says David, as he talks about one of the most unspoiled parts of the country. With warm days and cool nights the ripening of the grapes slows down, and the fruit becomes high in sugar. He rarely has to chaptalize (add sugar to) his wines.

The winery, built of native stone and wood resembles a miniature Rhine castle. David is planning to add turrets to make it look more like a real castle. The wine cellar is underground. There is a tasting room, deli, and a large deck for picnicking or just enjoying the view. "It's a great place to visit, " says David Morrisette. "We usually get 200 to 300 people on a typical weekend and 1000 per day in the fall." Most of the Chateau Morrisette wine is sold at the winery.

The Chateau Morrisette wines are made in a traditional European style. Jacketed stainless steel tanks are used for fermentation, and French and American oak are used for aging. Seyval Blanc and Vidal are blended for their white table wine. Their dessert wine, Sweet Mountain Laurel, is a blend of native American grapes.

Little did the Morrisettes know when in 1978 they decided to plant a vineyard that instead of an investment of $50,000 it would eventually come to almost 1 million. With all of the adverse climatic conditions David Morrisette is forging ahead with his expansion plans. He has engaged Steven Warner, an enology graduate of Fresno State University in California as winemaker. This will enable David to handle more of the administrative details and promotional activities.

In the next two years wine production at Chateau Morrisette will be increased to 40,000 gallons – about 18,000 cases per year. It takes a real pioneer to grow grapes in the Blue Ridge Mountains of Virginia.

David Morrisette, a bachelor, likes to cook and experiment with recipes to complement Chateau Morrisette wines.

TOURS
➡

Chateau Morrisette Winery, *P. O. Box 766, Meadows of Dan, VA 24210*
Directions: *(Near Roanoke) On Route 777, near milepost 172 on Blue Ridge Parkway, 3.5 miles north of Marby Mill.*
Visitation: *Daily, 10 a.m. to 5 p.m.*
Principals: *W. F. and D. W. (David) Morrisette*
Wines Produced: *Riesling, Chardonnay, Seyval Blanc, Cabernet Blush, Merlot, Cabernet Sauvignon, Sweet Mountain Laurel*
1987 Production: *12,000 cases*

ONION PASTA

Serve with Chardonnay

There are many different kinds of onions as to size, and color of their skins. The warmer the climate the sweeter and milder the onion. This pasta dish features just the sweet onions for a different flavor treat.

2 lbs. sweet onions, thinly sliced
3 tablespoons extra virgin olive oil
1/2 teaspoon freshly cracked pepper
1/2 cup Chardonnay

1 tablespoon freshly chopped herb, such
   as oregano or thyme
Salt to taste
10 oz. linguine, cooked al dente

In a large skillet, sauté the onions in olive oil until the onions are a rich brown, stirring the onions frequently. Season liberally with cracked pepper (more may be added if desired). Add the fresh herb and the wine. Scrape the bottom of the skillet with a wooden spoon to loosen any onion particles and simmer the onion mixture over very low heat for 10 minutes. Add salt to taste. Serve over hot pasta. *Serves: 4 as a main course or 8 as a first course*

Author's note: If fresh herbs are not available, use 1/2 teaspoon of dried Italian herbs.

BRANDY AND WINE PORK ROAST

Serve with Merlot

The addition of grape brandy adds a little tartness to the pork roast.

2 1/2 lbs. boned pork center loin
1/2 cup flour
1 tablespoon vegetable oil
2 tablespoons butter
2 tablespoons grape brandy

3 medium carrots, split and cut into
   2 inch pieces
1 1/2 cups Merlot
1/8 teaspoon nutmeg
2 bay leaves

Salt and freshly ground pepper, to taste

Coat pork loin with flour. In a roasting pan not much larger than the roast itself, melt oil and butter over medium high heat. Brown meat on all sides. Remove meat from pan. Lower heat and add carrots, spreading evenly over bottom of pan. Place meat on top of carrots and add brandy and wine. Sprinkle meat with nutmeg and salt and pepper. Bring to a boil, cover pot tightly with aluminum foil and the the pot lid. Cook on very low heat for 3 hours, occasionally turning the meat.

Slice the meat thinly and arrange on platter. Cover with sauce and serve with the carrots. *Serves: 6*

CHATEAU NATUREL "What kind of wine do you like to drink?" This is the question Arthur Hodges asked his friends, neighbors, family and acquaintances for two years before deciding to make wine. As he found out, most of the people in the southern Virginia area, south of Roanoke where the Hodges reside preferred an off-dry or slightly sweet wine.

Arthur and his wife, Ercelle, grew up around Rocky Mount, Virginia. Arthur is a carpenter who lives in the country and has operated a farm for many years. He grew tobacco until the mid 1970's when the bottom dropped out of the tobacco market. Arthur had an interest in European wineries and wine in general; and this interest led to his decision to plant grapes.

In 1978, Arthur planted 18 different varieties of grapes on 8 acres. He decided to eventually make wine himself, and also to market his grapes to home winemakers, as well as the jam and jelly trade. Since the Hodges farm and vineyard is often subject to extremely cold winter climates and summer rains, the majority of Chateau Naturel's grapes are French hybrids and labrusca, with some vinifera – Chardonnay and Cabernet Sauvignon. Arthur also planted blackberries from which he makes wine.

Every winter, in addition to hilling up the soil around the base of the vines, Arthur sows a cover crop between the rows of vines for frost protection. After mid-May, when spring frosts are over, he plows the crop under. The cover crop also helps to hold moisture in the soil.

The old tobacco drying barn was converted into the winery in 1980. Arthur did quite a bit of the work himself. "If we don't have the equipment, we make it," he says as he shows a unique stand he designed for holding bottles during labeling. Stainless steel tanks are used for fermenting and aging. Quite a number of the wines, however, also received bottle aging.

The grape juice is pressed, cold clarified and stabilized in stainless steel tanks. Yeast is added for fermentation. Arthur Hodges uses no chemical additives in his winemaking. He has designed a special paddle to punch down the cap of his fermenting red wines.

The large variety of grapes raised on the farm gives Arthur an opportunity to do a great deal of blending, producing wines which go well with food. His White Burgundy is a blend of 40% Villard Blanc, 36% Cayuga White and 24% Aurora. The Villard Blanc and Aurora are both French hybrids, while the Cayuga white is an American hybrid developed in New York State in 1972. It has a Zinfandel base. Golden Green Eye, the other Chateau Natural white wine, is 100% Villard Blanc.

Born Wild is made from American hybrids which originally developed out "in the wild." This wine consists of 75% Catawba and 25% Delaware. It is an aromatic rose which is slightly sweet.

Vintner's Choice, a medium sweet (4% residual sugar) red table wine, consists of 51% Baco Noir, 30% Marechal Foch and 19% Cascade. All three of these French hybrids blend together to produce a red wine which ages extremely well. Arthur Hodges' Blackberry Wine is handled like a grape wine. Berries are crushed and juice is fermented and aged in stainless steel.

Most of the Chateau Natural wines are sold at the winery. However, there is some local distribution. Arthur and Ercelle Hodges want only modest growth for their winery. They may increase their plantings of vinifera. Their goal, however, is to produce quality rather than quantity serving the needs of the Rocky Mount region.

TOURS →

Chateau Naturel, *R.F.D. 4, Box 1535, Rocky Mount, VA 24151, 703-483-0758*
Directions: *From Route 220 between Roanoke and Rocky Mount, take Route 919, then east on Route 812, 2 miles to the winery sign*
Visitation: *By appointment*
Principals: *Arthur C. and Ercelle B. Hodges*
Wines Produced: *White Burgundy, Golden Green Eye, Virginia Villard Blanc, Born Wild, Rose Labrusca, Vintner's Choice, red table wine, Blackberry Wine*
1987 Production: *425 cases*

FISH IN CREAM

Serve with Virginia Villard Blanc

The coast of Virginia is famous for its fish. This recipe is quick to prepare and is usually served with a green vegetable and cheese bread.

2 lb. flounder, cut in pieces, or other fish	1 tablespoon water
1/2 cup flour	1/4 cup shortening
1 teaspoon salt	2 medium onions sliced
1/4 teaspoon pepper	1/2 cup light cream
1/2 teaspoon paprika	1/2 cup sour cream
1 egg	

Blend flour, salt, pepper, and paprika. In a soup plate beat egg with 1 tablespoon water. In a large frying pan over medium high heat melt shortening. Quickly, dip fish pieces in flour, coating them well, and then into the egg mixture.

Fry in melted shortening until brown on one side, turn and place onions on top of fish. Cook until underside of fish is brown. Remove and drain if necessary. Place fish pieces flat in a casserole. Mix cream and sour cream together. Spoon mixture on top of fish. Cover casserole and bake in preheated 425 oven for 20 minutes. *Serves 4*

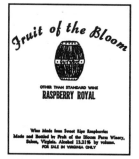

OTHER THAN STANDARD WINE
RASPBERRY ROYAL

Wine Made from Sweet Ripe Raspberries
Made and Bottled by Fruit of the Bloom Farm Winery,
Salem, Virginia. Alcohol 13.21% by volume.
FOR SALE IN VIRGINIA ONLY

FRUIT OF THE BLOOM WINERY "We are the Baskin Robbins of the Virginia wine industry," said Jim Guthrie about the 32 flavors of wine he produces. Some of the wines are made from grapes but most are fruit and blossom wines. "It doesn't have to be grape to be great," Jim says with a twinkle in his eye.

For centuries our forefathers have been making fruit and blossom wines. In the old days it was always a treat to have a glass of elderberry or dandelion wine. That was a sign of hospitality. Many home winemakers have experimented with raisin wine and fruit wines. However, this is the first commercial establishment in Virginia to offer a variety of fruit and blossom wines in modern times.

Jim Guthrie was probably inspired by his mother, who made dandelion wine for the family and friends for many years. Jim, a candy distributor, started making home fruit wines in the early 1970's. He had bought a book on winemaking which was not very good since it did not give portions in the recipes. The first batch of raisin wine was terrible and he almost threw it out. His family begged him not to make any more. After aging for a year, however, the raisin wine won praises from family and friends. The winemaking bug had bitten the Guthries and for the next several years they continued their experimentations. All types of fruit were used as well as blossoms. "When nature gives you all this stuff, why not use it," says Jim.

In 1983, Jim and Barbara Guthrie applied for and received a winery license from the Federal as well as state governments. Fruit of the Bloom qualifies as a farm winery since the wine is made from farm products and 51% of the fruit, berries and blossoms are raised on property owned or leased by the Guthries. There is one thing Jim and Barbara cannot seem to grow – dandelions. They have to go to the neighbors yards and dig them up.

After they received their winery license, Jim and Barbara purchased $200 of equipment. Then after the first sample wines were approved, they added another $700 worth of equipment. Each year, more and more varieties of wines have been approved by the the state and federal controls, until there are now 32. The most recently approved wines were 4 sparkling wines, including raspberry and strawberry.

One of the latest wines produced by the Guthries is named Rocco, in honor of Roanoke County. It is made from elderberries, bananas and raisins. The latter two were added to provide extra body and glycerin. "The glycerin contributes to the wine's "legs" which are those oily streaks when the wine is swirled in a glass," Jim explained.

The winery is an addition to the Guthrie's ranch style home, which Jim had built for his candy business. The addition is now used exclusively for the winery since that is Jim's full time occupation. There are no fermentation tanks or oak barrels one would see in a normal winery. There are instead over two hundred 5 gallon plastic containers that hold the various types of wine while fermenting. If the wines have finished fermentation, they are aging in these plastic containers and are waiting to be bottled. Jim prefers the plastic containers because they are easier to sterilize than wooden barrels.

The winemaking process for most varieties is basically the same. Most of the ingredients are raised on the Guthrie's 3.5 acre property. There are apple trees in the front of the house and roses and berries in the back. A batch of wine begins with mashed fruit, sugar, yeast and "fermentation water." Fermentation water is usually made 24 hours in advance and contains raisins, lemon juice orange juice, and water. The lemon and orange juice provide the natural acidity needed for a balanced wine. After the fruit mixture finishes fermentation, the wines are aged for a year in the 5 gallon plastic vats. During this process the fruit particles settle to the bottom and clear wine remains on top. Most of the time there are over 200 vats full of fermenting and aging wine.

Blossom wine is made the same basic way, but instead of mashing the fruit, boiling water is poured over the petals to soften them. Then yeast, sugar and the fermentation water is added.

Fruit of the Bloom makes both white and red rose petal wines, as well as rose hip, dandelion and mint wines. There is also a garlic wine. One of the most popular wines has been J-Bee's Dry Amber which is a blend of rich dark honey, tangy lemons, sweet oranges and aromatic hops. Nacta-Gold, a honey and spice wine, consists of dark, rich honey, elderflowers, spicy ginger, tart lemons, cloves and rich bee pollen. Jim Guthrie also makes some American hybrid grape wines.

Barbara is very much involved in the winery, although she has a career of her own. Barbara is a freelance writer of romance novels and confession stories. Twenty five years ago Barbara was not sure if she could write, but started writing short stories for national magazines. Finally Barbara decided to take the time to write a 43,000 word novel. She had always wanted to do this and was surprised when the first publisher she contacted bought the novel. That novel, entitled *The Bridge Between* became a reality several years ago and her latest work is *Vintage Love* which takes place in a fictitious Virginia winery.

Since Jim, ironically, cannot drink wine, Barbara has become the official taster. Her palate is very sensitive to the nuances of fruit wines. The three Guthrie daughters, who are now grown, still help at the winery. There is also a sales room for home winemaking equipment and books on the subject. Many a resident of Roanoke County has taken up winemaking as a hobby with encouragement from the Guthries .

Fruit of the Bloom is not the run-of-the-mill winery, but it has a very loyal local following. It is not capital intensive. Jim Guthrie says, "It doesn't cost a lot to make wine. All it takes is four pounds of fruit, a couple of pounds of sugar, a packet of yeast and two and a half bushels of patience."

Barbara Guthrie is inventive with her cooking and likes to experiment with Fruit of the Bloom wines, either as an ingredient or as a complement to her food.

TOURS
➡

Fruit of the Bloom Winery, *4780 Vintage Lane, Salem, Virginia 24153, 703-380-2795*
Directions: *At Glenvar, on Route 11/460, 4 miles west of I-81 exit 40,*
2 miles east of I-81 exit 39
Visitation: *Monday through Saturday 10 a.m. to 6 p.m., Sunday 1 p.m. to 5 p.m.*
Principals: *Jim and Barbara Guthrie*
Wines Produced: *Unique Blossom and Fruit Wines, Some Grape Wines*
1987 Production: *850 cases*

BAKED FISH IN GARLIC WINE

Serve with Niagara White

The fish is marinated in garlic wine and then baked with a combination of tomatoes and green pepper.

1 lb. fish, filets or slices	1 16 oz. can tomatoes, chopped, or fresh
Salt and pepper to taste	tomatoes in season
1 cup garlic wine	1 large green pepper
3 tablespoons butter, melted	

Salt and pepper fish and put in shallow dish. Pour wine over it and let stand for 1 hour. Remove fish from dish and place in baking dish containing the melted butter. Pour tomatoes over the top. If using fresh tomatoes, slice thin and place evenly over fish. Slice green pepper thin and place on top of tomatoes.

Put fish in preheated 400 degree oven and bake 15 to 18 minutes or until done. Baste frequently with the wine in which fish was soaked. *Serves: 2*

NUT POUND CAKE

Serve with Sweet Raspberry Wine

This rich pound cake may be served plain with a glass of wine and fresh fruit.

1 lb. powdered sugar	1/4 teaspoon salt
2 sticks butter, softened	1/2 teaspoon vanilla extract
1 stick margarine, softened	1/2 teaspoon lemon extract
1 lb. flour	1/2 teaspoon almond extract
2 teaspoons baking powder	2 cups chopped pecans or black walnuts
6 eggs	

In a large bowl cream together sugar, butter and margarine. Add flour and baking powder and mix well. Then add eggs one at a time, beating slowly. Add salt and flavorings, mixing well. Fold in the nuts. Pour into a greased and floured 10 inch tube pan. Bake in a preheated 350 degree oven for 1 hour or until cake tests done. *Serves: 12*

ROSE BOWER

VIRGINIA
ROSÉ OGRADY
Tom O'Grady, Winemaker

Produced & Bottled by the
Rose Bower Vineyard & Winery
Hampden-Sydney, Virginia 23943

VINTAGE 1985   SEMI-DRY   ALCOHOL 11.5% BY VOLUME

ROSE BOWER VINEYARD & WINERY "I feel more like a sculptor than a farmer as I impose my vineyards on the landscape; I feel more like a painter than a cook as I blend and shape my wines each year. Yet winemaking is an art that requires the sort of creativity which achieves a standard rather than something entirely new – your work must delight a wide variety of palates. It must be both accessible and intriguing. Each year you invent something totally new which must nevertheless give peace and comfort to people's everyday lives, while it excites. To be a poet one needs paper, pencil and a library card – plus, of course, another job to keep bread on the table. To be a winemaker, one needs not only elaborate and expensive equipment and vineyards, but the cash flow from the sale of all the wines of the previous years – plus, often, another job to keep bread on the table. Like all art forms, the sale of one's work simply buys time and the privilege to make more." These are the thoughts of Tom O'Grady, owner of Rose Bower Vineyard and Winery.

Tom O'Grady, a graduate in literature from John Hopkins University and a teacher at that institution of higher learning, decided to join the "back to the land" movement of the early 1970's. He wanted to live and work in the country and accepted a teaching position at Hampden-Sydney College. He also purchased a farm with a unique 18th century farmhouse. The house was named Rose Bower.

The name, Rose Bower, was given to the house in the late 1760's and is taken from the popular Irish song of that period, "Come Back To The Rose Bower." Rose Bower was the secret name for Ireland and the song was directed to those Irishmen who had fled the country. Many of these people went to France and became winemakers or coopers. A great deal of the oak for French wine barrels came from Ireland at that time. The Irish also immigrated to the area around Farmville, Virginia. It was one such Irish family who in the 1760's built Rose Bower. The house has an unusually high roof, the style of which goes back to the early 1600's in England.

There is much tradition in the land and the house at Rose Bower. It is this tradition that has influenced Tom O'Grady's vineyard and winery.

The vineyard began as a nursery in 1973 to determine if grapes would grow in the Hampden-Sydney area. There were records of vineyards in the region in the later 1800's. The small experiment proved successful and Tom and his wife Bronwyn, who teaches at Longwood College in Farmville, decided to plant a vineyard in 1974.

The vineyard was originally intended to supplement the O'Grady's income since Tom was and still is a part-time teacher and Poet-in-Residence at Hampden-Sydney College. He also had developed a taste for wine and thought he might pursue making wines on a small scale for their own use.

Tom O'Grady found similarities between the Burgundy plateau and the Piedmont region of Virginia and decided to plant his vineyard in the Burgundian style. The vineyard is sculptured along the rolling hills of the land. In the summer it is like viewing waves of green. There is a gazebo in the middle of the vineyard which is often used for picnics and winery functions. Two lakes were also built for temperature moderation. There is also a wind machine in the vineyard.

Tom planted the vineyard with French hybrids and vinifera. Today there are ten acres of grapes with a plan for some expansion. Although, originally Tom O'Grady only wanted to make some wine for home consumption, he soon realized that the type of wine he wanted to make required extensive knowledge and more facilities than his meager dug-out basement would provide. He proceeded to consider winemaking as a commercial venture and began an extensive reading program on wine production and winemaking techniques. The O'Gradys visited many wineries, both in this country and in Europe. They also hired consultants and began an experimentation program. "You never finish learning. It is a constant apprenticeship," says Tom O'Grady.

Since Tom is of Irish descent he wanted to create an estate-bottled winery using the name of the 18th century house, Rose Bower, as a brand name. Over the years other influences of the 18th century have crept into the winemaking at Rose Bower. There is barrel fermentation; siphoning of the wine whenever possible rather than pumping; greater lees contact; and use of natural clarifying agents such as egg whites and skimmed milk. "Ours was the first vineyard and winery in this area since the 18th century and one of the first in Virginia in the modern era," said Tom. "We felt the need to approach the whole project with an air of American pioneerism."

In 1979 the winery became a reality. Part of it is still in the dug-out basement of the house. Most of the barrel aging is done there because of the natural coolness. An additional farm building has been utilized for the winery.

Rose Bower's Chardonnay is barrel fermented – a portion in toasted French Limousin oak and another portion in American Wisconsin oak. The two batches are then blended together. The Riesling contains 15% Gewurztraminer for complexity. Once about every five years, the O'Gradys are fortunate enough to have some botrytised Riesling grapes and are able to make a Late Harvest Riesling. This was first produced in 1980 – the first of its kind to be made in the South.

Tom O'Grady was also the first to produce a nouveau style wine in the South. He has continued to do so each year. The Marechal Foch grape, a French hybrid which Tom says has Pinot Noir and Riesling in its ancestry, is used for the nouveau style wine. The grapes are left on the skins for 18 hours, then pressed lightly, placed in a stainless steel tank and inoculated with yeast. After fermentation the juice is pressed from the grapes and the wine goes into barrels where it goes through secondary or malolactic fermentation. The wine is then racked, cold stabilized, filtered and bottled. The entire process takes seven weeks and the wine is released at Halloween – the earliest release of a nouveau type wine.

The Cabernet Sauvignon as well as the Claret (a blend of 60% Chancellor and 40% Cabernet Sauvignon) are fermented on the skins for 8 to 10 days in open fermentors. The cap is punched by hand. The juice is lightly pressed to retain the fruity quality of the wine. Rose O'Grady is a blended rose wine made from barrel-aged Chelois and Vidal. The finished wine contains 3.5 % residual sugar. The Le Bateau Rouge is a sweetened blend of Cabernet Sauvignon and Chancellor. It is crushed by "foot stomping" and made in the style of a classic port.

Tom is very active in the local wine community and organizes a number of festivals at the winery each year to celebrate the new releases or the harvests. There are also a number of barrel tastings. All of these events are accompanied by music, craft exhibits, food and of course wine. He also teaches a wine appreciation class twice a year.

Throughout all of his winemaking activities, Tom has continued to contribute to his literary profession. He translated into English the works of the Nobel prize winning Czechoslavakian poet, Jaroslav Seifert. In the summer of 1987, he travelled to France to give a reading of his poetry.

Both Tom and Bronwyn O'Grady want the winery to grow modestly over the next few years. Tom says, "We continue to experiment slowly with vines and with wines, but with no desire to make a generalization until the next century dawns."

Bronwyn O'Grady enjoys cooking whether it be for Tom and their two young children or for a winetasting event. They particularly enjoy summertime meals in the gazebo that sits in the middle of the vineyard.

TOURS
➡

Rose Bower Vineyard & Winery, P.O. Box 126, Hampden-Sydney, Va. 23943, 804-223- 8209

Directions: *From Farmville take Rte. 15 south to Worsham, right on Route 665, 2 miles to second fork in road and bear left on Route 604. Continue 3 miles past Hampden Riding Stables, then right on Route 686, go 1 1/2 miles to red entrance sign on the right.*
Visitation: *April through December, Saturday and Sunday, 1 p.m. to 5 p.m.*
Principals: *Tom and Brownyn O'Grady*
Wines Produced: *Seyval Blanc, Marechal Foch, Vidal, Chardonnay, Johannisberg Riesling, Cabernet Sauvignon, Hampden Forest Claret, Rose O'Grady, Le Bateau Rouge, Le Bon Sauvage, Blushing Bride Wedding Wine*
1987 Production: *1500 cases*

BEEF FONDUE WITH SHIITAKE MUSHROOMS

Serve with Marechal Foch or Claret

This is a dish the O'Gradys traditionally prepare at the release of their Nouveau style Maréchal Foch wine. In fact the meat is cooked in the wine and the sauteed mushrooms served alongside. The real treat of the meal is the sauces that accompany the meat and mushrooms. The meal is accompanied by festive candle light and Autumn decorations, and usually is Halloween dinner. It is important for the success of this dish to use a reasonably heavy red wine as the cooking medium and to season the meat twelve hours before cooking. A tossed salad and freshly baked bread complete the meal.

3 lbs. beef ribeye or tenderloin	Fresh parsley sprigs
Salt, pepper and garlic powder	1/4 lb. butter
1 lb. fresh Shiitake mushrooms	1 750ml bottle red wine
1 teaspoon garlic powder	

To prepare beef for the fondue, cut beef into 1 inch squares and season with salt, pepper and garlic powder. Just before serving, slice mushrooms discarding the stem. Sauté mushrooms in butter with 1 teaspoon garlic powder for about 10 minutes over low heat.

To serve: Arrange raw meat on a large platter surrounded with fresh parsley. At the table, heat the wine in a fondue pot until just before boiling. Dip each piece of meat separately into the wine and cook it for a few minutes. It should be medium rare. The meat may then be dipped into various sauces, as you desire. The mushrooms are served along with the meat and may also be dipped into the sauces.

Mustard Sauce:

1/2 cup American mustard
1/4 cup English mustard
1/2 cup French mustard
2 tablespoons Worcestershire sauce
1 teaspoon garlic powder

Ketchup Sauce:

1/2 cup regular ketchup
1/4 cup barbecue sauce
2 tablespoons Worcestershire sauce
1 teaspoon garlic powder

Mix each sauce in small bowl and serve with beef fondue.

Soy Sauce:

1/2 cup soy sauce
3 tablespoons Worcestershire sauce
1 teaspoon garlic powder

Mayonnaise Sauce:

1 cup mayonnaise
3 tablespoons Worcestershire sauce
1 teaspoon garlic powder

Mix in small bowl and set aside. Serve all of these sauces with the beef fondue.
Serves: 8 to 10

COUNTRY CHEESE CAKE

Serve with Le Bon Sauvage

There are many variations to one of Virginia's favorite desserts – cheesecake. This version which is baked, also includes blue cheese for an extra flavor twist. For best results the cake should be prepared the day before it is to be served.

Crust:

2 cups graham cracker crumbs
1/3 cup plus 1 teaspoon granulated sugar
1/4 cup melted butter

1/4 teaspoon ground cloves
1/4 teaspoon nutmeg

In a bowl mix these ingredients together until the crumbs hold together. Press the mixture into a 9-inch spring-form pan. Set this aside while preparing filling.

Cheese filling:

3 8 oz. pkgs. of softened cream cheese
2 eggs, well beaten
1/3 cup sugar
1 1/2 cups sour cream

1/2 teaspoon salt
1/4 cup aged blue cheese, shredded
1 20 oz. can cherry pie filling

Blend the cream cheese, eggs, sugar, sour cream, salt and blue cheese together and pour into the prepared crust. Bake in preheated 375 degree oven for 45 to 55 minutes, until firm. Let stand for 1 hour in the oven. Remove from oven and let stand 1 more hour at room temperature. Remove the spring-form pan and place in refrigerator overnight. Before serving spread the pie filling on top of cake. *Serves: 10*

STONEWALL VINEYARDS "If you can grow peaches you can grow grapes," Betty Bryan says smiling as she points with pride to the 7 acre vineyard which comprises Stonewall Vineyards. It was not as easy as the sweep of her hand indicated. There was a great deal of work and experimentation behind this vineyard and its accompanying winery.

In 1966 Howard and Betty Bryan purchased their farm east of Lynchburg in Appomattox from Betty's father, John Alvis, Jr. Betty's parents own another farm a few miles away and reside there. At the time the Bryans purchased the property, farming was far from their minds since Howard, a captain in the Marine Corps, was headed for Vietnam. The Bryans regarded the purchase of the farm as an investment.

When the Bryans and their two daughters moved to Appomattox County in 1971 they wanted to find a use for the land. Both Betty and Howard had and still have full time occupations – Betty is an elementary school teacher and Howard is a product manager with a nuclear engineering company.

The trend toward grape planting in the early 1970's plus several business trips to Germany convinced Howard that they should plant grapes and establish a vineyard. Since there was not a great deal of information on grape growing in Virginia at the time, the Bryan's decided in 1972 to put in a test plot of grapes. They planted French hybrids and some Chardonnay. There were some losses to winter kill and the deer. In subsequent years the deer problem has been alleviated by an electric fence and two dogs.

After years of experimentation with various varieties of grapes, the Bryans decided to expand their vineyard in May of 1980. They had a big planting party for relatives and friends which resulted in the planting of 2500 vines of French hybrids and some Chardonnay. In 1984 they planted another section of the vineyard, bringing the total acreage to 7 acres. They intend to plant some Chardonnay vines this year.

The years of vineyard experimentation resulted in the selection of a trellising system which resulted in the most satisfactory crop for their growing conditions. Stonewall Vineyards uses a bilateral cordon training system on low wires. A low wire system provides good ventilation beneath the trellis during the growing season and permits quick drying of moisture on the grapes due to humidity or rain. This system is also recommended in areas where the trunk has to be covered for frost protection which is the case in many areas of Virginia.

Today Howard and Betty grow 80% of the grapes they use. They lease another 2 vineyards and purchase any additional grapes within Virginia.

During all of the years that the Bryans had been growing grapes Howard had been experimenting with winemaking in their basement. In 1983 the Bryans decided to build a winery and put their wines on the commercial market. The winery was designed by Howard with the help of Jacques Recht, an enology consultant, of Ingleside Winery. In 1987 they doubled the size of the winery, a brick colonial style building.

Howard, whose professional life has been concerned with industrial filters, is a most meticulous winemaker. He likes to ferment his wines slowly, using stainless steel tanks for the white and red fermentation. The red are fermented in open top fermentors, with the cap being punched down periodically. Reds are aged in French oak. "American oak does not impart the flavor," Howard commented. If necessary sweet reserve – natural, unfermented grape juice -- may be added to the wine, if the sugar content of the grapes is not high enough. Sugar content is a function of how ripe the grapes are when they were picked. Nature and the problems of weather often times dictate the ripeness of the grapes.

Stonewall Vineyards' Verdelet, a rare wine in the United States and of limited supply at the winery is a white wine. It comes from a delicate tiny pink grape that is crushed within two hours of picking to preserve its delicate fruit flavor. The wine is finished completely dry.

The Chambourcin, a light bodied red wine, is made like a white wine. There is no skin contact and a white wine yeast is used. After fermentation in stainless steel tanks, it is aged in French oak for 3 months.

The Cayuga White is made in a German style and finished semi-dry. The grape is an American hybrid of Skyler and Seyval Blanc. At the recent prestigious Virginia Wine Festival this wine won a bronze medal in April 1987.

Cabernet Sauvignon blended with some Chambourcin and Merlot is the blend used for Stonewall Vineyards' Claret. It is made in the dry Bordeaux style and aged for one year or more in French oak. The Claret also is an award winner.

The Bryans also make an old fashioned wine they call Pyment. It is a spiced honey wine which is a blend of Vidal Blanc juice and honey. Cloves, peppercorns and oil of Bergamot – a citrus fruit grown in the Middle East are added for spiciness. The wine is made according to a 14th century recipe from England. Pyment is particularly good served hot.

Stonewall Vineyards is a family affair. Howard Bryan is in charge of the winemaking and Betty is in charge of the vineyards. Katherine, the oldest daughter, prunes and does many of the vineyard chores, while her younger sister, Heather, often operates the tractor. Heather also cooks many of the meals for the winery and vineyard helpers. At busy times, however, some outside help is necessary.

The Bryans plan to increase their production to about 4000 cases per year, but still remain small enough to continue with their jobs. After the girls are out of school they might make the winery their full time occupation. For the present, however, they want to keep up the quality of their award winning wines.

Betty Bryan and daughter Heather often combine efforts to prepare meals, especially when there is a busy time at the winery. The following recipes can be used as the basis of an informal dinner.

TOURS
➡

Stonewall Vineyards, *Route 2, Box 109A, Concord, VA 24538, 804-993-2185*
Directions: *15 miles east of Lynchburg. From Route 460 in Concord, north 6 miles on Route 608, left on Route 721, winery on left*
Visitation: *April thorough December Tuesday through Saturday 1 p.m. to 7 p.m. Rest of year open every Saturday.*
Principals: *G. Howard and Betty A. Bryan*
Wines Produced: *Vidal Blanc, Verdelet, Cayuga White, Chardonnay, Chambourcin, Claret, Pyment*
Production: *1700 cases per year*

HOT CHICKEN SALAD

Serve with Chardonnay

This is Betty Bryan's grandmother's recipe and has been a favorite for covered dish suppers which are popular in the rural sections of Virginia. Serve this dish for lunch or a light supper with a fresh spinach salad .nixed with an herb dressing.

3 cups chopped cooked chicken	6 hard boiled eggs, chopped
3 cups chopped celery	1 (10 3/4 oz.) can cream of chicken soup
1 cup mayonnaise	4 tablespoons grated onion
1 cup chopped almonds	2 tablespoons lemon juice
1 cup bread crumbs	1 teaspoon white pepper.

Butter a large (3 quart) casserole dish. In a bowl combine all ingredients. Pour into casserole. Bake in a preheated 350 degree oven for 45 minutes. *Serves: 8*

OATMEAL BREAD

The Bryans often serve this bread with cheese at their wine tastings. The bread may also be frozen for later use. If a smaller amount of bread is desired, simply cut all ingredients in half.

4 cups oatmeal
1/2 cup oil
1 cup granola
4 tablespoons salt
1/2 cup molasses
1 cup honey

6 cups boiling water
4 pkgs. yeast
4 cups warm water
4 cups bread flour and additional flour to make dough (This recipe will take about 5 lbs. of flour in total)

In a large bowl combine oatmeal, oil, granola, salt, molasses, honey and boiling water. Mix well and set aside until lukewarm, about 2 hours.

Dissolve yeast in warm water and add to oatmeal mixture. Then add 4 cups of flour and mix well. Continue adding flour until dough can be kneaded. Turn dough onto floured board and knead well.

Place dough in a greased bowl, cover with a cloth and let rise in a warm place until double in bulk. Punch dough down and shape into loaves as desired -- 4 9x5-inch loaf pans or 8 French bread pans. Return to warm place and let rise until double in size.

Bake in preheated oven for 30 to 45 minutes, depending on size of pans used. Bake until loaves are golden brown and "tap hollow." *Makes: 8 small French loaves or 4 9x5-inch loaves*

LEMON BISQUE

Serve with Cayuga White

This recipe originated with Swannie Bryan, Betty's mother-in-law, who uses it often for her dinner parties. It is not a soup as the name implies.

1 large can condensed milk
2 cups graham cracker crumbs
1 1/2 sticks butter, melted
1/2 cup sugar

2 (3 oz.) pkgs. lemon gelatin
2 cups boiling water
2 cups cold water
1/4 cup sugar

Place the can of condensed milk in the freezer to get the milk very cold, but do not freeze it.

Mix graham cracker crumbs, melted butter and 1/2 cup sugar and put all except 1/2 cup of the mixture in the bottom of a flat 3 quart dish. Reserve 1/2 cup for topping.

Dissolve the lemon gelatin in 2 cups boiling water. Add the 2 cups cold water. Let gelatin congeal to the consistency of heavy cream. Beat gelatin until light and fluffy. Set aside.

Beat ice cold milk until stiff and gradually add 1/4 cup sugar. Fold milk into beaten gelatin. Pour over crust. Sprinkle remaining crumb mixture on top. Keep refrigerated until ready to serve. *Serves: 6 to 8*

EMIL'S Many Virginia winemakers have come from Europe in the past ten years. This is also true for Chefs de Cuisine and Urs Gabathuler is no exception. This young Swiss chef has built an excellent reputation for his cuisine.

Urs Gabathuler was born in Switzerland and decided early in life that he wanted to be a chef of some renown. As is the custom for training chefs in Europe, he became an apprentice at the Hotel Romanshorn in Romanshorn, Switzerland. There he learned cooking and food service from the chopping block to the table. After finishing his apprenticeship, Urs worked in several first class hotels in Switzerland. It was while working in one of the hotels that he met and married his wife Michelle.

In the late 1970's the Gabathuler came to the United States because they felt that with this vast land there would be better opportunities for Chefs de Cuisine than in their own country. Switzerland, which is known for its cuisine and the training of chefs, has become overcrowded with professionals in that field.

One of Urs first jobs in the United States was as assistant to the Conventions Coordinator at the Omni Hotel in Atlanta. He remained there for two years. In the early 1980's, the Gabathulers moved to Virginia where Urs took over the Rutledge Inn, a country inn and restaurant in Amherst, Virginia. While there he greatly improved the reputation of the restaurant and was featured in a full page article in the Washington Post.

Urs and Michelle had always wanted a place of their own. During the time they were in Amherst they explored the Virginia countryside whenever they could. They made several trips to Lynchburg and liked the community. The Gabathulers felt that a restaurant featuring basically Swiss and French Continental Cuisine would fill a niche in the Lynchburg restaurant market. In 1984 Urs and Michelle acquired Emil's Restaurant.

Emil's today is known as a restaurant with two faces – a rotisserie where lunch and dinner features fine Continental cuisine, and a Cafe for casual dining. There is also a carry-out bakery and deli, plus a small wine shop. A full bar and cocktail lounge complete the complex. The building is situated so that the cafe and lounge are separate from the rotisserie. One large kitchen serves both areas.

The atmosphere of the cafe with its blond furniture and green plants is light and cheery. White tablecloths, carpet, and soft lighting set the mood for more formal dining.

The menus are different in the two sections of the restaurant. The rotisserie's menu highlights many of the Swiss specialties Urs has developed over the years. The cafe, on the other hand, also has some of these specialties, but in a lighter vein. Sandwiches from the deli are included in the cafe menu.

Urs and Michelle have been very successful in their restaurant venture and have opened another restaurant across town. It is in the style of the cafe. Michelle, who spends quite a bit of her time taking care of their four small children, is also involved in the restaurant. She helps with the administrative work and enjoys meeting many of the clientele.

Emil's, *Boonsboro Shopping Center, Lynchburg, Virginia 24503, 804-384-3311*
Directions: *Take Main Street Exit off U.S. 29 Expressway, go north and west on Main Street for 5 miles to Rivermount and Boonsboro (Route 501), in Boonsboro Shopping Center*
Principals: *Urs and Michelle Gabathuler*
Meal Times: *Monday through Saturday, Lunch: 11 a.m. to 4 p.m., Dinner: 4 p.m. to 10 p.m.*

The following recipes not only use Virginia seafood, but also reflect some of Urs' international experience and cuisine.

SEAFOOD MONTICELLO

Serve with Virginia Chardonnay

Urs Gabathuler created this recipe when he was asked to participate in the Annual Governor's Seafood Contest. Urs was one of twelve chosen to participate. The objective of the contest was to show how many different ways Virginia seafood could be prepared. In this recipe seafood has been combined with fresh ripe tomatoes.

8 oz. sea scallops	2 fresh green peppers, diced
12 clams	3 cloves garlic, minced
4 Filets of fresh sole	2 cups Riesling
4 jumbo shrimp	2 dill sprigs
5 tablespoons chopped shallots	Salt, cayenne pepper, parsley, oregano,
4 oz. butter	thyme, basil and marjoram
4 medium tomatoes, diced	Rice, cooked

In a medium saucepan sauté 2 tablespoons shallots in 2 oz. butter. Add diced tomatoes, green pepper, and garlic. Cook until tomatoes start giving up their juice. Deglaze the pan with 1 cup of wine and let simmer. Reduce liquid but do not overcook. Season with salt, cayenne pepper, oregano, thyme, basil and marjoram.

In a large skillet, sauté 3 tablespoon shallots in 2 oz. butter. Add seafood and saute. Do not overcook. Deglaze pan with remaining wine and add the tomato sauce. Simmer for about 10 minutes. Arrange a ring of rice on a platter, pour seafood onto rice. Arrange clams around the rice and decorate with dill. *Serves: 4*

SCALLOPS BOMBAY

Serve with Virginia Gewurztraminer

This recipe was inspired by a trip Urs and Michelle Gabathuler took to India in 1977. Shrimp are usually the ingredients for a seafood curry. In this recipe, however, marinated scallops are used.

1 1/2 lbs. sea scallops
Salt and pepper
1/2 teaspoon Worcestershire sauce
Juice of 1 lemon
3/4 teaspoon curry powder, or
    more to taste
2/3 cup chopped shallots

3 tablespoons butter
Flour
1 cup Riesling
1/3 cup whipping cream
Cooked rice, whipped cream rosettes and
    curry powder for serving

Place scallops into a small bowl and marinate with salt pepper, Worcestershire sauce, lemon juice and curry. In a large pan sauté shallots in butter until soft. Powder scallops with flour, adding enough flour until marinade is mostly absorbed. Add scallops to the pan. Over medium heat saute for 2 minutes. Then add wine and simmer for 5 minutes, or until scallops are almost done. Remove scallops and reduce wine by half. Return scallops to pan, add cream and stir lightly.

On warm plates arrange rice in ring shape. Put scallops in the middle and pour sauce over top. Garnish with a rosette of whipped cream which has been lightly powdered with curry. *Serves: 4*

BEEF STROGANOFF A LA SWISS

Serve with Virginia Cabernet Sauvignon

This recipe is one of the Gabathuler's favorites and is very popular in Switzerland.

1 1/2 lbs. beef tenderloin, diced
Salt, pepper, paprika
Flour for dusting, plus 1 tablespoon
    for sauce
Vegetable oil
5 tablespoons butter
2/3 cup chopped shallots

1 4 oz. jar pimientos, julienned
2/3 cup pickles, shopped
2/3 cup red wine
2/3 cup beef stock or bouillon
3 tablespoons sour cream
Cooked noodles for serving

Season beef with salt, pepper and paprika. Dust meat lightly with flour. Saute meat quickly in a little oil in a hot skillet. Meat should be slightly underdone. Remove meat from pan. Add butter to skillet and melt it. Stir in shallots, pimiento, pickles and 1 tablespoon flour. Whisk in the wine and reduce slightly. Add beef stock and simmer for 2 minutes or until thickened. Add sour cream and stir thoroughly. Return meat to pan just before serving. Do not let meat simmer any more. Meat should not be completely done. Serve on warm plate with noodles. *Serves: 4*

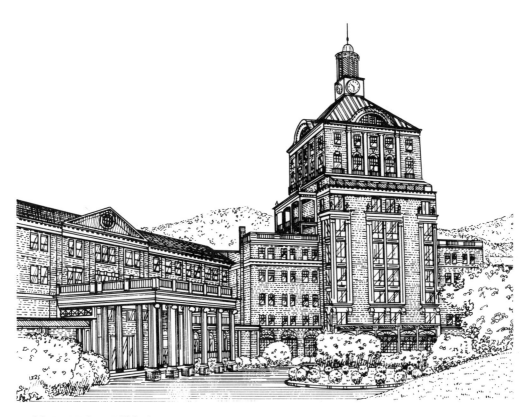

THE HOMESTEAD The five star Homestead hotel has been a favorite American resort for well over one hundred years. Its six hundred guest rooms can comfortably accommodate 1000 guests and its kitchen facilities can provide meals for these guests and the drop-in diner in their seven eating facilities. The Homestead has been host to generations of spa-goers, vacationers, golfers and skiers. It has also hosted thousands of conferences and conventions, including the Business Council. Each spring The Homestead hosts the annual Virginia Wine Weekend, which includes judging of Virginia wines and a nine course banquet in celebration of the new wines.

Bath County, the Warm Springs Valley and Hot Springs, where The Homestead is located, is steeped in early Virginia history. Settlers from Pennsylvania seeking new homesights first mapped out the Warm Springs Valley in the early 1700's. The first records of the area were in a 1750 diary of Dr. Thomas Walker, who on his way to Kentucky, discovered the warm mineral waters which had been used by the local Indians for hundreds of years.

The first inn in Hot Springs was constructed in 1766 by Thomas Bullitt who was in charge of nearby Fort Dunwiddie, a military installation visited by George Washington some ten years earlier. It seems Bullitt was so overwhelmed by unsolicited requests for room and board from people passing through the area on their way West, that he decided to construct an inn, and called it The Homestead.

In 1832, Dr. Thomas Goode acquired control of the inn and the bath-house which had been built to accommodate the vast number of people taking advantage of the 108 degree water. By 1846, Dr. Goode had opened a modern hotel which he called The Homestead, after its predecessor. After Dr. Goode's death in 1858, the property passed from owner to owner but the prestige of the health resort increased.

A group of businessmen, including M.E. Ingalls, then President of the C & O Railroad, became interested in the resort and purchased it in 1891. By 1914 the Ingalls family had gained controlling interest of the company and renamed it the Virginia Hot Springs, Inc. The Ingalls family is still the sole owner of The Homestead. The present member of the Ingalls family in charge of The Homestead is Daniel Ingalls. He recently gave up an administrative position at Apple Computer to take over the family corporation.

Upon taking over The Homestead in 1891, the investors remodeled it and then built the Spa -- now called the Bath House -- the following year. That same year a branch line of the C & O Railroad was built from Covington to Hot Springs. It operated until the 1950's when it was abandoned.

On July 2, 1901, The Homestead burned to the ground from a fire which started in the bake shop. Only the spa, casino and cottages were saved. By the spring of 1902 The Homestead was rebuilt and the next year the west wing was added. The year 1914 saw the addition of the East wing and in 1920, the tower section was completed.

In the 1930's, The Homestead became the social spa of America's elite, led by Mrs. Cornelius Vanderbilt. Many of the wealthy people of that era came to spend one to two months at The Homestead "taking the baths."

World War II changed the status of The Homestead. For several months it became the internment camp of the Japanese diplomats stationed on the East Coast, until they were traded for our diplomats in Tokyo. From that time on, The Homestead became prominent in national and international affairs.

Conventions have always been a large part of the activities at The Homestead. In 1973 the south wing was added with 197 guest rooms and a conference center able to accommodate 1100 people. There are smaller meeting rooms and numerous dining and banquet facilities available.

Besides the mineral waters and spa activities, there is an abundance of sports available at The Homestead. In 1893 the first golf course in America was built there. This original six hole course, of which the first tee is still in use, has since spawned three magnificent 18 hole golf courses. Sam Snead, a local boy, learned to play golf at The Homestead and was the professional at the Cascades course. Nationally recognized golf tournaments are frequently held at The Homestead.

In 1959, The Homestead, with the aid of the invention of the snow gun for artificial snow manufacturing, introduced Southern skiing. Although the winter weather is cold enough for snowfall, prevailing atmospheric conditions do not always comply. There are five slopes, a ski lodge with shops and a national ski patrol. For winter sports enthusiasts there is also an olympic-size ice skating rink.

One of the most important ingredients of The Homestead's successful operation is the exquisite cuisine. Albert Schnarwyler is the executive chef. He is from Lucerne, Switzerland and has been with The Homestead for 25 years. Upon coming to the United States more than thirty years ago, he worked in restaurants in New York, Las Vegas, St. Louis and several other cities. However, it was the quiet lifestyle in the mountains of Virginia that first attracted him to The Homestead. He even married a Virginia girl and they are parents of a teenage daughter.

The food style at The Homestead is Continental with regional Virginia specialties. The menus are changed daily for all of the eating establishments. Chef Schnarwyler has a staff of 80 to prepare as many as 1000 meals at each meal time.

Fresh local ingredients are utilized whenever possible. Mountain trout, a specialty of The Homestead, is raised twenty miles away. In season, produce comes from the area, as does the poultry. One of The Homestead's trucks goes to Washington twice a week for food supplies. The truck also picks up supplies from international sources, especially flown into the Washington area for The Homestead.

All breads, rolls and pastries are baked on the premises. There are 6 bakers and 8 pastry chefs. "We can make it better and cheaper than store-bought," the chef commented. All desserts are also made in-house.

Chef Schnarwyler commented on people's food habits at a resort. They are not calorie conscious and do not want to experiment with new food ideas. "People are here to relax and enjoy their meals," he says. Chef Schnarwyler observes a trend toward lighter eating, evidenced by the fact that over the last 18 months, fish consumption was up and beef was down by 50%.

An integral part of the yearly activities at The Homestead is the Virginia Wine Weekend in early April. There are seminars, wine competitions, an open tasting of Virginia wines and a nine course banquet lasting four hours. The affair starts on Friday afternoon and concludes with a Sunday champagne brunch, where the winners of the wine competition are awarded medals. The 1987 winner of the Best-of-Show was the 1984 Cabernet Sauvignon from Ingleside Plantation Winery.

The Homestead, an architectural beauty in the mountains of western Virginia, stands proudly as a symbol of excellence in resort facilities and cuisine. Located in tranquil Bath County where nary a traffic light exists, The Homestead continues to promote one of Virginia's pioneer industries – the Virginia wine industry.

DINING
➡

The Homestead, *Hot Springs, Virginia 2445, 703-839-5500*
Directions: *In center of Hot Springs*
Principals: *Virginia Hot Springs, Inc.*
Meal Times: *There are seven eating facilities at The Homestead. Their daily hours are as follows:*
Cafe Albert: *Breakfast - 9 a.m. to 11:30 a.m.   Lunch - 11:30 a.m. to 6 p.m.*
Cascades Club: *Lunch - 11:30 a.m. to 4 p.m., beverages and snacks until 6 p.m.*
Casino: *Buffet lunch in season - 12 noon to 2:30 p.m.*
Sunday Champagne Brunch - 11 a.m. to 2:30 p.m. in season
Homestead Dining Room:
Breakfast - 7:30 a.m. to 9:30 a.m., Dinner - 7 p.m. to 8:30 p.m.
The Grille: *Buffet Breakfast - 7 a.m. to 9 a.m., Sunday - 7 a.m. to 9:30 a.m.*
Lunch - 12 noon to 2 p.m.,   Dinner - 7 p.m. to 10 p.m.
Lower Cascades Club
Light lunch - 11:30 a.m. to 4 p.m.
Sam Snead's Tavern
Lunch - 11:30 a.m. to 5 p.m.,   Dinner - 5 p.m. to 9:30 p.m., limited menu 9:30 p.m. to midnight

The following recipes by Chef Schnarwyler are for popular dishes at The Homestead. The Chef's forthcoming book entitled *Dining at the Homestead will be available in 1988.*

SWISS BARLEY SOUP

Chef Schnarwyler's native country was the inspiration for this soup. Maggi is a concentrated beef flavoring base, available in most gourmet sections of the supermarket.

3 strips lean bacon	Salt
3 oz. smoked ham	Freshly ground white pepper
1 medium onion	Freshly ground nutmeg
1 small leek	1 cup half-and-half
1/4 celery stalk	1/2 teaspoon Maggi
3/4 cup barley	1 tablespoon fresh, chopped parsley
10 cups chicken broth	

In separate batches finely dice the bacon and ham. Peel and dice the onion. Thoroughly wash the leek and dice it. Dice the celery.

Sauté the bacon in a 5 quart saucepan over medium heat until most of the fat is melted, but the bacon has not browned. Add the ham, onion, leek, celery and barely, and cook stirring occasionally for 3 minutes. Pour in the chicken broth, season with salt, freshly ground pepper and freshly ground nutmeg. Bring to a boil and reduce heat to simmer. Adjust lid of pan, if necessary, to maintain a gentle simmer. Cook for 1 1/2 hours, stirring occasionally. Then add the half-and-half and simmer for 30 minutes more. Add the Maggi, adjust seasonings, if necessary. Stir in chopped parsley and serve. *Serves: 6 to 8 (Makes about 8 cups)*

BAKED MOUNTAIN TROUT WITH TARRAGON STUFFING

Chef Schnarwyler prefers the Italian flat leafed parsley for this dish. At The Homestead this dish is usually accompanied by boiled Parisienne potatoes and a tossed green salad.

2 cups fine white bread crumbs	2 tablespoons butter
2 1/2 cups half-and-half	1 tablespoon finely chopped shallots
2 teaspoons fresh chopped tarragon	1/4 cup dry white wine
2 tablespoon chopped fresh parsley	1/3 cup whipping cream
1/4 teaspoon salt	1 1/2 cups beurre blanc
1/8 teaspoon freshly ground white pepper	Fresh tarragon strips
8 fresh trout, weighing 10 to 12 oz. each	

In a mixing bowl, combine bread crumbs, half-and-half, salt, pepper, tarragon and parsley. Mix well and then refrigerate for 1 hour. The mixture must be a smooth paste. If not, add more half-and-half a few drops at a time.

Rinse trout thoroughly and using a boning knife butterfly them by splitting the trout open along the belly. Carefully remove the entrails, all bones, the head and gills. Then trim about 1/4 inch off the belly flaps. Open each trout and place skin side down on work surface. Season lightly with salt and pepper and spread 3 tablespoon of the tarragon stuffing in center of one half of the trout. Fold trout back together.

Preheat oven to 375 degrees. Butter a large baking dish with 1 tablespoon of butter. Cover the bottom of the baking dish with the shallots. Lay trout into the dish and pour wine around the trout. Dot fish with remaining butter and cover loosely with aluminum foil. Then place dish in the middle of the oven and bake for 15 to 18 minutes or until the fish springs back when lightly touched.

When fish is done, remove dish from oven and drain cooking liquids into a saucepan. Set baking dish aside in a warm place to keep fish warm. Add 1/3 cup whipping cream and reduce to 2 tablespoon over medium high heat. Blend this into the beurre blanc.

Gently peel skin from the trout, working from side to side. Reheat the fish for 2 minutes in the oven if necessary. Top with sauce and serve garnished with tarragon leaves. *Serves: 8*

Author's note: Since the shallots and wine are already incorporated in the dish; in this instance, the beurre blanc is basically a white cream sauce made with either chicken or fish stock.

BAKED VIRGINIA SMITHFIELD HAM WITH HOMESTEAD SOUTHERN FRUIT DRESSING

The six-month cured, country-style, smoked Virginia ham is the chef's preference rather than the regular cured ham of nine to twelve months. The milder cure leaves more moisture in the ham and is less salty, he emphasized. However, if a longer cured ham is preferred, it should be soaked in water overnight to draw off some of the salt.

This recipe for Virginia ham boils the ham first, and then browns it in the oven. The fruit dressing is made separately and baked in its own dish.

1 whole smoked Virginia ham, weighing 15 to 20 pounds	1 dozen or more whole cloves
1/2 to 3/4 cup light brown sugar	2 cups dry sherry

Fruit Dressing:

1 16 oz. can sliced yellow cling peaches (or halves)
1 16 oz. can sliced pears (or halves)
1 16 oz. can pineapple chunks
1 16 oz. can apricot halves
3 oz. raisins

8 oz. walnuts
5 slices white bread, toasted
6 oz. light brown sugar
1 teaspoon vanilla
8 oz. butter, melted

Wash the ham thoroughly under running cold water and then set it in a stock-pot or roaster, skin side down. Set the pan on the burner and add cold water to cover the ham by a depth of 2 to 3 inches. Bring water to a boil and then reduce heat to simmer. Cook the ham for 20 minutes per pound. Halfway through the cooking time change the water completely. Keep a check on the ham during the cooking time to see that is is covered with water at all times.

When the ham is cooked remove it from the pan and let it rest for 30 minutes. Discard the cooking water. With a paring knife trim the skin and excess fat from the ham, leaving 1/4 inch of fat. Sprinkle the top of the ham with the light brown sugar, dot with cloves and set the ham back into a roasting pan.

Preheat oven to 325 degrees.

Add the sherry to the ham in the roasting pan and set it into the oven to bake until it is well browned and glazed (about 15 to 20 minutes), basting twice during the period.

While the ham is baking, prepare the fruit dressing. Drain the peaches, pears and pineapple chunks in a colander and put them into a mixing bowl. (If using peach and pear halves, slice them.) Drain the apricots and reserve. Add raisins and walnuts to the bowl. Toast the bread, cut into 1/2 inch cubes, and add them to the fruit along with 4 oz. brown sugar and the vanilla. Blend together with a spatula, using gentle strokes so that the fruit is not crushed.

Use some of the melted butter to lightly butter an 11x7x2-inch baking dish. Pour the fruit mixture into the baking dish and arrange reserved apricots in a single layer on top. Sprinkle with remaining brown sugar, pour the melted butter evenly over the top of the casserole. Place in preheated 300 degree oven and bake for 30 minutes.

When the ham has finished baking, remove it from the oven and let it rest uncovered for 15 minutes before slicing. Slice and serve with warm fruit dressing. *Serves: 14 to 18*

HOTEL ROANOKE - REGENCY ROOM In 1882 the railroad came to the small community called Big Lick, one of the gateways to the West. Big Lick was named for the nearby salt deposits. Bison used to congregate at this salt lick on their way west through the Cumberland Gap. Indians also congregated there because they hunted the Bison.

It was a big event for this small valley community surrounded by farms when the headquarters of the Shenandoah Valley Railroad was moved from Hagerstown, Maryland to Big Lick. The reason for the move was the merger of the Shenandoah line with the Norfolk and Western. The citizens were so pleased with this newly formed corporation that they wanted to rename the town in honor of the president of the Norfolk and Western Railroad. He declined the honor and the name Roanoke, an Indian word for money, was chosen instead.

With the coming of the railroad headquarters, Roanoke experienced a boom in population – from 3,000 to 5,000. There were seven blacksmiths, nine hotels, twelve saloons, ten doctors and six lawyers. The town also had six churches, 258 private dwellings and a jail.

Norfolk and Western officials decided that if Roanoke was to be an important railroad town it needed a good hotel. The company invested $45,000 for this project. They purchased a 10-acre tract on a knoll overlooking the city. Construction started in the late spring of 1882 and the hotel had its grand opening on December 25, 1882.

The original building which still exists today was constructed of wood in the Tudor style. There was also a great deal of wood used on the inside – hand-rubbed English walnut, carved oak moldings, and cherry and ash panelling. The furniture, much of which is still in use today, was of Honduras mahogany. The inside was and still is elegant. The hotel had the first elevators in the town of Roanoke.

There were other firsts at the hotel, too. The first bathrooms in which one could bathe in a porcelain or zinc tub; the first sewer line in town ran from the hotel; the first electric bell and voice tubes used for communications among various departments and guests. Each guest room had a bell that was connected to a central station in the office. One ring was for the bellboy, two for the chamber maid, three for ice water and four for hot water.

On July 1, 1898 the third floor of the hotel caught fire causing it to close temporarily. Six months later it was reopened with a large party. The fire was to be the forerunner of change. During the next 83 years the hotel was rebuilt and renovated more than a half a dozen times. As the comforts and necessities of life progressed, they were added to the hotel. In 1937, the Hotel Roanoke was one of the first in the world to be air conditioned.

Over a hundred years old, the Hotel Roanoke, proudly standing on top of a knoll, is still one of the most elegant establishments in the state of Virginia.

Douglas Davis is the Executive Chef of the Regency Room of the Hotel Roanoke. A native of Florida, he attended the University of Florida and trained at a number of first class hotels along Florida's coast. Davis did an internship with Chef Peter Meyer, former chef of Movenpick Hotels in Zurich, Switzerland. He also worked for the Marriott Corporation in Houston and Dallas before becoming Executive Chef of the four star Regency Room.

The cuisine of the Regency Room is Continental interspersed with traditional Southern favorites.

DINING
➡

Hotel Roanoke, *19 N. Jefferson Street, Roanoke, Virginia 24026, 703-343-6992*
Directions: *From I-81, take I-581, 2 blocks north of downtown exit*
Principals: *Hotel Roanoke/ Virginia Holding Corporation*
Meal Times: *Regency Room Breakfast: 7 a.m. to 11 a.m. Monday through Saturday Lunch: 11:30 to 2:30 Monday through Saturday Dinner: 5 p.m. to 10 p.m. Sunday through Thursday Weekends: Sunday Breakfast: 7 a.m. to 10:30 a.m. Sunday Brunch: 11:30 to 3 p.m. Friday and Saturday Dinner: 5 p.m. to 11 p.m. Music for dancing is provided each night at dinner*
Reservations recommended

BREAST OF CHICKEN WITH LOBSTER

This unusual dish of chicken and lobster is enhanced with sour cream sauce.

2-8 oz. chicken breasts	1 pint chicken stock
1 teaspoon thyme	3 tablespoons white roux
1 teaspoon marjoram	1/3 cup white wine
1 teaspoon basil	1 tablespoon lemon juice
1 lobster tail, split	1/3 cup sour cream
Paprika	Salt and pepper to taste
1 tablespoon olive oil	

Bone and skin chicken breasts and flatten with a mallet. Mix together the thyme, marjoram and basil, and sprinkle on the inside of the meat. Roll half of the lobster tail in each breast and place them seam side down on a buttered sheetpan or cookie sheet. Sprinkle the chicken breasts with paprika and drizzle on a small amount of oil.

Bake in a preheated 350 degree oven for 30 minutes or until the meat is firm when squeezed. Meanwhile make the sauce: In a saucepan boil chicken stock with roux until slightly thickened, but very satiny and smooth. Add the white wine and lemon juice and simmer 10 minutes. Take pan off the heat and add sour cream until melted. Add salt and pepper to taste. Ladle sauce on plate and place chicken on sauce. *Serves: 2*

Author's note: To make white roux take equal amounts of butter and flour. Cook over low heat, stirring constantly, until blended and smooth. Do not brown.

VEAL CHAMPIGNON

These sautéed veal medallions on a satin sauce of wild mushrooms are served with angel hair pasta. The dried wild mushrooms are available in gourmet shops.

1/4 cup Cepes	1/2 quart demi-glace
1/4 cup chanterelles	Salt and pepper, to taste
1/4 cup dried morels	16 veal medallions, about 3 oz. each
1 small shallot chopped	1 tablespoon onion juice
1 tablespoon olive oil	1 teaspoon salt
1/2 cup brandy	1 teaspoon white pepper
1 quart whipping cream	2 cups flour
	Olive oil

Place mushrooms in a bowl and add enough hot water to just cover them. Soak the mushrooms for 20 minutes or until soft. Strain them and chop fine. Also strain the liquid through a coffee filter to eliminate any sand. Reserve for sauce.

Sauce: In a large saucepan sauté the shallots in 1 tablespoon olive oil until wilted, (do not brown.) Add mushrooms and cook until dry. Flame with brandy. Add the cream and soaking liquid. Reduce by half, about 15 minutes. Simmer and add demi-glace. Add salt and pepper to taste and more brandy, if desired. Simmer the sauce and whirl in the butter gradualy until absorbed.

Veal: Dredge the veal in the onion juice and salt and pepper both sides. Dip the veal in flour and shake off the excess. Sauté each piece in olive oil for about 30 seconds. This may have to be done in several batches. Drain and arrange on plates over the sauce. Garnish with angel hair pasta. *Serves: 8*

Author's note: Demi-glace as its name implies is a half glaze. It is made by roasting veal bones with vegetables and spices. These bones are then put into a kettle with water and cooked for several hours. The water is reduced to a small quantity.

LA MAISON In this day and age of high priced real estate it is almost unthinkable to have a huge plantation home of the 18th century type remain standing in all its splendor almost adjacent to a busy metropolitan airport. That, however, is the case in Roanoke. Today this colonial home of yesteryear houses La Maison, a well-known restaurant in the Roanoke Valley.

This valuable land was once owned by King George II of England. In 1748 he granted almost 1300 acres to a man named Mark Evans, who in turned willed the property to his son Peter.

In the 18th century the Roanoke Valley appealed to the early settlers because of its wide open spaces. This made farming much easier. In the midst of this valley stood the Evans property which became known in the local area as "The Barrens."

In the subsequent years the land was sold and subdivided several times. In 1923 the Coulter family purchased the remaining 84 acres of the original land grant. Elbert Murray Coulter, who was the founder of the National Business College in Roanoke, was excited about the prospect of having a home in the country.

The Georgian style of American architecture was decided upon for the facade and interior of the house. However, it is larger than most homes of that type existing in the surrounding area in the 18th century. In the 1920's and 1930's there was a revival of Georgian architecture and the Coulter home was designed in that style.

The outside of the home is brick with lovely large white columns. The downstairs living, dining and entertainment rooms are all large – reminiscent of another era. The gardens were lovely and still are present today.

Today the "mansion" houses the La Maison du Gourmet restaurant operated by Pete Karageorge. Pete who was born in Greece comes from a long line of restaurateurs and has wide experience in the culinary field.

Continental cuisine is served at La Maison, with an emphasis on fresh seafood.

DINING
➡

La Maison, *5732 Airport Road, Roanoke, VA 24012, 703-366-2444*
Directions: *Southeast of airport and I-581*
Meal Times: *The restaurant is open each day from 11 a.m. to 11 p.m., serving lunch and dinner. Dinner service starts at 5 p.m.*
Principals: *Pete Karageorge*

SCOTCH SHRIMP AND SCALLOPS

Flaming, using brandy or whiskey adds another flavor dimension to the dish. In this case the Scotch combines well with seafood. The La Maison basic cream sauce may also be used for other dishes.

1 1/2 tablespoons butter
4 medium shrimp. peeled and deveined
3 oz. scallops
1 tablespoon currants
1 1/2 oz. Scotch whiskey

1/3 cup snow peas, blanched
2 oz. reduced cream, (recipe follows)
1 cup cooked rice
1 teaspoon roasted pinenuts
Chopped parsley

In a medium size skillet heat butter over medium high heat. Add shrimp and scallops and saute quickly until almost done.

Add currants and Scotch whiskey and flame it. (If this is your first experience with a flambe, use a long match and keep your head back.) When the flame begins to die down add the snow peas and the reduced cream. Heat thoroughly.

Place a small mound of rice on each plate. Pour seafood mixture around the rice. Sprinkle with pinenuts and parsley. Garnish with lemon.

Reduced cream sauce: Makes: 1 pint

2 cups heavy cream
2 oz. cream cheese
1 oz. butter

1/4 teaspoon cracked pepper
1/4 teaspoon salt

In a small saucepan combine all ingredients, stirring constantly with a wire whisk. Bring, slowly to a boil, reduce heat and cook until cream begins to thicken and cream cheese is melted. *Serves: 2 as an appetizer*

SEAFOOD AND LINGUINE IN LEMON CREAM

If crabmeat is not available, small pieces of lobster may be substituted.

3 tablespoons butter
6 shrimp, peeled and deveined
4 oz. scallops
4 oz. crab meat
1/2 teaspoon dill weed
Salt and pepper to taste

2 tablespoons chopped scallions
Juice of 1 lemon
4 tablespoons chopped tomato
4 oz. reduced cream
6 to 8 oz. linguine, cooked al dente

In a large skillet heat butter over medium high heat. Add shrimp and scallops; season with dill and salt and pepper. Sauté until barely cooked 2 to 3 minutes. Add crabmeat, scallions and lemon juice. Cook until lemon juice is reduced by one half. Add tomato and reduced cream. Heat through, but do not boil. Pour sauce over pasta. Toss and serve. *Serves: 2*

MARTHA WASHINGTON INN In the 17th century, Abingdon became known as one of the gateways to the West – the gateway to that far away new frontier known as Tennessee. Today the charming town of Abingdon with 5,000 residents is regarded as the cultural and crafts center of Southwest Virginia. It could also be called the western gateway to the Virginia wine country.

Although Abingdon has several houses dating to pre-Revolutionary days and a few other dating to pre-Civil War days, none is more famous than the complex of buildings known as the Martha Washington Inn. The center building was constructed as a private residence in 1832 for Colonel Francis Preston and his wife Sarah Buchanan Preston.

The Colonel was born in Botetourt County, Virginia in 1765, graduated from William and Mary College, studied law and served in Congress from 1793 to 1797. Upon his retirement he settled at the Saltworks which today is known as Saltville. He then served as a member of the Virginia General Assembly representing the then distant area of southwest Virginia.

During the War of 1812 Francis Preston was commissioned a colonel. He gathered together a regiment and marched his men across the state to Norfolk. After the war he came back to Saltville and later moved to Abingdon where he had built his home.

Mrs. Preston, too, had a distinguished lineage. She was the daughter of General William Campbell, the leader of the Battle of King's Mountain – a battle fought near Abingdon. Mrs. Preston was also a niece of Patrick Henry.

The original home was a three story brick face building with a curving staircase that connects the three floors. The staircase and the large entrance hall are still in existence today. The public rooms of the mansion are parlors to welcome guests just as they did 150 years ago. The Preston family records indicate that there were several smaller buildings on the property, a kitchen, smokehouse, storage buildings, privies and "negro houses."

In 1858 the Holston Conference of the United Methodist Church purchased the Preston home from Thomas Preston for $21,000, an exorbitant sum at the time. The property became Martha Washington College in 1860.

Despite the interruption of the Civil War, the college survived. At times it was used as a hospital for both sides and at others it provided a refugee for Confederate soldiers who were being hunted by the Yankees. It is said that even to this day on a moonlit night strains of violin music can be heard on the third floor. They are the melody a young girl played to ease the pain of her wounded Confederate lover whom she had hidden in the attic when the Yankees took over the hospital. The soldier died, but the girl kept playing the melody in his memory.

The college buildings were also used as a training barracks for the Washington (County) Mounted rifles. The most famous member of the regiment was a young attorney, John S. Mosby, from the nearby town of Bristol. Part of Abingdon was burned during the Civil War, but Martha Washington College remained standing.

In 1919 Martha Washington College was consolidated with nearby Emory and Henry College in Emory, Virginia. The nearby college assumed the indebtedness of Martha Washington College and continued to operate it. In 1923, the school became a junior college but continued to decline.

This decline in enrollment and The Depression forced the college to close its doors in 1932. The building stood idle until 1935 when George S. Barnhill became the first of several owners to operate the property as an inn. The Martha Washington Inn and the Barter Theater became a major summer attraction drawing people to the Virginia Highlands from all over the East. During its various ownerships, the Martha Washington Inn received many renovations, including new kitchen facilities.

The passage in 1975 of the "liquor by the drink" referendum added another renovation to the Inn. Recognizing the financial potential of this opportunity, the hotel management converted the basement storage area, a part of the main house, into a lounge. Business was good and the facility has been enlarged twice since 1975.

In April of 1984, the United Coal Company purchased the property from a local partnership. The Inn was closed for one year during which time extensive renovations took place at the cost of $11 million. Today, the Martha Washington Inn -- this grand old lady -- stands as not only a symbol of southwest Virginia history and hospitality, but is a beautiful inn which combines fine antiques with modern facilities.

As in days past, the dining room of the Inn known as First Lady's Table again serves many traditional Southern specialties, along with an international menu. Rich Pense, Chris Feldlester and Lisa Mullin are in charge of supervising the preparation of the vast menu at the Martha Washington Inn. The wine list is extensive and features Virginia wines. The house wine is Montdomaine's Chardonnay and Cabernet Sauvignon.

DINING

Martha Washington Inn, *150 West Main Street, Abingdon, Virginia 24210,*
703-628-3161
Directions: *One half mile north of Exit 8 of I-81, in the center of town, near the Barter Theater*
Principals: *United Coal Company*
Meal Times: *First Lady's Table (Main Dining Room) Breakfast 7 a.m. to 10 a.m. Lunch 11:30 a.m. to 2 p.m. Dinner 5 p.m. to 10 p.m. (Monday through Saturday) Dinner 5 p.m. to 9 p.m. (Sunday)*
Special:
Friday Night Seafood Buffet: 5 p.m. to 10 p.m. Sunday Breakfast Buffet: 7 a.m. to 10 a.m. Sunday Brunch: 11:30 a.m. to 2 p.m.

MARTHA'S SPOON BREAD

Cornmeal and all versions of corn bread have been a staple at dining tables of Virginia since colonial days. Spoon bread is softer than corn bread and is usually served with a spoon, and eaten with a fork. The term may have come from the Indian word for porridge "suppawn." One of the traditions of the Martha Washington Inn has always been spoon bread, particularly at their holiday buffets.

1 1/2 cups yellow cornmeal	4 tablespoons butter
1 teaspoon sugar	5 eggs
1 1/3 teaspoon salt	2 cups milk
1 1/2 cups boiling water	1 teaspoon baking powder

In a large bowl, mix cornmeal, salt and sugar. Pour boiling water over the mixture and stir to blend. Add melted butter and mix. Beat the eggs and add the milk to them. Combine the two mixtures and add baking powder. Pour into a greased deep-sided baking pan (souffle dish) and bake for 30 to 40 minutes in a preheated 350 degree oven. *Serves: 10*

MARTHA'S APPLE DUMPLINGS WITH BOURBON SAUCE

This is a fancy version of a baked apple which has always been a favorite dessert in Virginia. The easy to prepare sauce is an added taste treat.

4 6-inch square pieces of puff pastry	1/2 teaspoon nutmeg
4 medium size tart apples, peeled cored	1 tablespoon cinnamon
and cut into quarters	1/8 teaspoon salt
1 cup sugar	1 1/2 tablespoons butter

Place the 4 quarters of each apple in the center of each piece of puff pastry. Mix together the sugar, nutmeg, cinnamon and salt. Sprinkle some of the mixture over each apple, dividing the mixture evenly. Put butter flakes on top. Fold opposite corners of puff pastry together, pinching the edges so that they will stick together. Bake for 20 minutes in a preheated 325 degree oven. Serve with Bourbon Vanilla Sauce.

Bourbon Vanilla Sauce:

1 small package instant vanilla pudding mix	1 oz. bourbon
2 1/2 cups cold milk	

Place pudding mix in a medium size bowl add milk and beat until the consistency of a thick sauce. Since more milk than the prescribed directions is added, the mixture will be thinner than pudding. Fold in the bourbon. *Serves: 4*

Shenandoah Valley Region

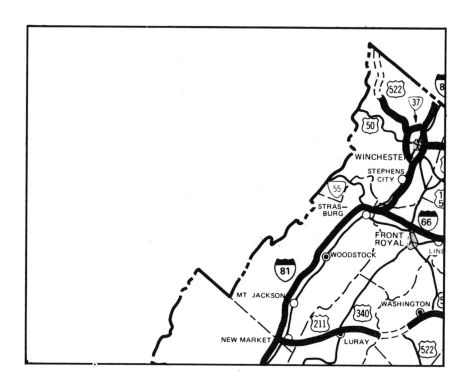

WINERIES:

Deer Meadow Vineyard

Guilford Ridge Vineyard

Shenandoah Vineyards

Tri-Mountain Winery & Vineyards

Winchester Winery

RESTAURANTS:

Edinburg Mill Restaurant

L'Auberge Provincial

My Father's Mustache

Parkhurst Inn Restaurant

Wayside Inn

DEER MEADOW VINEYARD If he were wearing a red suit and if it were the right time of year, Charlie Sarle could easily play the role of Old St. Nick. A man in his fifties, with a jolly smile and a twinkle in his eye, he proudly points to the winery he has literally built by himself. The project has been a long one, but he is finally getting his license, will be crushing his first grapes in the fall of 1987 and making his first wines.

A native Virginian, Charles Sarle was born and raised in Alexandria, Virginia and lived in Fairfax County and Indianapolis, Indiana most of his life. For 30 years of his professional life Charlie was a mechanical engineer specializing in engines and turbo machinery. His last position was with Wallace and Murry.

In 1959 Charlie Sarle and his wife Jennifer purchased a 120 acre farm southwest of Winchester. There was a 200 year old smoke house on the property which they refurbished into a weekend retreat and vacation home. The Sarles planted Christmas trees on the property and for many years operated a Christmas tree farm. It was one of the first such farms in the area. The sale of the trees paid for the farm and maintained the taxes for many years.

When Charlie took early retirement in 1982, many of the pine trees had been cut and sold. For years, the Sarles had planned to grow grapes and build a winery when they eventually retired to the farm. It was a natural progression for them. They had an interest in wine and Charlie had been a home winemaker for 10 years.

In 1983, Charlie and Jennifer planted 5 acres of grape vines, 4 1/2 of French hybrids and 1/2 an acre of Chardonnay.

The vineyard has both good soil, mostly shale which is quite high in acid, and good drainage. There are good growing conditions with a pond on the property and the nearby mountains for frost protection. At 1100 feet elevation the property is in a thermal band which also aids in protection from extreme winter cold and frost.

In order to make his vinifera vines more durable and resistant to extreme weather conditions, Charlie Sarle planted root stock first. This root stock grew for two years to establish a firm and large trunk. After two years of growth he grafted the varietals onto the root stock. With this method the vine has a large trunk up to the first wire and the graft is higher above the ground to avoid winter damage.

To protect his vineyard from the deer, Charlie Sarle left a natural fence of 10 to 20 foot pine trees midway through the vineyard. The deer are accustomed to travelling through this path between the vines. The perimeter of the vineyard is protected by an electric fence.

Shortly after he planted the vineyard, Charlie decided to start building the winery. Although he used his bulldozer, it took him one month to dig the foundation. He kept hitting rock. Charlie felled trees on the property, took them to a saw mill and had boards cut for the construction of the winery. It has taken one year of hard labor to build the two story building which houses the winery.

There is a large tasting room on the second floor with a view of the vineyards and Massanutten Mountain in the background. The natives of the area fondly refer to the mountain as a "mass of nuttin'." Charlie loves the view from the winery. At night he can stand on his property and not see a single electric light in any direction. It almost makes him feel like an early Virginia pioneer.

Charlie Sarle has two stainless steel and two large concrete fermenting tanks which are glass lined and will be used to settle the white wines and to ferment the reds. He has designed and built his own hydraulic grape press. The winery also contains other inventions which are not the normal equipment in a standard winery, but are unique to Charlie and his design of the winery.

The Sarles will also use some different winemaking techniques when they do their first commercial crush this fall (1987). They will ferment the red French hybrids – Marechal Foch and Chambourcin – with 30% whole berry clusters for complexity. They may do some blending of the two for an early released young red wine. They also plan to use an American hybrid to make a "Golden Blush" wine.

If the meticulous handcrafting of his winery is any preview to his winemaking, Charlie Sarle, a true 20th century pioneer in the Virginia wine industry, will certainly find a niche in the market.

Jennifer Sarle likes to cook, but with the busy life of vineyard work and helping Charlie when necessary, she prefers dishes which are simple to prepare.

TOURS ➡

Deer Meadow Vineyard, *Mountain Falls Route, Winchester, VA 22601, 703-877-1919*
Directions: *From Winchester take Route 50 west for 3 miles to Route 608, turn left (south) and continue for 6.5 miles to Route 629 on left, go 1 1/2 miles to private lane on right. Follow lane through the woods turning left at the "Y."*
Visitation: *April through November, Friday, Saturday and Sunday, 1 p.m. to 4 p.m., Other times by appointment*
Principals: *Charles and Jennifer Sarle*
Wines Produced: *Seyval Blanc, Chardonnay, Marechal Foch, Chambourcin, Golden Blush*
1987 Production: *1000 cases*

GYPSY STEAK

Serve with Marêchal Foch

This recipe has been a Sarle family favorite for 15 years. It is wonderfully versatile since it can be prepared with beef, pork or chicken. The Sarles especially like it with venison.

2 lbs. beef tenderloin
Salt, pepper, garlic powder, paprika
   and rosemary
1 tablespoon butter
4 slices bacon, diced

1 large onion, sliced
1 large green pepper, cut into strips
4 oz. fresh mushrooms, sliced
   (or canned if fresh are not available)
1/2 cup dry red wine

Slice tenderloin into serving size medallions, about 1 inch thick and sprinkle with salt, pepper, garlic powder, paprika and rosemary.

In heavy skillet over high heat, quickly sauté meat in butter to desired doneness, adding more butter if necessary. Remove meat from skillet and reduce heat to medium. Add diced bacon to skillet and cook until crisp. Drain all but approximately 1 tablespoon of fat from skillet. Add sliced onion, green pepper and mushrooms to the bacon and stir-fry until the vegetables are tender crisp. Pour wine over vegetables and continue cooking, stirring, for another minute. Return meat to the skillet long enough to heat, but not to cook. Serve with rice. *Serves: 4*

HAM LOAF

Serve with Chambourcin

This is a wonderful way to use leftover ham. The loaf is also good the next day for sandwiches.

1 lb. ham, ground	2 tablespoons minced onions
1/2 lb. ground pork	2 eggs
1/2 lb. ground veal	2 cups corn flakes, crushed
1 teaspoon salt	1 cup milk
1 tablespoon chopped green pepper	

In a large bowl combine all ingredients. Pack into a loaf pan and bake in preheated 350 degree oven for 1 hour. *Serves: 6*

CARROT CAKE

Serve with Golden Blush

Jennifer Sarle says it takes just a few minutes to mix this cake. In the summer she serves it with some fresh fruit.

1 cup flour	1 teaspoon cinnamon
1 cup sugar	3/4 cup vegetable oil
1 cup grated carrots	2 eggs
1 teaspoon baking soda	1 2 cup chopped nuts
1 teaspoon baking powder	Dash of salt

In a large mixing bowl combine all ingredients until well blended. Pour into a greased and floured 8x8-inch baking pan. Bake in preheated 350 degree oven for 35 to 40 minutes or until center of cake springs back when lightly touched or a toothpick inserted in center comes our clean. Allow cake to cool, then frost with cream cheese icing.

Icing:

3 oz. cream cheese, softened at room temperature	1/2 lb. powdered sugar
	2 tablespoons butter, melted

Combine icing ingredients and beat until smooth. Spread on cake. *Serves: 8.*
Author's note: For a little more tang add 1 tablespoon lemon juice to the icing.

GUILFORD RIDGE VINEYARD In 1971, with 4 acres of vineyard, Guilford Ridge was the second largest vineyard in the state of Virginia. Since there was a trend toward grape growing in the state at that time, John Gerba decided to plant 2400 vines on his farm south of Luray. The farm of 85 acres in Page Valley, a part of the Shenandoah Valley, includes an apple orchard in red and golden delicious apple trees.

John Gerba, who has a Masters Degree in City and Rural Planning from Yale, works full time for the EPA and lives in Washington during the week. Weekends, however, are spent at the farm where Harland Baker is in charge of the vineyards and is also the cellar master. Harland who handles the day-to-day activities, has a Masters Degree in Drama from Brandeis University.

The vines originally planted on the Guilford Ridge farm were all French hybrids. In recent years, minor amounts of Chardonnay, Riesling, Cabernet Sauvignon and Pinot Noir have been added.

The early years were spent in experimentation with trellising systems, vineyard management and experimental winemaking. The farm proved to have good climatic conditions for grape growing. It is at 1100 feet elevation and its microclimate is influenced by nearby Shenandoah River and Massanutten and Blue Ridge Mountains. There was some background of grape growing and winemaking in the region before Prohibition and also in the early 1940's.

Until the early 1980's the bulk of the grape crop was sold mainly to home winemakers. At about that time John Gerba found he was losing the home winemakers market for his grapes as the number of vineyards and wineries in Virginia began to multiply.

In 1983, after much winemaking experimentation, John and Harland decided to establish their own winery.They are advocates of blending wines to achieve complexity and will only produce a varietal wine if one of the grape varieties is exceptional. John's grapes are primarily French hybrids, but he and Harland use some of his vinifera to increase the complexity of the blends. Each grape variety is fermented and aged in separate lots and then blended to make the final wine. Blending may occur before, during or at the end of the aging period. All reds are aged in oak as are some of the white. John and Harland handcraft their wines with meticulous attention to detail.

Page Valley Red is composed of seven varietals, although primarily Chambourcin, Baco Noir, and Cabernet Sauvignon. There are two versions of this wine on the market – one is rather assertively oaked and the other is lighter and fruitier in character. The Page Valley White, to be released this year, consists of five varietals including Seyval Blanc and some Rayon d'Or, a fruity tasting grape which has enjoyed popularity in France as a blending wine.

In 1983 John and Harland did make a varietal wine. It was one of the exceptional vintages they had been looking for. The grapes – Chelois, a red French hybrid -- were picked with botrytis. Botrytis is a mold which gathers on the skin of the grape as a result of a period of warm weather and high humidity. This "noble rot," as it is known in Europe, does not rot the skin of the grapes but causes the juice to become concentrated and high in sugar – much like a raisin. The result is a natural sweet, highly flavorful dessert wine. These conditions have not occurred since 1983.

The Guilford Ridge Vineyard and Winery is also involved in several theatrical and musical productions that take place in the vineyard each summer and fall. Harland Baker is in charge of all of the productions. He also writes some of the scripts. Usually these theatrical events are all day affairs including picnics and winetasting. Harland also conducts an annual "Wine Taste Tour of the Blue Ridge."

John Gerba will add more vinifera acreage to his vineyard, but plans to keep the winery small. They love to experiment with all phases of winemaking, particularly with blending techniques.

Harland, who is in charge of the entertainment and food at the winery enjoys cooking – from the simplest of dishes to his luscious cheesecake.

TOURS
➡

Guilford Ridge Vineyard, *Route 2, Box 117, Luray, VA 22835, 703-778-3853*
Directions: *From light at Main and Broad Streets in Luray, go 4 miles south on Route 340, west 1 mile on Route 632 to vineyard entrance*
Visitation: *By appointment and scheduled events*
Principals: *John Gerba, Harland Baker*
Wines Produced: *Page Valley Red, Page Valley White, Late Harvest Chelois*
1987 Production: *200 cases*

STEAKS WITH GLAZE BRIAN

Serve with Page Valley Red

This is a nice change from the usual broiled steak. The glaze adds to the flavor of the meat.

2 steaks, beef, ham or venison	2 tablespoon Dijon mustard
1/2 cup red wine	1 tablespoon grape jelly
2 tablespoons soy sauce	1 tablespoon vinegar

Pan fry steaks to your desired doneness. If there is excess fat in the pan, pour it off. Deglaze pan with 1/2 cup wine. Boil the liquid down to 3 tablespoons. Add soy sauce, mustard, jelly and vinegar. Heat and spoon over the steaks. Serve immediately. *Serves: 2*

Author's note: For additional flavor use of one the fruit vinegars.

QUICK STROGANOFF

Serve with Page Valley Red

Beef stroganoff is usually considered to be a Russian dish. However, the sauce is thought to have either a German or Dutch influence. The cuisines of both countries influenced Russian cooking during the 16th and 17th centuries. Today there are many variations of beef stroganoff and it is served in most western countries.

1 lb. beef tenderloin, 1 inch thick	1/2 cup sherry
2 tablespoon butter	3/4 cup heavy cream
1/2 cup chopped green onion	1 to 2 tablespoons sour cream
3 to 4 large mushrooms, sliced	2 tablespoons chopped parsley
Salt and pepper, to taste	

Trim any fat from tenderloin before frying. In a heavy skillet pan fry steak to medium rare. (A little butter may be added to grease the skillet or some of the trimmed fat may be used for greasing the skillet.) Remove meat and set aside.

Pour off any excess fat from the skillet. Add 2 tablespoons of butter and sauté onions and mushrooms for about 10 minutes over low heat.

In the meantime, slice steak into thin slices and salt and pepper to taste. Remove mushrooms and onions from pan. Add sherry and boil down to about 3 tablespoons. Reduce heat and add heavy cream. Also add the juice from the sliced steak. Boil gently until sauce is thick. Add sliced steak, onions, and mushrooms. Heat through. Remove from heat and stir in sour cream and parsley. Stir to blend. Serve with noodles, spaetzle, or rice. *Serves: 2*

GUILFORD RIDGE CHEESECAKE

Serve with Late Harvest Chelois

There are many versions of cheesecake. This no bake, easy to make method is enhanced with the addition of grape jam and jelly.

1 1/4 cup graham crumbs	3/4 cup sour cream
2 tablespoons sugar	3 teaspoons vanilla extract
5 tablespoons butter, melted	Grated rind of 1 lemon
1 1/2 cups sugar	Grated rind of 1/2 orange
1/4 teaspoon cream of tartar	3 tablespoons Grand Marnier
1/3 plus 2 1/2 tablespoons water	1 cup grape jam
5 egg whites	1 cup grape jelly
24 oz. cream cheese, at room temperature	

Combine crumbs, sugar and butter in a small bowl. Blend well. Spray a 10 inch spring-form pan with PAM. Press crumbs firmly over bottom of spring-form pan. Chill.

Combine sugar, water, and cream of tartar in a saucepan. Bring to a boil and boil rapidly until syrup registers 236 degrees on a candy thermometer (or until it spins a 2 inch thread when dropped from a spoon).

Meanwhile, in a large bowl, beat egg whites until stiff peaks form. Then pour hot syrup in a thin stream over egg whites while beating constantly. Continue beating until very stiff peaks form.

Beat cream cheese and sour cream until light and fluffy. (Egg whites do not have to be cleaned from beaters.) Beat in vanilla. Add lemon rind, orange rind and Grand Marnier. Beat to blend. Blend in 1/4 of the egg white mixture, then fold in rest of the egg white mixture, blending until no streaks remain.

Heat jam in small saucepan over low heat until thin enough to spoon.

Spoon about 1/4 of cheese mixture into prepared pan; drizzle lukewarm grape jam over cheese mixture. Continue to layer cheese mixture and jam. Top layer should be cheese. Freeze overnight or until firm.

Two or three hours before serving, heat grape jelly in small saucepan over low heat until it can be poured. Pour over frozen cheesecake. Return cheesecake to freezer for an hour.

Remove from freezer. Remove sides of spring-form pan. Keep cheesecake in a cool place for one or two hours before serving. *Serves: 12 to 16*

VIRGINIA
SHENANDOAH VINEYARDS

Virginia
SEYVAL BLANC
White Table Wine
Very Dry
1985

Seyval Blanc, made from 100% Seyval Blanc grapes,
is a soft yet substantial wine, lightly aged in Oak.

PRODUCED AND BOTTLED BY
SHENANDOAH VINEYARDS, EDINBURG, VIRGINIA, USA

SHENANDOAH VINEYARDS Thomas Wolfe once said, "You Can't Go Home Again." He probably meant you cannot return to the same situations – but you can go home again and start a brand new career. Emma Randel did that after being away almost 35 years.

Emma French Randel grew up on a farm in Shenandoah County. Little did she realize when she went away to college that nearly forty years later she would be back not as a farmer, but as one of the leading vintners in the state of Virginia.

After graduating from high school she studied at Duke University where she received a degree in economics. After college, Emma's career path took her to Washington, D. C. where she met her husband James Randel, a petroleum engineer. The Randels moved to New Jersey where James became a vice president of Public Service Electric and Gas Co.

During the time the Randels were living in New Jersey, James became interested in wine and started making wine at home. He purchased the juice from vineyards in Pennsylvania.

In 1974, after James had a heart attack, the Randels decided to spend some time on the family property in the Shenandoah Valley. The quiet setting was a perfect place for recuperation. The farm, which dates back to pre-Civil War days, also contains the old log cabin where Emma's mother was born. It has been completely restored. In past times the farm was primarily an apple orchard and later became pasture for cattle.

It was while the Randels were visiting in Virginia in 1974 that the idea of growing grapes first occurred to them. They read about Virginia's new wine industry and assessed their land for climate, soil and location with the possible idea of growing grapes. James and Emma thought that it would be a good retirement occupation, since at some point they planned to move to Virginia permanently.

Two years later after extensive studies were completed, the Randels planted 5,000 vines on 7 1/2 acres of rolling hillside. Mostly French hybrids were planted because they had proved to be heartier. In subsequent years, there were more plantings of French hybrids as well as vinifera to bring the the total vineyard acreage up to 45 acres. Today there are 12 varieties of grapes being grown at Shenandoah vineyards.

James and Emma Randel had every intention of producing wine when they planted the first vineyard. They figured that three years after planting there would be enough mature grapes to make wine. However, grape growers heard of their intended winery and started bringing them grapes to use.

Plans for the winery had to be speeded up. The old barn, which dates back to the Civil War, was converted into the winery and a full-time winemaker was hired. The winery opened to the public in 1979.

James Randel unfortunately passed away in June of 1985. Emma decided to continue with the winery project and make it her full time career. She moved to Virginia and took charge of the operations. Along with Jack Foster, Shenandoah's winemaker, they are producing award winning wines. At the April 1987 Virginia Wine Festival Competition Shenandoah Vineyards won three medals – two bronze and a silver. The silver was awarded to the 1983 Cabernet Sauvignon.

Jack Foster makes 10 to 11 different wines each crush – vinifera as well as French hybrids.The hybrids are produced as varietals while also being used for blends. He ferments the Shenandoah Chardonnay in stainless steel and then ages it in French oak. The Cabernet Sauvignon, the driest wine made at Shenandoah is aged in French oak for about two years. The Chambourcin and the Shenandoah Ruby receive American oak aging. Both of these wines are fermented off-dry. The Shenandoah Ruby is aged in oak for a short time and is released 9 months after crush. The result is a light and fruity red wine. Jack feels that each oak adds a different flavor component to the wine. "Oak to wine is like adding spice to food," he commented.

The winery is open all year around and about 75% of the wine is sold at the winery. Each fall on the Sunday after Labor Day Emma hosts a Harvest Festival for about 2500 visitors who enjoy visiting the vineyards, winery and picnic facilities.

Emma Randel intends for Shenandoah Vineyards to grow. The winery has the capacity to handle 70,000 gallons (28,000 cases per year). With the addition of new vineyards in Virginia, the supply of grapes will be increasing and expansion of winemaking will be feasible.

Emma often gives food and wine seminars and enjoys creating recipes for the Shenandoah wines.

TOURS ➡

Shenandoah Vineyards, *Route 2, Box 323, Edinburg, VA 22824, 703-984-8699*
Directions: *Take Edinburg exit (Exit 71) off I-81, west on Route 675, heading away from Edinburg, right at first road, Route 686, 1.5 miles to wine barrel sign on left*
Visitation: *Daily 10 a.m. to 6 p.m., closed Easter, Thanksgiving, Christmas and New Year's Day*
Principals: *Emma F. Randel*
Wines Produced: *Seyval Blanc, Vidal Blanc, Johannisberg Riesling, Chardonnay, Chambourcin, Cabernet Sauvignon, Shenandoah Blanc, Shenandoah Rose, Shenandoah Blushing Belle, Shenandoah Ruby*
1987 Production: *4000 cases*

CHAMBOURCIN BEEF

Serve with Chambourcin

The use of both chuck steak and top rump in this recipe adds to the complexity of flavors, as does the slow cooking. The black olives give this dish a Mediterranean flavor.

1 lb. chuck steak	1 750 ml bottle Chambourcin wine
1 1/4 to 1 3/4 lb. lean boneless shoulder	1 small sprig rosemary
of beef or top of rump	1 bay leaf
2 tablespoons flour	2 cloves garlic, peeled and left whole
3 tablespoons olive oil	1/2 lb. button mushrooms
1 lb. medium onions, quartered	2 tablespoons tomato paste
Salt and pepper to taste	4 oz. small black olives

Heat oven to 325 degrees. Cut meat into pieces weighing about 3 oz. each.

Dust meat with flour. In a large heavy frying pan or dutchoven, heat 2 tablespoons of oil. Add meat pieces and brown lightly. Add onions and brown them. Season with salt and pepper to taste and add wine. Reduce heat slightly and simmer gently to reduce liquid to about half. Add enough water to cover ingredients sparingly. Stir well and add the herbs and garlic.

Transfer ingredients to a casserole; cover top with a sheet of foil and press down tightly with the cover of pan to seal in moisture. (Also cover with lid of casserole of dutchoven, if used.) Place in oven and cook for 3 hours without lifting the lid.

Wipe mushrooms, trim stalk, and cut into quarters. Sauté mushrooms in remaining tablespoon of oil. After 3 hours remove casserole from oven and strain contents through a colander into a large bowl. Return the meat to the casserole. Add the mushrooms.

Remove the fat from the sauce. Stir in tomato paste and olives. Pour over meat. Cover and return to oven for 30 minutes. Serve with sauteed potatoes. *Serves: 6*

CURRIED CHICKEN

Serve with Seyval Blanc

Curry powder is probably the world's earliest spice blend. Curries which are native to India were made without red peppers before the early 16th century. When Columbus discovered America and found the red pepper family that spice was brought to India by the Portuguese and added to the curry blend. Early colonial Virginia cookbooks contained recipes for curries. The spice was brought to Virginia by the seafaring traders who had travelled to the Far East.

2 teaspoons margarine	1/4 cup raisins
1 large onion, chopped	1 medium tomato, chopped
1 clove garlic finely chopped	2 tablespoons curry powder
4 chicken breasts (pieces), skinned, boned, cut in 1/2 inch strips	Salt and pepper to taste
	1/2 cup Seyval Blanc
1/2 cup scallions, chopped	1/3 cup heavy cream

Heat margarine over medium heat in large skillet. Add onions and garlic and cook until onions are wilted. Remove onions and garlic from skillet, leaving margarine and juices. Add chicken and cook until the chicken loses its raw look, about 2 minutes. Add onions, garlic, scallions, raisins, tomato and curry powder. Salt and pepper to taste. Stir to distribute curry evenly. Cook over medium heat for 2 minutes.

Add wine and simmer until wine is reduced by about half. Add heavy cream and cook over medium heat until curry is hot, about another minute. Serve hot over rice.
Serves: 4

TRI-MOUNTAIN WINERY AND VINEYARDS

Tri-Mountain Winery is located in the cradle of 3 mountain ranges – Blue Ridge, Massanutten, and Great North. Although the winery gained a reputation in Virginia in the early 1980's, no wine has been produced since 1984.

Joe Geraci, of Italian decent, started planting grapes for commercial use on his 112 acre farm in 1973. He had always had grapes on the farm for his own winemaking. It was an Italian family tradition to make wine.

Originally from New York, Joe Geraci moved to Alexandria at an early age. In the 1950's he purchased a farm near Middletown and not long afterwards built Dinosaur Land, a major tourist attraction a short distance from Middletown. Tourists from far and near remember the large Dinosaur standing in front of his theme park.

In the mid 1970's when he saw other Virginians successfully growing grapes and making wine, Joe decided to join the state's newest agricultural venture. He planted 15 acres of grapes with 18 varieties, including some table grapes. In subsequent years he added more vineyard acreage bringing the total to 24 acres of vinifera and French hybrids. A 4 acre lake was constructed on the farm to moderate the temperature for the vineyards and reduce frost damage.

In 1980 Joe retired from his business operation to devote full time to the farm and a possible winery. Unable to sell all of the grapes he was growing, Joe Geraci decided in 1981 to build a winery and produce wine. He had been making his own table wine for many years. An old barn was converted into the winery and a winemaker was hired. In the early 1980's the Tri-Mountain wines received several medals in state wine festivals.

A variety of French hybrids and vinifera wines were produced and some are still being sold at the winery.

Joe Geraci passed away in January of 1987 at the age of 76. He had been in failing health for some time. as a result, the winery had not been productive for two years and had been up for sale. Upon his death his four daughters inherited the winery. Joann Leight, who lives closest to the winery, is now the president. As of this writing, the sisters intend to hire a winemaker and do a crush in the fall of 1987. Their intention is to keep the winery in operation themselves or find a suitable buyer who will. That is what Joe Geraci would have wanted.

Joann Leight and her sister Gloria Talbott both enjoy developing recipes using wine. Since both are employed full time – Joann is a teacher and Gloria is a secretary in the Fairfax County School system -- they like recipes which are easy to prepare and utilize precooked ingredients.

TOURS
➡

Tri-Mountain Winery & Vineyards, P. O. Box 391, Middletown, VA 22645, 703-869-3571
Directions: From I-81, exit 77 (Middletown), east on Rte. 627 for 1 mile, winery on left
Visitation: March thru December, Wednesday thru Sunday, 11:30 a.m. to 4:30 p.m.
Principals: Family Corporation - the daughters of Joe Geraci
Wines Produced: Riesling, DeChaunac, Seyval-Aligote, Vidal, Chardonnay, Cabernet Sauvignon, Massanutten White, Blue Ridge Rose, Tri Mountain Red, Great North Mountain Concord
1987 Production: 2000 cases

JOANN'S BEEF STEW

Serve with Massanutten White

Joann Leight prefers to cook this stew in a crock pot, while she is at work. The slow cooking enhances the flavors of the ingredients. The same recipe may be cooked in an ovenproof casserole in a 300 degree oven for 2 1/2 to 3 hours.

2 lbs. beef stew meat, cut into cubes	3 stalks celery, diced
1/2 cup flour	2 onions, chopped
2 tablespoons oil	3 carrots, sliced
2 quarts water	1 pkg. frozen peas
2 envelopes Beef Stew Seasoning mix	Salt and pepper to taste
6 potatoes, diced	1/2 cup white wine

Dust meat with flour. Heat oil in large skillet over medium high heat, add meat and lightly brown on all sides. Set aside. Put water into crock pot. Add seasoning mix and stir well to blend. Then add vegetables, meat, salt and pepper. Cook on low for 8 hours. About 30 minutes before serving, add wine. Thicken gravy if needed. *Serves: 5 to 6*

Author's note: If cooking in the oven, use only 3 to 4 cups of water. The shorter cooking time will prevent the ingredients from absorbing some of the liquid.

GLORIA'S SPAGHETTI SAUCE

Serve with Tri-Mountain Red

The addition of coffee to the sauce gives it an extra taste dimension and smooths out the acid of the tomatoes.

1 lb. ground turkey	1/8 cup prepared coffee
1 tablespoon olive oil	1/4 teaspoon oregano
1 32 oz. jar of prepared spaghetti sauce	1 teaspoon mixed Italian spices
with mushrooms	2 tablespoons dried parsley
1 16 oz. can tomato sauce	2 tablespoons dried onion
1/2 cup red wine	1 bay leaf, crumbled
1/2 cup water	

In a medium size dutchoven heat olive oil over medium high heat. Add turkey and brown well, breaking up the meat pieces. Then add spaghetti sauce, tomato sauce, and the rest of the ingredients. Bring to a boil, cover and simmer for 1 hour. Remove the lid and continue simmering the sauce for another 30 minutes. Serve over cooked spaghetti. *Serves 8 to 10*

WINCHESTER WINERY Their operation may not be anywhere near as large as their counterpart in California, but Steve and Scott Smith have often been referred to teasingly as the "Ernest and Julio" of the Winchester area.

Their winery, Winchester Winery, is located on the family farm, Cedar Lane Farm. Scott and Steve's father, Ray, purchased the property in 1974 after he retired from an engineering career. The elder Smith had owned a mechanical engineering firm in Rockville, Maryland for many years. He wanted to do something different and thought farming and living in the country would provide a change of pace for the family. It was also a good investment.

The farm was, and still is, primarily in hay. In 1976, however, the Smiths planted 5 acres of grapes on their 93 acre property. Thirteen different varieties were planted to determine which ones would be suited for their soil and climate. The vineyard was also considered an experimental one for home winemaking.

Even with winter temperature fluctuations, the climate proved to be favorable for grape growing. The same was true for the soil composition. The Smiths had planted mainly French hybrids, since at the time they did not know how vinifera would fair on their property. In recent years they, like so many other vineyards in Virginia were hit by the droughts of 1985 and 1986.

There are now 18 acres in grapes, including Riesling and Chardonnay. Scott, who manages the vineyards, plans to expand to 35 acres and plant some Cabernet Sauvignon.

For years, the Smiths sold their grapes to other wineries. Since their grapes were being used for some medal winning wines, it seemed only natural that they would want their own winery. In 1983 and 1984 they designed and built a two level winery building. The bottom level houses all of the winemaking equipment and the upper one is for office space and a tasting room. There is a large glass window in the tasting room which gives the visitor an excellent view of the winery operations.

Steve Smith attended Penn State and also took some enology courses at the local community college in Middletown. He is the winemaker. His grape growing experiences have been a great asset to him. "Wine is made in the vineyard. If you have good grapes, you're on the road to good wine," is Steve's philosophy.

Steve makes Winchester Winery's Chambourcin, a French hybrid, in the Bordeaux style.The red wine is aged for 1 year in small American oak casks after fermentation. Eventually he plans to produce a Cabernet Sauvignon.

Winchester Vidal Blanc, which is fruity and made in a German medium dry style, was a medal winner in 1986. The Johannisberg Riesling is medium dry, also made in a German style, while the Seyval Blanc is completely dry and produced in the style of a Chablis. Steve Smith makes the Winchester White from the Rayon d'Or French hybrid – a fruity, spicy grape which ripens well in cooler regions. The Rayon d'Or is all grown on the property. Each year the Riesling is completely sold out before the next vintage is ready for release.

Raymond Smith is still involved in the farm and winery operation, although only on a part time basis. Steve and Scott are in charge of the vineyard and the winery. Kim, Steve's wife, is also active in the winery. She helps with hospitality and administration.

Kim enjoys cooking and likes to experiment with entrees to complement Winchester Winery's wines.

TOURS
➡

Winchester Winery, *Box 188, Mt. Falls Rt., Winchester, VA , 703-877-1275*
Directions: *From intersection of Routes 50 and 37, just west of Winchester, go 2.8 miles to Route 608, left on Route 608 and 4.2 miles to the winery of the left*
Visitation: *Wednesday through Friday: 12 noon to 6 p.m.*
Saturday and Sunday : 10 a.m. to 6 p.m., Other times by appointment
Principals: *Stephen R. Smith, Scott Smith and Raymond F. Smith*
Wines Produced:*Seyval Blanc, Vidal Blanc, Johannisberg Riesling, Chambourcin, Winchester White, Winchester Rose*
1987 Production: *2200 cases*

CHINESE CHICKEN WITH SNOW PEAS

Serve with Vidal Blanc

This quick to prepare and colorful meal, works best when all ingredients are ready to cook and the sauce is made. Serve with rice.

1 lb. chicken breasts, skinned and boned	1 1/2 cups snow peas
1 tablespoon cornstarch	1 medium carrot
1 tablespoon soy sauce	1/4 cup diced green onion

Sauce:

1 tablespoon sugar	2 tablespoons soy sauce
1 tablespoon vinegar	2 tablespoons white wine
1/2 tablespoon cornstarch	2 to 3 tablespoons vegetable or peanut oil

Cut chicken into bite size pieces and marinate in the combination of cornstarch and soy sauce for 30 minutes. Remove tips and strings from snow peas. Shave carrot into pieces about 2 inches long. Combine sauce ingredients.

In a large skillet, electric frying pan or wok heat oil to almost sizzling. Stir fry chicken until just done, 2 to 3 minutes. Remove chicken. Drain oil from pan leaving 1 tablespoon. Quickly stir fry snowpeas, carrots and onions. When barely tender, return chicken to pan and mix with vegetables. Add sauce ingredients to pan, quickly stir to blend and thicken juices. Serve with rice. *Serves: 4*

Author's note: If more sauce is desired add 1/2 cup chicken broth to sauce mixture. Cook about 1 minute longer to heat sauce. *Serves:4*

CHAMBOURCIN SPAGHETTI SAUCE

Serve with Chambourcin

Everyone has a favorite spaghetti sauce. This one, however, has an added dimension with the use of pepperoni and chili powder.

1 to 2 tablespoons olive oil	2 oz. pepperoni
1 medium onion, diced	1 tablespoon oregano
1 medium green pepper, diced	1 teaspoon chili powder
2 cloves garlic, diced fine	2 bay leaves
1 lb. lean ground beef	1 tablespoon sugar
1 16 oz. can tomatoes with liquid	Dash of basil
1 15 oz. can tomato sauce	Dash of thyme
1 6 oz. can tomato paste	Pepper to taste
1 cup water	1/4 cup dry red wine

Put just enough oil in bottom of dutchoven to barely cover bottom – like a very thin film. (This prevents meat and onions from sticking to pan.) Heat pan over medium high heat and add onions, green pepper, garlic and ground beef. Cook meat until it loses the pink color. Drain off the fat. Add all remaining ingredients, except the wine. Simmer sauce for 45 minutes. Add wine and continue to simmer for 15 more minutes. Serve with pasta. *Serves: 4*

EDINBURG MILL RESTAURANT The Edinburg Mill and the family who owned it have been a part of the history of the Shenandoah Valley since before the Revolutionary War. For 139 years the mill helped feed the people of the Valley and today, in modern times, it is still providing meals not only to the Shenandoah Valley residents, but to the many tourists who stop for a meal, be it a snack or a full course dinner.

On a fateful day in 1758, a party of savage Indians led by chief Bill Black attacked the settlement at Hawksbill near what is today Luray, Virginia. The Indians killed all residents except two young boys who were taken captive. One of those youths was George Bishop who possessed great hunting skills and gained the confidence of the chief. Since young Bishop stood proud and tall he soon became known to the Indians as "Grandstaff." Bishop was held captive for three years and finally escaped during a hunting expedition in 1761.

As a reminder of his capture by the Indians the young man chose to retain the name Grandstaff. He settled near Luray and later moved to Narrow Passage Creek near Edinburg. His grandson and namesake George was born in 1787 and grew up in Edinburg. He became active in the community and served in the War of 1812. Major Grandstaff returned to Edinburg, married and raised nine children.

In 1848 one of Major Grandstaff's sons built the Edinburg Grist Mill. When the Civil War erupted several years later the Shenandoah Valley became a battleground. The Valley was known as the grainery of the Confederacy. At that time the Edinburg Mill supplied much of the grain for the Southern forces. As the Union General Sheridan blazed his way through the South, the mill at Edinburg was one of his primary targets. Storming into town Sheridan and his men twice set fire to the mill. The fire was put out by Nellie Koontz and her sister Melvina Grandstaff, the grandaughters of the Major. The young ladies pleaded with the General to spare the mill. The girls charmed the General Sheridan, and Nellie received permission to ride his horse. She seized the opportunity and quickly sewed a Confederate flag to her petticoat, before riding off to warn the population of the Valley of Sheridan's impending attack.

The mill survived the Civil War and continued to supply grain to the Edinburg area. The charred remains of Sheridan's attack can still be seen at the front of the mill. Grain continued to be processed at the Edinburg Mill until it closed in 1978. In 1979, however, the building with some modifications reopened as a charming country restaurant. The original interior has been preserved and serves as part of the dining room. The current owners, Mr. and Mrs. Paul Bynum of Alexandria, Virginia also own the historic Seaport Inn Restaurant in that city.

The Edinburg Mill serves country style food, specializing in fresh seafood and home baked breads of all types.

DINING
➡

Edinburg Mill Restaurant, *Edinburg, VA 22824, 703-984-8555*
Directions: *Take Edinburg exit off I-81, go east to first major intersection, go 1/2 block south. Mill on the right.*
Meal Times:*Daily:Breakfast - 7 a.m. to 11 a.m. Lunch - 11 a.m. to 2 p.m. (Buffet style) Dinner - 5 p.m. to 10 p.m.*
Principals: *Mr. and Mrs. Paul Bynum*

SHRIMP AND SCALLOPS IN CREAMY WINE SAUCE

Serve with Seyval Blanc

Serve this mild seafood dish with saffron rice and a green vegetable.

3/4 cup julienned carrots	Flour
3/4 cup julienned celery	1/2 cup white wine
2 to 4 tablespoons butter	2 tablespoons lemon juice
2 cloves garlic, cut in large pieces	Salt and pepper to taste
16 shrimp	1 cup heavy cream
16 scallops	

In a medium size saucepan, blanch carrots and celery, until al dente. Drain and keep warm.

In large skillet over medium high heat melt butter and sauté garlic for two to three minutes. Do not let garlic brown. Remove garlic and lower heat. Add more butter if necessary. Dredge shrimp and scallops in flour. Sauté over medium heat until just done 3 to 4 minutes. Remove seafood from skillet and keep warm. Add wine to the skillet and stir to deglaze. Add lemon juice, salt and pepper, and mix well. Stir in cream and continue to cook until sauce thickens or coats the back of a spoon. Return seafood and vegetables to the sauce. Heat and serve. *Serves 4*

L'AUBERGE PROVENCALE L'Auberge Provençale is a French restaurant and country inn that occupies a restored farmhouse on a knoll near the town of White Post. The town and area is famous because over two hundred years ago a surveyor named George Washington was surveying the area and drove a white post into the ground as one of his markings. Many generations have passed, but the post remains. L'Auberge Provençale is in northern Virginia, about a 20 minute drive from Middleburg. The establishment is owned by Alain and Celeste Borel, a young couple who have been in the restaurant business for ten years.

Alain, a fourth generation chef from Avignon, France, owned two very successful French restaurant in Key West Florida until 1980. A friend told him about the beauty of the countryside in northern Virginia. He and his bride of a few months decided to take a look with the possibility of establishing a country inn and restaurant. Alain, who had just turned 30, was tired of the hustle of the resort community and had always wanted a country inn and restaurant. The Borels thought they would probably settle in Colorado, but wanted to peruse the East Coast first. The Borels liked the area around Winchester, since it is close to Washington and the immediate surroundings have tourist attractions. There are vineyards, horse shows, antiques and the Skyline Drive nearby. Besides, the area reminded him of the Loire Valley in his family homeland.

Alain and Celeste spent four months looking for suitable property. In the meantime they sold their businesses in Florida. The Borels found just the right place in northern Virginia – an old farmhouse named Mount Airy with 8 acres of rolling farmland. The house was built around 1750 and is partially constructed of stone.

In order to open an inn and restaurant in this agricultural community, the Borels had to obtain a special zoning ordinance from the County Board of Supervisors. At first there was a great deal of objection, since the farmers felt that a restaurant would hurt their agricultural environment. The first hearing turned down the request, but a second one several months later granted the zoning variance.

The Borels immediately began renovating the old farmhouse in March of 1981. They were extremely careful to retain the original architectural aspects of the house. Designs for moldings were copied from a neighboring house built in 1790. The decor on the inside is early American with a touch of country French. There are six rooms available for overnight guests two in the main house and 4 in a cottage, which has been constructed in the back. The cottage is the same 18th century architecture as the main house.

The decor of the three dining rooms is like a fresh spring day; tablecloths either match the draperies or the wall coverings. There are fresh flowers from the garden on the table. The china and silver are exquisite. The service is unhurried. "When you drive an hour and a half to a country inn for dinner, you want to relax and spend several hours dining," says Celeste.

Alain Borel grew up in the kitchen. His great-grandmother, his grandfather and his father were all chefs in the Provence Region of France. They owned a multi-starred restaurant in the south of France. Since he was thirteen, Alain has worked in restaurants in Canada and the United States. He has been a restaurant owner for over 10 years, having operated his father's restaurant in Key West, Florida at the age of 22. Not too long afterwards he became the owner of the restaurant called Chez Emile. Several years later he opened another restaurant in Key West called The Deck.

Celeste, who is from Philadelphia and attended the University of Pennsylvania, had also been in restaurant and bakery operations for a number of years. Today she is in charge of the wine list at the inn, oversees the bookkeeping, acts as hostess for the dining room and manages a staff of five. In addition she takes care of the their one year old son.

Most of the vegetables and all of the herbs used at L'Auberge Provençale are grown in the garden in back of the house. The Borels employ a full-time gardener. Alain has contracted with nearby farmers to obtain quail, partridge and lamb. Fresh seafood and other meats are brought in from Washington on a regular basis.

Alain Borel's style of cuisine is French with a touch of Provence. "We wanted to keep some of the style of Provence in our cuisine which would probably be termed 'cuisine moderne.' We emphasize fresh herbs, spices, and vegetables since they are associated with the cooking of the south of France. However, our sauces are not the heavy cassoulet type, but are more smooth and elegant," explains Alain.

The menu changes at least once a month or seasonally, and there are always daily specials according to the availability of ingredients. Everything, including the desserts, are made on the premises. It is no wonder that with the extensive menu selections Alain works a 12 to 14 hour day. The long hours have been part of his training and he loves it. That is what has made L'Auberge Provençale a success.

There is an extensive wine list – European, Californian and a nice selection from northern Virginia vineyards. The Borels are happy in the country. They have brought a little bit of France to this beautiful section of northern Virginia.

DINING
➡

L'Auberge Provençale, *P.O. Box 119, White Post, VA 22663, 703-837-1375*
Directions: *On US 50 going west, turn left onto US Route 340 (at three way traffic light), go south for 1 mile, sign on right*
Principals: *Alain and Celeste Borel*
Meal Times:*Dinner only 6 p.m. to 10:30 p.m. Sunday dinner 4 p.m. to 9 p.m. Closed Thursday*
Reservations: *advised*

LES MOULES AVEC HERBES DE PROVENCE

Serve with Semillon

A gathering of mussels with fresh herbs of Provence. "Provence is the garden of France where traditionally herbs are used with a heavy hand in most recipes. This dish brings out the fragrance and taste of all that is best in this region." The dish of mussels is usually garnished with sprigs of fresh herbs. Alain Borel created this recipe while vacationing at the seaside.

5 lbs. fresh mussels, washed and debearded	1/2 teaspoon chopped garlic
1 1/2 cups dry vermouth	1/4 teaspoon white pepper
1 teaspoon chopped shallots	Juice of 1/2 lemon

Fresh herbs as follows – dried herbs are not recommended

1 teaspoon tarragon	1/2 teaspoon thyme
1 teaspoon oregano	1/2 teaspoon parsley
1 tablespoon mint	1/2 teaspoon fennel, chopped

In a large stainless steel pot put all of the ingredients except the mussels. Bring to a boil. Add the mussels and cover the pot. When mussels open up, remove the pot immediately from the burner. **Do not overcook** the mussels, since they will become rubbery. Arrange mussels in serving dishes, discarding any unopened ones. Ladle some of the broth and herbs on top of each serving. Serve immediately. *Serves: 4*

Author's note: If you do not have fresh herbs in your garden check the gourmet food shops. Many now carry small packages of fresh herbs in their produce section.

LES CREVETTES A LA RUSSE

Serve with Chardonnay

The shrimp are sautéed with fresh ginger and scallions, and de-glazed with vodka. This dish is normally served with a fresh herb or spinach pasta.

24 large shrimp, shelled and deveined
Flour
3 tablespoons olive oil
1/2 stick butter
1 lemon
1 large clove of shallot, chopped
2 large cloves garlic, chopped

1 teaspoon grated fresh ginger
3 oz. vodka
1 tablespoon chopped parsley
1/2 bunch julienned scallions
1 cup shrimp stock made with
Salt and pepper to taste
    the shells or fish stock *

Dust the shrimp with flour. In a large skillet over high heat, heat the olive oil. Add shrimp, and saute on one side for 3 minutes. Reduce heat to medium, turn shrimp and cook for 2 more minutes. Add 1 tablespoon butter and the juice of 1/2 lemon. Cook for 2 more minutes. Remove shrimp and drain on rack or paper towel.

Wipe skillet, and add remaining butter, shallots, garlic and ginger. Cook until the ingredients sweat (do not brown), about 20 seconds. Add 2 oz. of vodka over high heat and flame it. When flame subsides add shrimp stock, remaining lemon juice and vodka. Reduce to 1/2 volume. Add parsley and scallions and cook until scallions are al dente. Salt and pepper to taste. *Serves: 4*

Arrange shrimp on plates. Pour sauce over shrimp and serve.

Author's note: * A simple way to make the shrimp stock for this recipe is to shell the shrimps several hours before cooking time. Place shells, 1 cut-up carrot, 1 chopped onion, 1 cut-up stalk of celery and some fresh herbs such as thyme, marjoram, parsley in a medium sauce pan. Cover with a mixture of half water and half dry white wine. Bring to a boil and simmer for 30 to 45 minutes, to extract the flavors from the shells, vegetables and herbs. Skim off any foam which collects on the top during cooking.

LES RIS DE VEAU AU PORTO ET AUX CAPRES

Serve with Chambourcin

Sweetbreads with vintage port and capers

Alain Borel created this dish which has an exotic flavor while he was chef-owner of Chez Emile in Key West, Florida. Many chefs have tried to duplicate this recipe, but have not quite succeeded. The sweetbread dish is one of Alain's well publicized specialties.

2 lbs. sweetbreads
2 quarts water
1 teaspoon salt
1/2 teaspoon pepper
6 bay leaves
3 oz. red wine vinegar
Flour for dusting sweetbread
Salt and pepper to taste

1 stick sweet butter, unsalted
Juice of 1/2 lemon
2 medium shallots, chopped
8 oz. port – Vintage, if possible, or Ruby
8 oz. concentrated veal stock
2 teaspoons baby capers
Salt and pepper to taste

Rinse sweetbreads in a bowl with slowly running water for 4 hours. Clean and devein.

In a large saucepan boil the 2 quarts of water with the 1 teaspoon of salt, 1/2 teaspoon pepper, bay leaves and red wine vinegar. Plunge sweetbreads into water, reduce heat and simmer for 20 minutes. Drain and let the sweetbreads cool. Using a heavy skillet as a weight, place the skillet on top of the sweetbreads for 1/2 hour until they are slightly flattened. Dust the sweetbreads with flour and salt and pepper.

Sauté sweetbreads in a heavy skillet in 1/2 stick of butter until slightly golden. Squeeze lemon juice over meat. Remove from heat. Remove sweetbreads from pan and place on a warm plate.

With a clean towel wipe the residue from the skillet and add 2 tablespoons butter and shallots and cook until soft. Add port and veal stock, and reduce by 1/2 over medium heat. Add capers, season with salt and pepper. Remove pan from heat and add the remaining butter. Arrange sweetbreads on plate. Pour sauce with capers around and on the meat. Serve.

This dish may be prepared in advance up to the time of sautéing the sweetbreads. *Serves: 4*

MY FATHER'S MOUSTACHE "Father had the money (as well as the moustache), son Mycal had the culinary experience and Mom had the junk," members of the Noel family will say when asked why they opened a restaurant. Father still has the moustache, Mike is the chef and Mom is still collecting almost anything and everything.

Arnold and Marge Noel decided in 1976 they wanted to move away from the city (Washington, D. C.) and enjoy a more relaxed lifestyle in the country. Arnold, or Pappy as he is known, had a long career as a professional photographer, 21 years of which were spent as a military photographer. In 1962 he joined U.P.I. and still traveled all over the world on assignments. Stationed in Washington, Pappy often covered the White House and his last assignment was acting as the advance pressman for President Ford. Arnold Noel is the past president of the White House News Photographers and a lifetime member of the organization. Pappy's work has been on the cover of National Geographic Magazine as well as in many other magazines and newspapers.

The Noels had purchased a country home near Front Royal and decided to move there in 1976. Marge had been haunting antique and second hand stores for 25 years. "I bought mostly junk, but attractive junk," she says. Not satisfied to take life easy during retirement, the Noels decided that they wanted to open a restaurant. When the large Victorian on South Royal Avenue was put up for sale, Marge could not wait to buy it. She had wanted that house since the early 1950's. It was in a terrible rundown condition, but the Noels all pitched in and restored it. One of the Noel sons is a carpenter.

The exterior of the house is in rare fishscale shingles. Inside there are a dozen rooms, many of which have been converted into dining areas. Nine coats of wallpaper had to be peeled off of some of the walls. The city building inspectors condemned the garage on the back of the lot. The Noels tore it down, but saved the tongue and groove lumber to panel one of the rooms. One of the dining rooms is "papered" in burlap potato and peanut sacks. The original kitchen of the house was enlarged and modern equipment was installed.

At last Marge had a place to put her "junk." The house is very tastefully decorated in memorabilia of days gone by. There is a red and white room, the coke room, decorated with coke sign and advertisements of the product. The doll room displays a collection of over 100 dolls. There is a cabinet in the hall containing at least five hundred items of miniature doll house furniture. The bar was constructed from wainscoting from a local church. There is an old German black oak sideboard and an old organ. All of the decorations add to the country atmosphere of the restaurant, and there is something to see in every nook of the house, including the bathrooms.

Some of the table settings are unusual, too. In the burlap room the water glasses are Mason jars. If a beer is ordered it too is served in a chilled Mason jar. Scotch is served in a wine glass and wine in a small tumbler.

Mycal Noel is the chef. He has no formal training, but learned cooking through experience at a number of restaurants. His style of cooking is country American, with emphasis on "everyday good food." Mycal's soups are all homemade and they are unique. All meats and seafoods are prepared fresh. Pappy Noel goes to Washington once or twice a week to buy fresh produce, meats and seafood for the restaurant. There is always a daily special on the menu and on weekends there are two or three.

For a family who wanted a quiet life in the country – that has not been the case. It has been hard work running a restaurant, but a lot of fun. Today Marge says, "Ten years after opening the restaurant, Dad is out of money, Mom is out of junk, but Mycal has more experience." The latter may be true, but Pappy is still doing some remodeling to the old house and Mom is still buying a knick-knack for here and there -- just the right touch to add to one of the rooms.

DINING
➡

My Father's Moustache, 108 South Royal Ave, Front Royal, VA 22630, 703-635-3496
Directions: *Front Royal may be reached by Route 50, I-66 or Route 50. Restaurant is located in center of Front Royal*
Meal Times: *Tuesday through Saturday,Lunch: 11:30 a.m. to 3 p.m. Dinner: 5:30 p.m. to 9:30 p.m. Sundays, 12 noon to 8 p.m. - Dinner service only Closed all holidays and the week between Christmas and New Year's. Reservations requested on weekends.*
Principals: *The Arnold Noel Family*

PUMPERNICKEL SOUP

Bread soups have been popular in many countries of Europe for years, especially Portugal, Spain, Russia and the Slavic countries. Russians regard soup as an important part of the meal and a great aid in digestion. Good bread is a prerequisite for any bread soup.

1 stick of butter	1/2 loaf of stale pumpernickel bread, cubed
2 medium carrots, peeled and finely diced	
1 large onion, finely diced	2 medium potatoes, peeled and cut into 1/2 inch cubes
2 stalks celery, finely diced	
6 cups beef stock	1/4 to 1/2 cup sour cream

Melt butter in a soup pot and add carrots, onion and celery. Sauté until soft. Add stock and simmer 30 minutes. Add cubed bread and stir until blended. Remove from heat. Add sour cream and stir until blended. Then add the cooked potatoes to the soup and heat through, but do not boil. Serve with a dollop of sour cream.

In the meantime, cook potatoes in a separate pot until done, about 15 minutes. Do not overcook them. Drain and save. *Serves: 8*

FRESH SALMON WITH SAUCE BEURRE BLANC

A beurre blanc sauce, literally a white butter sauce, is excellent with a poached fish. The sauce usually contains white wine and came into popularity with nouvelle cuisine.

4 6 oz. filets of fresh salmon
1/2 cup fish stock

1/2 cup dry white wine

Sauce:

2 tablespoons chopped shallots
1 cup very dry white wine
1/4 cup Champagne vinegar

2 1/4 cups whipping cream
1 cup butter at room temperature

Place filets in ovenproof pan. Pour stock and wine over the filets. Cover with buttered brown paper. Oven poach in a preheated 375 degree oven for 15 minutes or until fish flakes easily.

In the meantime prepare the sauce: Place shallots, wine and vinegar in a medium saucepan. Reduce over medium heat until shallots are moist and tender, about 6 minutes. Add cream and boil until the back of a spoon is coated, about 8 to 10 minutes. Remove from heat and add butter, bit by bit, stirring to incorporate. Keep sauce warm, but do not boil.

To serve place fish on plates, surrounded by the sauce. Serve with tiny new whole potatoes and whole baby carrots. Garnish with caviar and fresh dill.

Author's note: Use a whisk to incorporate the butter into the sauce. This may be done over warm heat. However, be careful not to let sauce boil, since the butter will separate.

PARKHURST INN RESTAURANT In 1978, George and Nita Weddleton traveled from California across the country to find their niche on a hilltop near Luray, Virginia. They made the trip across country in six months in a truck and trailer with their three children. "We took all of the back roads," said George Weddleton."We wanted our family to see the United States, not the freeways."

The Weddletons had become tired of the hectic life in San Francisco and wanted their children to grow up in the country. Both George and Nita have been involved in the food business for most of their careers. They owned a restaurant in San Francisco, as well as one in Nevada City, California near Lake Tahoe. George did take a sabbatical for five years when he had his own stained glass window business.

When George and Nita reached Virginia, they liked the lifestyle and started searching for either a restaurant to lease or some property to buy. They found the Parkhurst Motel as it was then called. Although the place needed quite a bit of renovation, the terms were favorable and they bought it.

The Parkhurst Motel was originally built in 1938 and rebuilt after a fire in 1940. On the outside it looks like a typical roadside motel of the middle of the century. It is no longer being used as a motel, but is strictly a restaurant. It took the Weddletons a year to remodel the building. There was no kitchen and no equipment. They purchased some used kitchen equipment from a restaurant that was going out of business. It took two weeks to scrub the stove, before it was in shape to be used.

Finally, after a year of hard work, the Parkhurst Inn Restaurant opened in July of 1979 – just in time for the gasoline crisis. Nobody wanted to drive out to the country for dinner. It was one mountain ridge further from Washington than most people at the time would go for a Sunday outing. A week after the opening the chef became discouraged and quit.

George took over the cooking and has loved it ever since. He is very fussy and pays attention to the tiniest details. Although he spent some time as a chef in an Italian restaurant in California, the cuisine at Parkhurst is international, with George's own unusual touches. Everything, including the desserts are homemade. The menu varies from day-to-day, depending on what is available fresh and also what George chooses to prepare that day. The daily menu is written on a portable blackboard and presented at each diner's table.

Fresh vegetables and herbs are grown in the garden behind the kitchen and are used on the menu when they are in season.

To supplement the restaurant business, the Weddletons have added a wine shop, just in front of the restaurant. It used to be a porch. The area is adorned with some of George's stained glass windows, which he still makes as a hobby. There is an impressive selection of wines in the shop as well as on the restaurant menu. Many Virginia wines are featured. They also plan to open a wine bar in the near future.

Once a month, George and Nita host the Page Valley Wine Tasting Society at their restaurant. There is usually a guest speaker and a selection of cheese, breads and pates to complement the wines.

It has been a struggle for George and Nita Weddleton, but they have brought international cuisine to one of the most beautiful areas of Virginia.

George Weddleton is the kind of chef you like to to have around. He does some basics and adds his own touches, turning the dishes into interesting taste experiences.

DINING
➡

Parkhurst Inn Restaurant, *Route 1, Box 442, Luray, Va. 22835, 703-743-4009 or 703-743-6009*
Directions: *On U.S. 211, 2 miles west of Luray Caverns. (Follow signs to Luray Caverns.)*
Principals: *George and Nita Weddleton*
Meal Times: *Wednesday through Sunday: Dinner,5 p.m. to 10 p.m.*
In summer and fall also Monday and Tuesday 5 p.m. to 10 p.m.
Reservations requested

OYSTERS PARKHURST

Serve with Seyval Blanc

Oysters are a Virginia favorite – on the half shell in stews, in casseroles, and baked as an appetizer.

1 dozen fresh oyster, cleaned and shucked reserve liquid	1/4 teaspoon oregano
1/2 cup dry bread crumbs	1/4 teaspoon garlic powder
1/4 cup Parmesan cheese	Pinch of black pepper
3/4 teaspoon basil	Pinch of thyme
3/4 teaspoon minced parsley	2 tablespoons olive oil
1/4 teaspoon salt	2 tablespoon Virginia Seyval Blanc
	1 tablespoon lemon juice

After oysters have been cleaned and shucked, reserve liquid. Take 12 half shells and scrub them well.

Combine first 9 ingredients and place 2 teaspoons of this crumb mixture on each half shell. Place one oyster with a little liquid on top of the crumbs. Combine olive oil, wine and lemon juice. Sprinkle liquid evenly over all of the oysters. Top with remaining crumb mixture.

Place the oyster shells on a cookie sheet and bake in a preheated 350 degree oven for 8 to 10 minutes. Serve with lemon wedges. *Serves: 3 to 4 as an appetizer*

FETTUCINE ALFREDO

The word fettucine comes from the Italian "fettuccia" meaning ribbon. These ribbon noodles are enhanced with a traditional cream sauce with a different twist – sour cream, which helps bind the sauce. Shellfish may also be added to this recipe

12 tablespoons butter	Garlic salt to taste
2 1/2 cups heavy cream	1/2 to 3/4 cup freshly grated
4 tablespoons sour cream	Parmesan cheese
Freshly ground pepper to taste	1 lb. fettucine, cooked al dente

In a large skillet over medium heat melt the butter. Add the heavy cream and the sour cream. Whisk to combine and heat. When very hot add enough grated Parmesan cheese to make a thick sauce. Add the fettucine and toss until well coated and the pasta is hot. Season to taste with garlic salt and freshly ground pepper.

For fettucine with shellfish, add to the sauce with the fettucine 1 cup cooked bay shrimp, 1/2 cup poached scallops and 1/2 cup cooked crabmeat. Heat through and serve on warm plates. *Serves: 4*

POPPY SEED BREAD

Makes: 2 loaves

Poppy seeds are used primarily in Austrian, Czechoslovakian and Hungarian cooking and baking. The tiny seeds of the large poppy are not round but kidney shaped. They have a nut like flavor and are popular sprinkled on rolls and breads. They can also be used in the baked goods as in this recipe. A light quick bread, the poppy seed bread can be used at meal time, as well as for breakfast toast.

2 1/2 cups flour	1/3 cup vegetable oil
1 cup sugar	1/3 cup olive oil
4 1/2 teaspoons baking powder	1 1/4 cups evaporated milk
1/2 cup poppy seeds	1 teaspoon vanilla extract
3 eggs	

Grease and flour 2 glass bread pans (9x5x3 inches). Preheat oven to 350 degrees. Sift together the flour, sugar and baking powder. Add the poppy seeds.

In a large bowl combine the eggs, the oils, evaporated milk and the vanilla extract. Beat well to combine ingredients. Slowly add the dry ingredients and blend well. Divide batter between the two pans.

Bake in preheated 350 degree oven for 45 to 50 minutes. Test for doneness with a toothpick inserted in center which should come out clean. Let cool 10 minutes and remove from pans to a wire rack for further cooling.

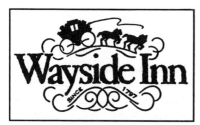

WAYSIDE INN In the late 1700's the stagecoach stops in northern Virginia were Harrisonburg and Winchester. However, a law was passed that a traveler could stop at night at any farmhouse along the way. Each time a traveler stopped at a farmhouse he would present the farmer with a little chit (voucher) which could then be presented to the government for payment.

A man named Wilkerson who lived in Middletown near Winchester got tired of people staying with him in his home and decided to build an inn. The Wilkerson Tavern, as the property was known in those days, opened in 1797. Although the name of the establishment and ownership have changed a number of times, the hostelry has been in operation for almost 200 years.

In the early 19th century the Wilkerson Tavern became a relay station for stagecoaches. It was a welcome stop for weary travelers who were greeted with hot food and drink, while a fresh team of horses was made ready for the continuation of their journey. The food was hot and waiting for the travelers because the Tavern employed a lookout for the stagecoach. This lookout was usually a young boy who ran and alerted the cook when he saw the coach in the distance. The cook immediately stoked up the fire and got the food ready.

The Inn remained unscathed during the Civil War since it served all comers – both Northern and Southern soldiers. Even though several battles were fought nearby including Jackson's Valley Campaign and the Battle of Cedar Creek, there was no damage to the Inn.

After the Civil War the Inn was purchased by Jacob Larrick who changed the property's name to Larrick Hotel. It sold again in the early 20th century

270

to Samuel Rhodes who added a third floor and wings on each side. Rhodes gave the place another name – the Wayside Inn.

In the late 1950's district businessman and antique collector, Leo Bernstein purchased the historic building and did some major renovations. He enclosed the coachyard between the original tavern and the old slave kitchen. The area became the Coachyard Lounge where guests may enjoy a cocktail and also be served a meal. Bernstein also did major renovations of the public and guests rooms, furnishing them with antiques of the early 19th century.

In October of 1985 tragedy struck the Wayside Inn. It was almost gutted by fire. Faulty wiring caused the fire which broke out at 3 a.m. All of the overnight guests and personnel were quickly evacuated. However, the fire did considerable damage and the Inn had to be closed for 1 year for rebuilding and renovations. Some priceless antiques were lost. "Others were salvaged and have been repaired and restored," said Joseph Sewell, the curator of the Inn and full-time employee who is in charge of restoration and acquisitions.

The Inn reopened in the fall of 1986 with a limited menu, since the kitchen had not been completely rebuilt. A large modern kitchen is now under construction. It is separate from the main building and the traditional Southern style menu will be restored. The Inn can serve 500 in several dining rooms and also has banquet facilities.

Irene Washington, the chef of the Wayside Inn, whose family has worked for the Inn for generations, shares some traditional Southern recipes.

DINING ➡

Wayside Inn, 7783 Main Street, Middletown, VA 22645, 703-869-1797
Directions: *Take Middletown exit from I-81 to the center of Middletown*
Meal Times: *Breakfast: 7 to 10 a.m., 7 days a week, Lunch 11:30 a.m. to 3 p.m., 7 days a week , Dinner 5 p.m. to 9 p.m., 7 days a week*
Principals: *Olino M. Portanova, general manager Wayside of Virginia, Inc.*

PEANUT SOUP

Although the peanut is native to Brazil, it has been an important agricultural crop for Virginia since the Civil War. Early Virginia settlers found that if they fed their pigs these groundnuts (the nuts form underground) the pork was particularly tasty.

1 3/4 cups light cream	1 cup creamy peanut butter
1 stalk celery, sliced	3 1/2 cups chicken broth or
1 carrot chopped	Dash of sugar
1 medium onion, chopped	2 14 1/2 oz. cans chicken broth

In large saucepan combine broth, celery, carrot and onion. Bring to boil; reduce heat to simmer. Cover and simmer for 15 minutes, or until vegetables are tender. Strain broth and discard the vegetables. Place peanut butter in the same sauce pan and gradually stir in the hot broth. (Mixture will be stiff at first, but will become smooth.) Add cream and a dash of sugar. Heat through, but do not boil. *Serves: 6*

271

PECAN PIE

Although the pecan tree is native to states further south than Virginia, Thomas Jefferson is probably responsible for starting the pecan industry in Virginia. He became enamored with the nuts when a friend sent him some from New Orleans. Jefferson proceeded to plant the nuts on his property and persuade his friend George Washington to do so also. Some of the trees Washington planted are still standing beside the Potomac at Mount Vernon. This traditional pecan pie has always been associated with Southern cooking.

Pastry:

2 cups flour
1/2 teaspoon salt

2/3 cup shortening
4 to 5 tablespoons ice water

In a mixing bowl cut shortening into flour with a pastry blender until mixture looks like fine crumbs. Make a well in the center, pour in 4 tablespoons ice water. Mix quickly with a knife and add more water if necessary to produce a firm, but not sticky dough. Roll dough to fit a 9 inch pie plate.

Filling:

3 eggs
2/3 cup brown sugar
1/4 teaspoon salt

1/3 cup butter or margarine, melted
1 cup dark or light corn syrup
1 cup pecan halves or broken pieces

Preheat oven to 375 degrees. In a bowl beat eggs, sugar, salt, butter, and syrup with a rotary beater. Cover bottom of pie shell with pecans. Pour egg mixture over nuts. Bake 40 to 50 minutes in 375 degree oven or until filling is set. *Serves: 8*

Bibliography

There is a plethora of books on wine of regions throughout the world. Few of these, however, deal with the particular conditions associated with the eastern United States, much less the state of Virginia. However, there are a few excellent ones that do provide considerable insight into wine development in the East. It was from those listed below that much of the historical and technical information for this book was derived. For readers wishing to pursue this fascinating subject further, each of the books listed identify a wide range of additional bibliographic material.

ADAMS, LEON D. *The Wines of America*. 3rd ed. New York: McGraw-Hill Book Company, 1985.

AMERINE, MAYNARD ANDREW. *Wine Production Technology in the United States*. ACS Symposium Series 145. Washington, D.C.: American Chemical Society, 1981.

CATTELL, HUDSON AND MILLER, LEE. *Wines of the East: I. The Hybrids; II. The vinifera; III. Native American Grapes*. Lancaster, Pennsylvania: L & H Photojournalism, 1979

HYAMS, EDWARD. *Dionysus: A Social History of the Wine Vine*. New York: The Macmillan Company, 1965.

LAWRENCE, R. DE TREVILLE. *Jefferson and Wine*. The Plains, Virginia: Vinifera-Wine Growers Association, 1976.

MORTON, LUCIE T. *Winegrowing in Eastern America*. Ithaca, New York: Cornell University Press, 1985.

PRYOR, ELIZABETH B. *Heaven's Favourite Gift: Vitaculture in Colonial Maryland, Virginia, and Pennsylvania*. Accokeek, Maryland: National Colonial farm Research Report No. 23, The Accokeek Foundation, Inc.

VINIFERA WINE GROWERS ASSOCIATION. *The Vinifera Wine Growers Journal*: Volumes 1 through 14, No. 1. The Plains, VA, 1974-1984

WAGNER, PHILIP M. *A Wine Grower's Guide*, Revised, New York: Alfred A. Knopf, 1985.

WAGNER, PHILIP M. *Grapes Into Wine*. New York: Alfred A. Knopf, 1986.

Winery & Restaurant Index

Recipe Index

HORS D'OEUVRES

Chevre Cheese Loaf, 66
Spices added to cheese and baked in a loaf, served with crackers

Champagne Oyster Loaf, 172
Hollowed out French bread with oyster filling

Hot Crab Dip, 167
Shrimp and cheese are combined for a hot dip, serving in chafing dish

APPETIZERS

Appetizer Pasta Angelina, 158
Shrimp and Virginia Ham are combined in a tomato, cream sauce and served over pasta

Brioche of Oysters, Sweetbreads and Mushrooms, 148
Individual hollow brioches are filled with a mixture of oysters, blanched sweet breads and mushrooms

Oysters Parkhurst, 268
Oysters in an herb, crumb mixture are baked on the half shell

Oysters Rappahannock, 178
Oysters and spinach topped with grated cheese are baked on the half shell

Sauteed Sea Scallops on Leaf Spinach, 191
Sauteed sea scallops served on spinach leaves with hazelnut butter

Scotch Shrimp and Scallops, 235
Flambeed with a basic cream sauce

Shrimp in Herb Butter with Angel Hair Pasta, 161
Shrimp and walnuts are sauteed and served over pasta

Tomatoes a la Reine, 77
Tomatoes stuffed with a vegetable mixture, served cold

SOUPS

Black Bean and Sausage Soup, 90
Variation of popular Southern soup recipe with Italian sausages

Book Gallery Minestrone, 151
Meatless, flavorful, hearty soup

Broccoli Soup, 69
Hot or cold broccoli cream soup

Crab Soup, 94
Clam broth and tomato base flavor this cream soup

Cream of Crab Soup, 183
Green peppers, celery and crab in a cream soup

Cream of Leek Soup, 122
Stilton cheese is a flavor component in this leek soup

Mushroom Soup, 147
Wine, herbs and some cream enrich this mushroom soup

Peanut Soup, 271
Traditional Virginia recipe with peanut butter and light cream

Potage Crecy, 79
A delightful and distinctive carrot soup

Pumpernickel Soup, 265
A hearty soup made in the Russian style with pumpernickel bread

Sausage and Greens Soup, 83
A soup of navy beans and greens flavored with ham

Sicilian Sausage Soup, 80
Italian soup with a tomato base

Swiss Barley Soup, 228

A traditional Swiss soup of barley, flavored with ham

Watercress Soup, 143

Watercress and potatoes are combined in a cream soup

MAIN DISHES: BEEF

Beef Birds in White Wine, 77

Beef birds with an herb, cheese stuffing cooked in Chardonnay

Beef Bourguignon, 69

Slow simmered beef with herbs and red wine

Beef Fondue with Shiitake Mushrooms, 216

A beef fondue with four different sauces

Beef Pot Roast, 114

A slow cooked roast with flavorful gravy

Beef Stroganoff a la Swiss, 224

Pickles and pimientos are added to the stroganoff

Beef Tenderloin and Snow Peas, 151

Stir fried beef with ginger and mushrooms

Blenheim Meatloaf, 107

Meatloaf using red wine

Chambourcin Beef, 250

A slow cooked roast enhanced by red wine, spices and black olives

Chambourcin Spaghetti Sauce, 256

Pepperoni, chili powder and red wine combine to add zest to spaghetti sauce

Filet Montross, 186

Bacon wrapped filet with red wine sauce

Flank Steak Marinade, 119

Red wine marinade with ginger

Goulash, 110

Beef stew with old world flavorings

Gypsy Steak, 242

Sauteed beef with stir fried mushrooms, green pepper and onions

Joann's Beef Stew, 253

Beef stew and vegetables slow cooked in a crock pot

Quick Stroganoff, 246

Beef stroganoff prepared by the traditional method

Steaks with Glaze Brian, 245

Pan fried steaks with wine sauce

Stufato with Cabernet Sauvignon, 105

An Italian recipe for beef roast cooked slowly with red wine

MAIN DISHES: LAMB

Navarin of Lamb, 58

Browned lamb stew is enhanced by herbs and Cabernet Sauvignon

Oakencroft Farm Pie, 133

Ground lamb and vegetables are topped with a crust of mashed potatoes

MAIN DISHES: VEAL

Calf's Liver with Balsamic Vinegar and Shallots, 85

Calf's Liver prepared simply with a tangy sauce

Jaegerschnitzel, 145

The sauce is prepared separately and then served over the sauteed veal

Les Ris de Veau au Porto et aux Capres, 262

Sweetbreads with vintage port and capers

Osso Bucoo, 143

Traditional Italian recipe for veal shanks

Veal Blanquette, 125

A French white veal stew

Veal Champignon, 233

Veal medallions and wild mushrooms with angel hair pasta

Veal Regency, 196

Veal, crabmeat and asparagus spears are topped with a bearnaise sauce

Veal Strips in White Wine and Cream, 73

Veal scallops are sauteed and prepared similar to a stroganoff

MAIN DISHES: PORK

Baked Virginia Ham with Homestead Southern Fruit Dressing, 229

Cured, boiled and baked Virginia ham with fruit dressing which bakes in separate dish

Brandy and Wine Pork Roast, 207

Brandy and wine add an interesting flavor combination to pork

Ham Loaf, 243

A wonderful way to use leftover ham

Pork Tenderloin with Rosemary, 137

Roasted pork tenderloin in the German style

Roast Loin of Pork with Fruit Stuffing, 161

Pork Roast stuffed with dried fruit, baked in apple cider

MAIN DISHES: POULTRY

CHICKEN BREAST:

Almond Chicken, 111

Stir fried chicken breasts with vegetables

Breast of Chicken with Lobster, 233

Chicken and lobster with sour cream sauce

Chicken Vidal, 58

Chicken breasts and mushrooms are served with a wine sauce and garnished with blanched grapes

Chinese Chicken with Snow Peas, 256

Marinated chicken breast pieces are stir fried with vegetables

Curried Chicken, 251

Chicken breasts are prepared in a cream curry sauce with white wine and raisins

Fools Chicken, 118

Chicken breasts wrapped with bacon and topped with a mushroom cream sauce

Grilled Chicken Breast on Beet Fettuccine, 191

Beet Fettuccine topped with grilled chicken breast and a light cream sauce

Spring Chicken, 100

Chicken breasts and ham with a wine-cream sauce

Tarragon Chicken, 62

Chicken breasts with tarragon baked in wine

WHOLE CHICKEN AND POULTRY:

Brunswick Stew, 202

Lima beans, okra, tomatoes and chicken combine to make a colonial stew

Chicken and Leek Pie, 201

Leeks, mushrooms and chicken in an early Virginia recipe

Chicken in Wine Sauce, 98

Baked chicken in wine sauce with mushrooms

Chicken Pot Pie, 188

Style of chicken pie prepared in colonial Virginia

Cloria's Spaghetti Sauce, 253

The addition of coffee enhances this sauce

Colonial Fried Chicken, 154

Moist, tender chicken the colonial way

Cornish Game Hens in Casserole, 200

Cornish game hens combined with vegetables and a white Burgundy sauce as per an early colonial Virginia recipe

Hot Chicken Salad, 220
Tasty combination of chicken, celery and almonds

MAIN DISHES: GAME

Rabbit with Almonds and Raisins, 123
Rabbit is simmered with spices and garnished with raisins and almonds

Welsh Rabbit with Beer, 202
A colonial Virginia recipe; actually a "rare bit" without the rabbit

Westmoreland Venison, 173
Marinated venison is cooked with herbs and Smithfield ham

MAIN DISHES: SEAFOOD

FISH:

Baked Fish in Garlic Wine, 212
Fish filets marinated in garlic wine and baked with tomatoes and peppers

Baked Fish with Spinach Stuffing, 80
A spinach stuffed fish in baked in white wine

Baked Mountain Trout with Tarragon Stuffing, 229
Boned trout stuffed with herb and bread stuffing is oven poached

Braised Salmon with Vegetables, 85
Salmon poached in wine with vegetables and black olives, accompanied by a wine sauce

Catfish, 128
Breaded catfish are baked in oven

Cioppino, 158
Traditional fish stew in the Italian style

Fish in Cream, 209
Pieces of fish are baked in a sour cream sauce

Fresh Salmon with Sauce Beurre Blanc, 266
Fresh salmon with a light white sauce

SHELLFISH:

Baked Scallops, 54
Scallops baked in oven seasoned with wine

Camarao Pernambucana, 175
Typical Brazilian shrimp dish with coconut

Chesapeake Bay Medley, 172
Oysters, scallops and asparagus served with a wine sauce

Colonial Crab, 185
Crabmeat and Virginia country ham are combined for a quick entree

Curried Oysters, 167
Oysters and rice baked in a casserole

Deviled Eggs and Shrimp in Mornay Sauce, 132
Casserole of shrimp and deviled eggs with a light cream sauce

Eastville Inn Crab Cakes, 183
A firm, yet light crab cake

Fresh Sea Scallops in White Wine Sauce, 119
Sauteed scallops in wine sauce served with vermicelli

Hot Crab Open Face Sandwiches, 110
Broiled sandwich of crab mixture tops an English muffin

Les Crevettes a la Russe, 262
Flambeed shrimp sauteed with ginger and scallions

Les Moules avec Herbes de Provence, 261
Mussels in the traditional French style of the Provence

Mussel Soup, 72
Mussels are cooked in clam juice and white wine, served in soup bowls

Northern Neck Crab Imperial, 186
An unusual variation of Crab Imperial

Oakencroft Mussel Bisque, 132
Mussels cooked in wine and served with a cream sauce

Seafood and Linguine in Lemon Cream, 235
Seafood in a reduced tomato cream sauce served with linguine

Seafood Monticello, 223
Award wining recipe is a mix of Virginia seafood

Scallops Bombay, 224
Curry marinated scallops are combined with a cream sauce

Shrimp and Scallops in Creamy Wine Sauce, 258
Seafood dish includes celery and carrots

Virginia Crabmeat, Saute Randolph, 195
Crabmeat on patty shells topped with hollandaise sauce

PASTA

Cold Pasta Salad, 136
A colorful, flavorful pasta salad with many herbs

Fettuccine Alfredo, 269
Fettuccine Alfredo with a different twist

Fettuccine Alfredo Barchella, 62
A quick and easy preparation of classic Fettuccine Alfredo

Fettuccine St. Andre, 150
Soft, creamy cheese and mushrooms are the basis of this fettuccine casserole

Fresh Tomato Sauce, 61
Fresh tomatoes are quickly prepared into a light sauce which is served over pasta

Onion Pasta, 207
Sweet onions are the basis of a sauce to serve over linguine

Pasta Kalanty, 179
Sausages and asparagus in a sauce is served over red pepper pasta

Spaghetti Pie, 80
Pasta forms the crust and sausage is the filling of this unusual pie

PASTA DOUGH:

Beet Fettuccine, 192
A beet is part of the ingredients for basic pasta dough

BREADS

Baked French Toast, 88
French toast the quick and easy way

Corn Bread, 155
Traditional Southern corn bread

Martha's Spoon Bread, 238
A light fluffy type of corn bread

Oatmeal Bread, 221
Oatmeal, molasses and honey combine in this textured bread

Poppy Seed Bread, 269
A light quick bread with poppy seeds throughout

VEGETABLES AND ACCOMPANIMENTS

Cauliflower, 128
Steamed cauliflower with cheese

Kidney Bean Relish, 201
Beans are marinated in an herb vinaigrette

Mint Peas, 128
Peas steamed with mint leaves

Potato Salad, 154
Old fashioned potato salad with celery and pickles

Red Cabbage, 145
Red cabbage simmered in wine with spices

Risotto with Pinot Noir Blanc, 105
An old Italian recipe with wine and hot
    cream

Schwarzwurzel, 140
Black salsify, a European vegetable, with
    light, nutmeg flavored cream sauce

Stewed Tomatoes, 154
Mixture of crumbled biscuits and tomatoes

Wine Roasted Potatoes, 140
A German version of hot fried potatoes

CAKE AND PASTRY

Black Cav Cake, 180
A genoise is filled with chocolate mousse
    and iced with a butter, rum icing.

Bourbon Pecan Butterscotch Pie, 159
Bourbon and butterscotch chips are added
    to a traditional pecan pie

Carrot Cake, 243
Carrots and nuts abound in this cake

Chocolate Mousse Cake, 81
A chocolate mousse, which is a flourless
    cake

Country Cheesecake, 217
Baked cheesecake uses blue cheese for
    extra flavor

Nut Pound Cake, 212
Pound cake is enhanced by the addition of
    pecans or black walnuts

Pecan Pie, 272
A recipe from an old Virginia Inn

Zwetschenkuchen, 175
Austrian plum cake

DESSERT

Dutch Apple Baby, 88
A large pancake with stewed apple filling

Guilford Ridge Cheesecake, 246
An elegant, no-bake, freezer cheesecake

Lace Cookie Cups, 162
Baked cookies are shaped into cups

Lemon Bisque, 221
A light, custard-type dessert

Martha's Apple Dumplings with
    Bourbon Sauce, 238
Pieces of apples are baked in puff pastry
    with Bourbon sauce

Peach Wine Sorbet, 122
A slightly sweet, tangy sorbet

Peaches with Cabernet Sauvignon
    Blanc, 105
Marinated fruit

Pear Sorbet in a Tulip with Lemon
    Custard Sauce, 192
Pear Sorbet in a light cookie cup with sauce

Pears in Red Wine, 73
Pears poached in red wine.

Poached Pear in Wine, 202
Pears poached in port wine.

Raspberry Champagne Sorbet, 91
Fresh raspberries and champagne combine
    for a light, refreshing dessert

Raspberry Mousse, 162
A simple to prepare raspberry dessert,
    served in Lace Cookie Cups

Souffleed Banana Rum Pancake, 94
A light, fluffy banana, rum dessert

Very Fine Raspberry Creme, 137
Whipped raspberry creme